THE PAINTED ENAMELS OF LIMOGES

SUSAN L. CAROSELLI

The PAINTED ENAMELS *of* LIMOGES

A Catalogue of the Collection of the Los Angeles County Museum of Art

LOS ANGELES COUNTY MUSEUM OF ART

First published in 1993 by
Los Angeles County Museum of Art
5905 Wilshire Boulevard
Los Angeles, California 90036

Distributed in the United States by
Thames and Hudson Inc.
500 Fifth Avenue
New York, New York 10110

Distributed in all other countries by
Thames and Hudson, Ltd.
30 Bloomsbury Street
London WC1B 3QP

Edited by Mitch Tuchman
Designed by Scott Taylor
Photography by Barbara Lyter
Composed in Adobe Garamond
Printed by Typecraft, Inc., Pasadena, California
Bound by Roswell Bookbinding, Phoenix,
Arizona

LIBRARY OF CONGRESS
CATALOGING-IN-PUBLICATION DATA

Los Angeles County Museum of Art.
The painted enamels of Limoges : a catalogue
of the collection of the Los Angeles County
Museum of Art / Susan L. Caroselli.
p.   cm.
Includes bibliographical references and index.
ISBN 0-500-97406-3
1. Painted enamel—France—Limoges—Catalogs.
2. Painted enamel—California—Los Angeles—
Catalogs. 3. Los Angeles County Museum of Art—
Catalogs. I. Caroselli, Susan L., 1947–   .
II. Title.
NK5024.F82L565 1993
738.4'6'094466-dc20   92-31537
                                       CIP

COVER

Master of the Aeneid
Plaque: Naval Games in Honor of Anchises
1525/30
Cat. no. 4

PHOTO CREDITS

Figs. 1, 3, 11, 30: All rights reserved, The Metropolitan Museum of Art.

Fig. 6: Réunion des Musées Nationaux.

Figs. 7, 9: Copyright The Frick Collection,
New York.

Figs. 10, 17–18: By permission of the British
Library.

Figs. 12, 14, 40–41: © 1992 Museum Associates,
Los Angeles County Museum of Art.

Figs. 15, 24, 36–38: Phot. Bibliothèque
Nationale, Paris.

Fig. 16: © 1992 The Art Institute of Chicago.
All rights reserved.

Figs. 19–20: Robert D. Rubic, New York.

Figs. 22–23: © 1992 National Gallery of Art,
Washington.

Contents

THE RENAISSANCE IN France saw the creation of many monuments of painting, sculpture, architecture, and decorative arts, but perhaps no art form is more representative of that time than the painted enamels produced by a small group of relatively unknown artists in the city of Limoges in central France. Working in a new and difficult technique, the enamel painters turned out a range of work from devotional plaques to platters to hand mirrors. Artistically their value is enormous: we may trace clearly in the work of the enamel painters the paths of artistic influence operative on all French artists of the period—from the early realism of Flemish illuminators and panel painters, through the agonized spirituality of German printmakers, to the elegant secular sophistication of Italian mannerists working at Fontainebleau. But the enamels are even more valuable for the glimpses they provide into the daily life of Renaissance France, not only the world of the nobility but also of working men and women.

Prized in their time by patrons from Catherine de' Medici, the queen of France, to German burghers and Spanish priests, the painted enamels of Limoges enjoyed an enormous resurgence of popularity as a result of a Renaissance revival in mid-nineteenth-century France. They became a necessary component of every great European and American collection of the early twentieth century, including that of William Randolph Hearst. From his holdings my predecessor William R. Valentiner chose the group represented in this volume. That number has been recently increased by a generous donation of works of art by one of our trustees, the noted collector Hans Cohn and his wife, Varya.

Supported by a research grant from the National Endowment for the Arts, Susan Caroselli spent several years documenting the painted enamels in the collection of the Los Angeles County Museum of Art. She prefaces her catalogue with a comprehensive discussion of the technique, history, style, iconography, and patterns of collecting of painted enamels. I wish to thank Dr. Caroselli for her work and to add my thanks to those individuals and institutions mentioned by her in the acknowledgments.

MICHAEL E. SHAPIRO

Director
Los Angeles County Museum of Art

I FIRST WISH to thank the National Endowment for the Arts for its support of both the research and publication of this book with two generous grants. Additional funding for the production of the book was provided by the Andrew W. Mellon Foundation Publications Fund and Typecraft, Inc.

I had the privilege and pleasure of first studying the painted enamels of Limoges in the company of Philippe Verdier, who was completing the catalogue of the enamels in the Frick Collection when I began my duties there. Later Professor Verdier provided valuable advice and enthusiastic support as I began my research on the County Museum's collection. In Limoges the director of the Musée Municipal, Madeleine Marcheix, treated me with exceptional kindness, permitting me to examine the museum's extraordinarily comprehensive library and archive, built up by her over many years with obvious care and dedication.

I wish to thank other museum directors and curators who allowed me access to works of art and archives under their care. I received particularly generous assistance in Europe from Sophie Baratte at the Musée du Louvre; Alain Erlande-Brandenburg at the Musée du Cluny and Musée de la Renaissance, Écouen; Richard Beresford, Suzanne Gaynor, and Rosalinde Savill at the Wallace Collection; Anna Somers Cocks at the Victoria and Albert Museum; Hugh Tait at the British Museum; Julia E. Poole at the Fitzwilliam Museum; and in the United States from Roger M. Berkowitz at the Toledo Museum of Art; Michael Conforti at the Minneapolis Institute of Arts; Bernice Davidson and Edgar Munhall at the Frick Collection; Peggy Fogelman at the J. Paul Getty Museum; David Torbert Johnson at the Taft Museum; Alison Luchs at the National Gallery of Art; Jeffrey Munger at the Museum of Fine Arts, Boston; Ian Wardropper at the Art Institute of Chicago; and Patrick de Winter at the Cleveland Museum of Art. Private collectors Varya and Hans Cohn, Los Angeles, and Olivier Ziegel, Paris, were extremely cooperative. Mr. and Mrs. Cohn allowed me free access to the enamels in their fine collection and recently presented the museum with a large group of objects, including three enamels in this volume.

At the Los Angeles County Museum of Art, former director, Earl A. Powell III, and Peter Fusco, former curator of sculpture and decorative arts, first encouraged me to begin this catalogue, and the successive curators of decorative arts, Timothy B. Schroder and Leslie Greene Bowman, continued to support the project, as did Martin Chapman, associate curator in charge of European decorative arts. Other members and former members of the decorative arts staff were extremely helpful; they include Jeanette Hanisee, Martha Drexler Lynn, and Constantina Oldknow on the curatorial staff, and Jo Barzda, Amalia Jonas, Roger Jones, and Lori Kaplan on the secretarial staff. I am grateful also for the enthusiasm and support of many members of the Decorative Arts Council.

Bruce Davis, curator of prints and drawings, provided much helpful information on print sources, and Edward Maeder, curator of costumes and textiles, advised on matters of costumes and hairstyles as aids for the dating of the enamels and their sources. Mary Levkoff,

assistant curator of European painting
and sculpture, was a fund of information
about the French Renaissance. I thank the
staff of the Research Library, especially
head librarian Eleanor Hartman and Anne
Diederick, in charge of interlibrary loans,
for their assistance and for allowing me
to carry out a great deal of my research
during library reconstruction at a considerable inconvenience to them. Tom
Jacobson, head of grants and sponsorship,
and Dana Hutt, grants coordinator, of
the Development Office were responsible
for the successful grant applications, and
Mark Mitchell of the Business Office
handled the financial arrangements. Eric
Lindeen of the Management Information
Systems department was extremely helpful
in computer matters.

Special thanks must go to object conservators Sharon Blank, Andrea Morse,
Claudia Rubin, and Marie Svoboda of the
Conservation Center, who found time in
their busy schedules not only to clean
and restore the enamels but to take an
interest in them, which prompted a valuable exchange of information leading to
a better understanding on my part of this
exacting technique. Many members of
the Technical Services staff contributed to
this catalogue by their cooperation in the
deinstallation, transportation, and rein-
stallation of the enamels; I am particularly
grateful to Rory Waggoner, whose observations led me to the attribution of one
group of objects.

The members of the staff of the
Publications and Graphic Design depart-
ments at the museum have been enormously supportive. I wish to thank
especially Mitch Tuchman, editor in chief,
who allowed me the time to carry out my
research and writing and who made the
experience of being edited entirely pain-
less. Nancy Carcione, Randy Jacks, Carol
Pelosi, and head designer Sandy Bell
handled the many details of production.
Thanks also to Barbara Lyter of the
museum's Photographic Services Department, who, with the assistance of designer
Scott Taylor, ably carried out the time-
consuming and difficult task of photo-
graphing objects that were decorated on
every surface, and to Mr. Taylor, who
provided the elegant design of the catalogue itself. I am grateful to Museum
Service Council member Marcia Tucker
for undertaking the task of indexing
the book.

My gratitude goes also to a group
of individuals who contributed their
time and effort behind the scenes at the
museum and elsewhere, assisting me with
practical matters and providing advice,
evaluation, and especially encouragement
and support during this project. They
include Patrick Anderson, Betsy Kardos,
Bernard Kester, Paul A. Johnson, Janice
Leoshko, Elizabeth P. Loken-Egdahl,
Cecily MacInnes Welmers, Anne Morris,
the late Vivienne Greenwood Pagliai,
John Passi, Michael Stoughton, Nancy
Thomas, Jeremy West, and my parents,
Ruby and Joseph Caroselli.

SUSAN L. CAROSELLI

Associate Curator
European Painting and Sculpture
Los Angeles County Museum of Art

SEQUENCE

The entries in the catalogue are arranged
chronologically by the artists' periods of
activity; within each artist's oeuvre
enamels are also catalogued in chronological order.

DATES

A slash between two dates—for example,
1560/65—indicates that the work
was produced at an indeterminable time
between the first and second date.

DIMENSIONS

Dimensions are given in both centimeters
and inches. Unless otherwise indicated,
in two-dimensional objects height
precedes width and in three-dimensional
objects height precedes width precedes
depth.

BIBLICAL CITATIONS

Citations from the Bible are taken from
either the Authorized (King James)
Version or the English Revised Version,
as indicated by AV or ERV, respectively.

EXHIBITIONS AND LITERATURE

Exhibition and bibliographical references
are indicated in the text by a short form
consisting of the city and date of the
exhibition in the former case and the
author's name and date of publication in
the latter. Complete citations can be
found in the bibliography.

T HE CITY OF Limoges, in the geographical center of France, has been a source of luxury goods for nearly a millennium. Now almost universally associated with fine porcelain tableware and filled with showrooms displaying a range of ceramic objects from the exquisite to the ghastly, Limoges is rarely remembered for the enamel techniques that her artisans perfected and promoted for more than five hundred years. Of these techniques the least understood is the art of painted enamels. Visitors to the museums whose holdings include large collections of these works often mistake them for ceramics and have little, if any, knowledge of the exacting process of their creation. Most general discussions of enameling mention Renaissance painted enamels only briefly, and the few books devoted exclusively to the art form, such as Philippe Verdier's excellent catalogues of the collections of the Walters Art Gallery, Baltimore (1967), and The Frick Collection, New York (1977), are primarily studies of iconography.

Restorations of the great châteaux of the Renaissance, such as Amboise, Azay-le-Rideau, Blois, Chambord, Chenonceaux, and Langeais in the Loire Valley and Chantilly, Écouen, and Fontainebleau outside Paris, have re-created the ambience of those days with period furniture, tapestries, and some metalwork, glass, and ceramics. Conspicuous by their absence, however, are the painted enamels that were so popular, probably because most examples have now found their way into museum collections and because the restorers did not understand how these objects were displayed in their original settings. In the few châteaux where enamels are exhibited, it is in modern vitrines, such as a small group at Chantilly and a large collection from the Musée de Cluny, Paris, now on view in the Musée de la Renaissance established in the château at Écouen.

The painted enamels of Limoges were produced during a finite period of time — a little more than a century — in one place by a group of artists to whom the craft was restricted by royal decree. It is not surprising that they are a perfect manifestation of the specific culture that produced them, late medieval and Renaissance France during the reigns of the last of the Valois kings, from Louis XI to Henri III (1461 to 1589). They are

Opposite:

PIERRE REYMOND

Tazza:
Scene from the Book
of Proverbs (detail)
c. 1558

Cat. no. 10

also a virtual digest of fifteenth- and sixteenth-century two-dimensional European art: manuscript illumination, painting, book illustration, and especially prints. According to Verdier (1967, x), "Limoges enamels were instrumental in disseminating the aesthetic lesson and the sociological influence of European prints amidst the aristocracy and the rich merchant-class at the time of the Renaissance."

The collection of painted enamels in the Los Angeles County Museum of Art contains works by most of the major enamel painters (*peintres-émailleurs*) of Limoges, from the earliest identifiable artist, the so-called Monvaerni Master of the fifteenth century (cat. no. 1), to the later sixteenth-century masters of the Courteys family (cat. nos. 20–23, 25–41). The group of forty-five enamels includes pieces from famous series now dispersed throughout Europe and America, such as the *Aeneid* series (cat. nos. 3–4) and two versions of the tale of Cupid and Psyche (cat. nos. 20–22) by Pierre Courteys, and a unique complete set of calendar plates by Martial Courteys (cat. nos. 29–40). Largely unpublished, the Los Angeles enamels represent a range of styles—early and late polychrome and grisaille work—and types—plaques, vessels, and plates.

The decorative arts are distinct from the "fine" arts of painting, sculpture, and architecture in that they are usually commissioned or acquired for their owner's immediate use and pleasure, and not as a legacy to the future. We can more easily learn the truth about a culture from the earthenware from which a man eats than from the portrait he calculates will bring him posthumous glory. Rarely does an era find as complete an expression of itself as does Renaissance France in the painted enamels of Limoges. Its history, social structure, beliefs, and tastes are all preserved in their durable beauty "tel que l'ambre une fleur" (like a flower in amber), in the words of poet, connoisseur, and art critic Théophile Gautier.*

ENAMEL

Enamel is similar in composition to glass: both are basically silica and a fluxing agent, which allows the ingredients to fuse when fired at a relatively low temperature. The most common fluxing agents used by ancient, medieval, and Renaissance enamelers were soda, potash, lime, lead oxide, and borax. The addition of most of these compounds made the enamel easier to work, but the finished product was friable and consequently susceptible to deterioration and decomposition.

To produce colors, the enameler added a small amount of metallic oxide or carbonate to the colorless flux, or *fondant*, when it was heated to a molten state. Only these substances

---

*From a sonnet to the enamel painter Claudius Popelin, published in Falize 1893–94, 517–18.

could withstand the firing temperatures necessary for the adhesion of the enamel to its metal support; thus the artist's palette was limited to the range of colors produced by these additives. Ancient and medieval enamels were executed primarily in colors containing a large amount of tin or, less commonly, lead, which functioned as an opacifier. Only a few hues of opaque enamel were available—white, black, several shades of green and blue, violet, yellow, iron red, and a pink suitable for flesh tones—and not every culture that produced enamels achieved even this limited range.

In the fourteenth and fifteenth centuries glassmakers were learning to paint on clear glass in translucent colors rather than assembling pieces of colored glass. The appropriation of their techniques and recipes gave enamelers a much larger palette. Since the clear fluxes varied in composition—some contained lead, others were alkaline (containing salts consisting primarily of potassium or sodium carbonate)—they reacted differently to an added colorant. The addition of copper oxide to the lead-glass flux, for example, produced a translucent green, while the same oxide yielded a translucent blue when combined with a leadless, alkaline flux. In the latter case even a variation of the amount of colorant had an effect: a small amount of copper produced turquoise, a larger amount dark blue (Michaels 1964–65, 22). Black was a mixture of fragments of colored glass with manganese, cobalt, and iron oxide. (Under magnification, or where a layer of enamel is very thin or damaged, the black of the Renaissance painted enamels is revealed as a translucent mulberry color applied thickly enough to seem an opaque black.)

The fusion of all the ingredients at about 700°C (1300°F) produced a crystalline form of enamel that shattered when it cooled. To prepare the enamel for use, it was necessary to grind this substance, an exacting task that was performed with the enamel submerged in pure water to keep the tiny particles from being blown away by stray air currents or even the breath of the artisan. Ground too fine, the enamel would lose its reflective properties and the color would be dull; ground too coarse, the enamel would coat its metal support unevenly, causing streaking, puddling, and possibly bubbling from moisture or air trapped in the particles (and the metal thus exposed would be susceptible to oxidation). The ground particles of enamel, once thoroughly dried, were finally ready for whatever procedure was to be employed.

ENAMEL TECHNIQUES

The major enamel techniques are cloisonné, champlevé, and painting, the first two integrally related to metalworking. In cloisonné the areas of colored enamel are separated from one another by metal strips called cloisons soldered to a metal base; in champlevé (raised-field) the enamel is placed in recesses that have been cast or worked in the surface of the metal. Painting with enamel involves mixing the powdered enamel with water and a binder such as gum arabic or tragacanth and applying it with a spatula, brush, or pointed tool to a metal support. All other enamel techniques are variations of these three processes: *plique-à-jour* (literally, "braid letting in daylight") is cloisonné enamel without a metal backing; encrustation is essentially champlevé enamel that has not been filed flush to the metal surface; and *basse-taille* (low-relief) is a combination of champlevé and painting, in which translucent enamels are laid over an engraved or incised metal field. The firing of the piece to fuse the enamel to the metal is the common denominator. This was done in the medieval and Renaissance eras in kilns heated to 600–850°C (1100–1550°F) by wood or charcoal; the piece was placed on a support of iron or clay and protected from impurities by a sleeve, or muffle.

THE EARLY HISTORY OF ENAMELWORK

The history of enamelwork has been discussed in detail in hundreds of books and articles dedicated to this medium. It is sufficient to mention here that the process of fusing enamel to metal was discovered in the Near East as early as the thirteenth century B.C. (Cold enamels, that is, enamel set into, rather than fused to, a metal framework, have been found dating to the Mycenaean culture of the nineteenth century B.C.). There is no written or archaeological evidence to suggest that the craft was practiced in Greece after the end of the third century B.C., and in Rome, a center of glassmaking, the art of enameling was, curiously, unknown. The Greek rhetorician Philostratus of Lemnos, attached to the Roman imperial court in the early third century A.D., made only a brief reference to an art form practiced by the northern tribes, noting that "the barbarians of the outer sea pour these colors into bronze molds [and] the colors become hard as stone, preserving the designs." Indeed, the earliest true enamels have been found on the edges of the Roman empire, in Britain, Belgium, the northern Caucasus, and Syria (fig. 1).

FIGURE 1

Vase, provincial Roman (found in central France), third century A.D., champlevé enamel on blackened bronze, height 12.1 cm (4¾ in.), diameter 11.4 cm (4½ in.), The Metropolitan Museum of Art, New York, Fletcher Fund, 1947.

At some point, possibly before the formation of the kingdom of the Franks by Clovis in the early sixth century, the craft died out in northern Europe. It was not until the late eighth century in Italy and the tenth century in France and Germany that Western European craftsmen began to execute enamels to decorate liturgical objects and furniture. Earlier enamels in church treasuries have invariably been identified as Byzantine in origin, mostly liturgical objects of cloisonné enamel and gold, brought back from Byzantium by merchants, pilgrims, and crusaders. Their opulent beauty encouraged local artisans to attempt to duplicate them; although lacking the material (gold in particular), sophistication, and skill to do so, the Europeans nevertheless had the ingenuity to develop the colorful and exuberant champlevé technique. This was brought to a high standard by artists in the Rhine and Meuse valleys, culminating in the work of Eilbertus of Cologne (active c. 1130–40), Godefroid de Claire of Huy (active c. 1145–73), and Nicolas of Verdun (active 1181–1205). Monastic communities in these areas, particularly Cologne and Stavelot (near Liège), had close relationships with their brother and sister houses in central France, where the production of champlevé enamels soon became the primary industry of the city of Limoges.

The first three decades of the twelfth century saw the ascendance of Limoges as the premier source of enamelwork for all Europe. This was due not only to the skill and prolificacy of her artisans but to the situation of the city itself—an already thriving economy as an administrative and, therefore, market center during the Merovingian and Carolingian eras, its fortuitous location on many trade and pilgrimage routes, and the propinquity of several extensive (and wealthy) monastic foundations, particularly the abbey of Saint-Martial in Limoges itself and the abbeys of Solignac, Grandmont, a center of monastic reform, and Sainte-Foi in Conques, an important pilgrimage site. The workshops of Limoges turned out incense burners, censers, crucifixes, monstrances, ciboria, pyxes, paxes, croziers, reliquaries (fig. 2), tomb slabs, and portable altars for churches and monasteries; caskets, bookbindings, beakers, and basins suitable for liturgical or domestic use; and jewelry and ornaments for caps, gloves, sandals, and mantles for personal adornment. The enamels were disseminated throughout France and to Germany, Poland, Sweden, Austria, Spain, Italy, and England, where other schools of enamelwork developed.

FIGURE 2

Reliquary Chasse with Scenes from the Passion of Christ, France (Limoges), thirteenth century, champlevé enamel on gilded copper, 38.9 x 42.7 x 14.3 cm (15 5/16 x 16 13/16 x 5 5/8 in.), Walters Art Gallery, Baltimore.

As the robust Romanesque style, so perfectly characterized by the substantial and energetic champlevé enamels of Limoges, gave way to the graceful Gothic, a more delicate and sophisticated variant of enamelwork began to achieve popularity—the use of jewel-toned translucent enamels over gold and silver, ideal for brilliant accents to the period's masterpieces of liturgical metalwork (fig. 3). French centers other than Limoges came to the fore, as did others in Spain and Italy, Paris and Siena being the most celebrated in the fourteenth and fifteenth centuries. Limoges continued to produce champlevé, but as the demand dropped, so did the quality. The industry ended abruptly with the sack and near-destruction of the city by the English troops of Edward, the Black Prince, in 1371.

THE TECHNIQUE OF PAINTED ENAMELS

For the technique of painting in enamel we have three sources of information: a small number of medieval accounts describing cloisonné and champlevé that provide useful information on the production and working of enamel; the testimony of nineteenth-century connoisseurs, many of whom were enamel painters themselves; and the evidence supplied by modern conservators and conservation scientists.

One of the earliest sources is *De diversis artibus* (translated as *On Divers Arts*), an early twelfth-century (c. 1122) treatise and how-to text by "Theophilus," which most authorities believe to have been the pseudonym of the Benedictine monk and goldsmith Roger of Helmarshausen. In the third book the author describes the steps of making a chalice, and the short chapters 53, 54, and 55 (Theophilus 1979, 125–28) address the manufacture of enamel decoration for the vessel. Theophilus provides no recipes for colors, however, merely instructing the artisan to use powdered ancient glass of the desired color as a sort of "starter." The most useful sources of enamel-color recipes are a text by Blaise de Vigenère, printed in Paris in 1615 (cited at length in Gauthier 1972, 17–24), and a manuscript written by René François of Limoges, also in the early seventeenth century (published in 1855 by Maurice Ardant), both reproducing far older recipes for a great variety of colors.

Very little written information survives from the period of production itself, and that is found in the writings of Italian artist-theoreticians. Only Leonardo da Vinci discusses painted enamels specifically: three times in his *paragone*, the ongoing debate over which art form was superior (Richter 1970, vol. 1, 58, 93, 95), and three times in his analysis of painting practices (Richter 1970, vol. 1, 369–70) he mentions painting on copper with enamel (*colori di vetro*, literally, "glass colors") as a means of producing a work of art that would last far longer than a painting on canvas, panel, or stucco and would be superior to sculpture because it could depict perspective. He describes the technique of an early polychrome plaque as "a picture painted on thick copper covered with white enamel on which it is painted with enamel colours and then put into the fire again and baked" (Richter 1970, vol. 1, 370). His knowledge is hardly surprising, since he lived the last years of his life, from 1516 to 1519, in Amboise in the circle of the newly crowned François 1 (r. 1515–47), a patron of the enamel painters of Limoges. Giorgio Vasari and Benvenuto Cellini also mention enameling, Cellini at some length in his *Trattato dell'oreficeria* (1568), but it is *basse-taille* work, a Tuscan specialty.

The painted enamels of Limoges are most fully discussed by nineteenth-century connoisseur-historians such as Maurice Ardant, Alfred Darcel, Jules Labarte, and Jean-Joseph Marquet de Vasselot and connoisseur-enamel painters such as Louis Bourdery, Édouard Garnier, and Claudius Popelin, who worked in the revived Renaissance tradition to produce enamels of great technical virtuosity. Unfortunately, since these artists and their colleagues did not have sophisticated means of analyzing the Renaissance enamels, they attributed their own practices and materials to their predecessors. Thus the books and articles of the revival period, roughly 1840–1914, present sometimes conflicting technical information, the authors describing the Renaissance procedure in terms of their own techniques. Nevertheless the writings of Popelin (1866, 1881) and Bourdery (1886, 1888, 1897 [with Lachenaud]) do contain much that is accurate and helpful. Among twentieth-century works on enameling in English, Herbert Maryon supplies a very detailed account of enamel painting (1971, 192–98; the first edition was published in 1912), but it is basically a how-to guide for the modern painter.

The use of more sophisticated instruments of observation and analysis in the second half of this century has led to a clearer understanding of what the craft involved. Technical articles such as those by Peter Michaels (1964–65) and Rika Smith, Janice Carlson, and Richard Newman (Smith 1987) have provided valuable information about the medium and the procedure of painted enamels that assists the art historian in questions of attribution, dating, and authenticity.

Although painted enamels seem far removed from cloisonné and champlevé work, in which the metal is a highly visible, if not dominating, element of the design and technique, metal—in this case, copper—was crucial for the production of these pieces. It functioned as the support for the enamel just as fully as canvas is the support for paint, and its preparation as a surface was as exacting. The copper used in such quantity in the ateliers of Limoges was probably from Spanish mines. Due to the proximity of the city to the pilgrimage routes to Santiago de Compostela, there was a great deal of commercial traffic in both directions, and a number of Limoges enamels found their way into Spanish collections and treasuries. There also seems to have been some direct relationship between Limoges and Spain: in 1479 the bishop of Limoges, Jean I Barthon de Montbas, urged the faithful to contribute to the hospice at Roncesvalles in the Pyrenees, five miles from the French border and the famous pass of the same name, and two years later the abbot of Saint-Martial in Limoges wrote to the kings of Spain requesting donations to his hospital (Marquet de Vasselot 1921, 13 n. 2).

In the earliest painted enamels the artist began with a copper plate hammered into a slightly convex surface, which was roughened so that the initial coat of enamel would adhere securely. The front of the plate was covered with a ground color; the earliest enamel painters used a dark color, but white soon became more common. The back was also coated with enamel—residue, failed color batches, or whatever was handy in the workshop; this counter-enamel (contre-émail) retarded oxidation of the copper and minimized the rate of expansion and contraction of the plate during heating and cooling, thus preventing the cracking of the enamel on the front surface. The plate was then fired for the first time to fuse both the ground and the counter-enamel to the copper: the front would be a regular, glazed surface, the back usually uneven and slightly rough due to the inferior quality of the counter-enamel.

Although a few plaques have been found in which the initial design was engraved into the copper itself (suggesting the influence of basse-taille enameling), the enamel painter usually traced the contours of his composition on the ground in black or red enamel; once fired, these slightly raised lines functioned as tiny cloisons to facilitate the separation of colored enamels. They also gave the plaque the appearance of a woodcut, fittingly so, since many of the early enamels were based on prints.

The colors were then applied to the plaque. This presented the enamel painter with a challenge, since the colors changed when fired. It required considerable experience to know what amount of which additives and what degree of grinding would produce the desired color on a finished piece. Whether the enamel was translucent or opaque, whether it had been made with lead or leadless flux, the melting point was the same. The even fusion of the edges of the areas of color on most early painted enamels indicates that, after the ground and underdrawing were fired, all the colors were applied and fired at one time (Michaels 1964–65, 26), although, to minimize bleeding, one color was allowed to dry before the next one was put down. As a wider range of colors, with a wider range of chemical composition and reaction, was adopted, it became necessary to fire certain colors and gold ornamentation at a lower temperature. From the ground color to the final details in gold, a piece might be fired as many as eight or nine times (although hardly the twenty suggested by some of the nineteenth-century authorities).

Often drops of opaque white enamel or beads of translucent colored enamel over tiny pieces of silver foil, called *paillons* or *clinquants* were applied to the plaques to represent jewels or the petals of flowers for a richer decorative effect. Details in black or iron red and gold highlights were added last, by mixing powdered enamel or gold with powdered colorless flux and firing the plaque very briefly, so that the areas would remain sharply delineated instead of fusing with the layers of enamel beneath them.

Since the enamel painter's limited palette did not provide anything approaching a natural flesh tone, it was here that the artists best demonstrated their ingenuity. The early enamel painters worked in opaque white enamel over a dark ground. The thinner the white enamel, the more of the ground showed through, so modeling could be achieved with a range of gray tones. More distinct contour lines or facial features could be produced by removing the white enamel in a process known as *enlevage*, a "lifting" of the enamel with a small tool, often a very fine needle (*enlevage à l'aiguille*) or even the handle of the brush or tool used in the application of the enamel. For the modeling of faces, hands, and nude bodies the Monvaerni Master (active 1461–at least 1485), the earliest identifiable enamel painter of Limoges, relied less on varying thicknesses of white than on the use of "washes"—thin layers of red, gray, or black finely powdered enamel suspended in clear flux, applied over the white ground, and fired. The slightly later Master of the Baltimore and Orléans Triptychs (active c. 1475–c. 1500) used a more complex method that yielded subtle results: over the white ground he put a layer of iron red and then a layer of translucent dark blue, which combination gave the appearance of a lustrous black; over that he applied the opaque white, which he manipulated by additions and *enlevage* to produce a range of violet-gray tones or black lines or dots.

Members of the Pénicaud family and a majority of the early anonymous masters adopted another method for flesh tones. By mixing translucent mulberry with opaque white they obtained a semi-opaque lilac (*violacé*), which they laid over a dark translucent layer, sometimes blue, sometimes mulberry, occasionally black. Subtle modeling was achieved by varying the thickness of the lilac layer, and features and details were delineated by *enlevage*. After this enamel was fired, a final coat of opaque white was applied for subtle highlights; this too was lifted to vary the tone and reveal the black contour lines and dots in the layer of lilac.

By the end of the first quarter of the sixteenth century a number of technical changes had occurred. The use of a clear flux for a counter-enamel seems to have originated in the atelier of Jean 1 Pénicaud (Marquet de Vasselot 1921, 13 n. 3). Painters had begun to put metal foil on the surface of the copper to heighten the brilliance of the translucent colors painted over it. Enameling over foil was precarious: since the enamel did not fuse to the foil, it was attached to its support only at the edges and could thus easily be dislodged (Texier 1842, 265). The use of borax to promote adhesion of the enamel to the foil introduced an additional hazard, which unfortunately could not have been foreseen: the borax absorbed moisture from the atmosphere and decomposed, leaving a fine grayish, humid powder (Marquet de Vasselot 1921, 14).

Conservation scientists have identified the factors that render enamels, particularly these early polychrome works (c. 1470–c. 1530), more fragile than their makers realized. These range from simple damage, such as fractures of the enamel and corrosion of the copper support, to inherent vice common to glass and enamel, crizzling (surface crazing), "weeping," and spalling (chipping or scaling), which are caused by chemical deterioration of the enamel itself when exposed to moisture in the atmosphere.

In the 1530s the painters of Limoges began to work primarily in grisaille on copper plates and vessels. The more elaborate forms—footed bowls, candlesticks, ewers, covers with finials—were often made from several copper forms soldered, pinned, or screwed together. In the case of most ewers and candlesticks the copper form was complete before the enamel decoration was applied; many footed vessels and finials, however, give evidence that the pieces were decorated separately and then assembled. As with the simple plaques, it was necessary for every surface to be covered with enamel, in order to control the rate of expansion of the metal, but the backs and undersides were no longer coated with an inferior-quality counter-enamel. The same ground color, a deep mulberry that appeared black, was applied to every surface, and so-called secondary surfaces were as elaborately decorated as the front or top. Obviously, such objects could not sit on their bases or undersides during firing; three or four small circular holes in the enamel of many of the plates, along the inner rim on the underside, suggest that they rested on pins or saggers in the kiln.

To create a grisaille design, the painter covered an area of fired ground color—the mulberry "black" or a dark blue—with a layer of opaque white enamel thin enough to appear gray because of the darkness of the ground beneath. Contour lines and hatching were produced in the wet enamel by *enlevage*. After another firing, more white was added to create highlights; that too was fired. Flesh tones were still created by the red-wash technique developed by the earliest masters, and other details and decorations were added in gold and an occasional accent of color—iron red was particularly popular for inscriptions. These final elements were fired at lower temperatures to avoid destroying the previously applied layers of enamel and to preserve the crispness of the surface additions. This accounts for the grainy texture of most flesh tones: the red particles were not fired at a temperature high enough to permit them to fuse completely with the colorless flux in which they were suspended. Also, the gold, red, and other colors applied in this way are more fugitive and hence more subject to loss from rubbing or other normal wear. Fortunately a higher concentration of lead, which resisted moisture, in white enamel and flesh tones seems to have spared the grisaille works from the glass-related diseases mentioned above (Smith 1987, 103–4).

In the 1560s the enamel painters rediscovered the polychrome technique, and fewer vessels and more plaques were produced. Some artists continued to paint grisaille enamels, which they then covered with translucent colors; others returned to the procedures of the early sixteenth century, abandoning the dark ground for a bright white, often with large areas covered with foil, to enhance the shimmer of the translucent colors applied over it. This more liberal use of white enamel and changes in the color formulae seem to have increased the stability of the enamels from this phase of painting. A larger palette of colors was now available, but flesh tones were still produced by the red-wash method, one constant in a continually developing technique.

A HISTORY OF PAINTED ENAMELS

The development of painted enameling is still to be traced back to its inception. The application of translucent enamel to an incised metal surface, *basse-taille* or *lavoro di basso-rilievo* (bas-relief work), was a first step toward the painting technique. Although the earliest dated example of translucent enameling is Italian—a chalice made for Pope Nicholas IV between 1288 and 1292 by Guccio di Mannaia (San Francesco, Assisi; Lightbown 1987, 59)—the technique seems to have developed independently and simultaneously in France, culminating in the elegant Parisian enamels of the fourteenth century (although some were probably executed in northern France or Flanders). *Basse-taille* enamels were found in Limoges in

the fifteenth century and may have contributed to the development of the painting technique, but it is the mid-fifteenth-century Low Countries—Flanders, Brabant, and the
duchy of Burgundy—that are usually given the credit for the development of painted
enamels. The so-called *Ara Coeli* medallion (fig. 4) in the Walters Art Gallery, Baltimore
(inv. no. 44.462; Verdier 1967, cat. no. 1), may be the earliest extant example. Executed in
white enamel and gold on a blue ground fused to silver, it is dated about 1425. Verdier
(1967, 2) suggested that the artist was the youngest of the talented Limbourg brothers,
Arnold, who was recorded as a goldsmith in Nijmegen in 1417. The inventory of Philip the
Good, duke of Burgundy (1419–1467), whose court was in Bruges, mentioned other articles "enameled in blue, with figures enameled in white" (Verdier 1961, 27). The technique
traveled to Venice, where blue and white enamel and gold were used to decorate silver,
brass, and copper ewers, basins, and other domestic and liturgical objects (fig. 5).

An exquisitely painted self-portrait medallion of the celebrated illuminator Jean
Fouquet (c. 1420–c. 1481) of Tours, now in the Musée du Louvre, is another mid-fifteenth-
century forerunner of the painted enamel, produced much closer to Limoges. Although
in a different technique from the *Ara Coeli* medallion—it is painted in gold on black
enamel and has no counter-enamel—it is important as a very early example of *enlevage à
l'aiguille*, which would be used by all the enamel painters of Limoges. The first true painted
enamels in Limoges were probably made in 1470/75. A few early examples can be dated by
the circumstances of their donation, such as a reliquary given by Jacques Lallemand to the
abbey of Grandmont in 1479 (now in the church at Saint-Sulpice-les-Feuilles), a gilded

silver statue of Saint Sebastian, incorporating a coat of arms and scenes from the life of the saint in painted enamels.

The first enamel painters may have been descendants of the Limousin enamelers and goldsmiths who had carried on the profitable champlevé industry in earlier centuries. Some of the earliest masters were probably trained as glass painters; their technique shows none of the tentativeness of a beginner in a very exacting medium, and the style of many early enamels echoes that of glass painted in the first half of the century. Other enamel painters began as manuscript illuminators; some, such as the Master of the Baltimore and Orléans Triptychs, seem to have been working in the two mediums simultaneously (see cat. no. 2). There had been a thriving workshop of illuminators at the abbey of Saint-Martial in Limoges itself, but there was less call for the lavish, expensive books after the invention of printing. As Marvin Ross noted (1941, 25), some illuminators turned to hand coloring prints or book illustrations, but surely some others must have become enamel painters.

In other European cities enamelers were required to seek admission into the guilds of goldsmiths and jewelers, where they were treated as lesser artisans and by whose regulations their materials and practices were carefully controlled or restricted. In Limoges, however, coming as they did from the community of painters and being the suppliers of the city's chief export, the enamel painters were powerful enough to maintain a separate guild. The recurrence of surnames throughout the period of productivity is not just a result of the craft being handed down from one generation to another: according to royal edicts issued by Louis XI in the mid-fifteenth century, guild masters could only come from certain families who held the privilege by right of descent.

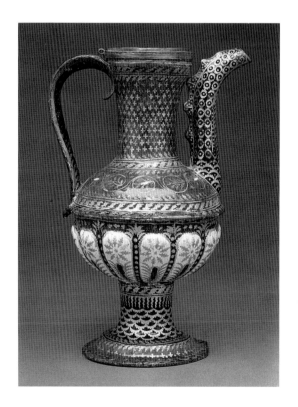

The earliest painted enamels from Limoges, small panels illustrating religious themes, were displayed singly or in triptychs (or an occasional diptych), usually in a setting or frame of wood with strips of copper molding, often decorated with interlacing in relief. The wood might be painted, gilded, or even covered with fabric or painted parchment.

There is no evidence of early enamel plaques being commissioned as stationary church altarpieces—their small size would have precluded that, although some framed groups were later used for this purpose (see comparative examples mentioned in cat. nos. 5–8). It may therefore be assumed that these works provided the focus for private devotions, in

settings as diverse as a small sleeping chamber in a private residence and a guildhall oratory. Their size and durability made them ideal as portable altarpieces. Identifiable coats of arms incorporated in the scenes (see cat. no. 1) reveal that the commissioners were primarily nobles and churchmen, at first local and then farther afield as the objects reached the court and were disseminated throughout France. One of the most important patrons of the enamel painters was the constable of France, Anne de Montmorency (1493–1567) (fig. 6), who probably became acquainted with their work through the offices of his younger brother Philippe, bishop of Limoges from 1517 to 1519.

Although we may now be able to identify a number of patrons of these early artists of Limoges, we cannot identify the artists themselves. In the early twentieth century Jean-Joseph Marquet de Vasselot performed the invaluable service of examining the unsigned and undated plaques of the early Limoges masters. He separated them into at least seven stylistic schools, to which he gave names based on fragments of inscriptions, patrons, major works, or stylistic characteristics, presenting in his many articles and his seminal book, *Les Émaux limousins de la fin du XVe siècle et de la première partie du XVIe* (Paris: Auguste Picard, 1921), the work of such curiously named artists as the Master of the Large Foreheads and the Master of the Violet Mantles.

The exact iconographical sources of the earliest painted plaques are difficult, if not impossible, to trace, but they were surely inspired by countless French books of hours and other illuminated manuscripts and early devotional woodcuts. Abbé Texier's remark (1842, 266) that the early enamels have a great deal of local color in details of clothing and architecture would seem to underscore the fact that the artists were using contemporary regional paintings and prints for their models in depicting the popular devotional scenes, most of them from the lives of Christ and the Virgin Mary.

The first enamel painter to be known by name was Nardon (Léonard) Pénicaud (c. 1470–1541), one of the few early masters who was known also to have been a goldsmith (Verdier 1977, 11). His many civic duties—consul, tax collector, captain of the district guards—demonstrated the high status of the enamel painters in the hierarchy of the city of Limoges. Pénicaud's grandiose, crowded, and unemotional religious plaques were often grouped in polyptychs (fig. 7), their translucent colors lavishly touched with gold details and patterns. Although more than forty of his enamels are extant, he left behind only one signed and dated work, a *Crucifixion* of 1503 (Musée de Cluny, Paris). His late Gothic style changed little during his four decades of activity, but a chronology of sorts can be established thanks to the gradual appearance of Renaissance architectural elements in his work and to a decreasing use of books of hours as models and an increasing use of prints, particularly those by Martin Schongauer.

No matter what the source of their iconography, the early masters tended to transform their models stylistically into a distinctly French expression, paralleling the manuscript illuminations and paintings executed in their own country—although perhaps "echoing"

would be a better choice of words, since the models displayed in the ateliers of Limoges were often several decades old. The work of the early masters, particularly the Monvaerni Master, Nardon Pénicaud, and the Master of the Large Foreheads, reflected a shift from the formal linearity of the Gothic to a marked realism that recognized, and seemed to celebrate, physical imperfections. First encountered in manuscript illumination in the late thirteenth century, during the time of Charles V of France (r. 1364–80), the tendency was partly due to the presence in Paris of more naturalistic Flemish and Dutch painters and partly to a growing fascination with individuality, expressed in the new art of portraiture (Avril 1978, 23–25). It is instructive to note stylistic parallels of early enamel plaques to stained-glass windows of the first half of the fifteenth century, especially obvious in the long, thin, often ugly figures and the distinctive broken drapery folds.

In the 1520s the enamel painters of Limoges began to depict secular themes, inspired by the proliferation of illustrated printed works of classical literature. Such enamels, freed from any religious associations, could be displayed as *objets de vertu* or incorporated into the decorative scheme of an interior. Series of portraits or episodes from ancient mythology or literature in rectangular, round, oval, or diamond formats were suspended from gilded leather hangings or framed in the carved wooden paneling or wainscoting of a *cabinet* or larger room (fig. 8), or, in the case of later two-sided plaques, in the panels of a door (see, for example, a two-sided oval of Ceres and Minerva in the Frick Collection [inv. no. 16.4.30; Verdier 1977, 170–73]). Evidence of this type of display exists for the royal residences of Fontainebleau, Chambord, and the Château de Madrid in the Bois de Boulogne (Texier 1842, 284). The inventory of the possessions of the queen mother Catherine de' Medici, made immediately after her death in 1589, recorded the existence of a "cabinet des émaulx" in the Hôtel de la Reine, Paris, in which thirty-nine oval plaques and thirty-two rectangular portraits, a foot in height, were set into the gilded *boiseries* of the room (Bonnaffé 1874, 14, 155–56, nos. 842–43).

Jean I Pénicaud (c. 1480–after 1541), thought to be Nardon's younger brother, effected a transition from the Gothic to the Renaissance, being the first to copy the prints of Albrecht

Dürer. He is also credited by some as the creator of the grisaille technique, which was quickly adopted by all the enamel painters of Limoges in the early 1530s. The popularity of grisaille enamels was probably due to a combination of cultural, artistic, and practical factors. There was the influence of the elegant sobriety of Spanish fashion and a new solemnity ushered in by the Reformation. Added to this was the artistic impetus of relief sculpture of marble and stucco, especially as practiced by Italian artists and their French followers working at Fontainebleau and other châteaux; the grisaille technique in painting (including painting on enamels) was in imitation of this. Finally, it should be noted that by this time the enamel painters were working almost exclusively from black-and-white woodcuts and engravings, which may have prompted an imitation of the techniques and effects of printmaking. To be sure, the development of the grisaille technique did coincide with stylistic changes. Grisaille in itself was nothing new: manuscripts in grisaille had been commissioned by the kings of France and the dukes of Berry and Burgundy as early as the mid-fourteenth century and throughout the fifteenth (Evans 1969, 273). But the models for the enamel painters at this period were almost exclusively German woodcuts and engravings, and it is likely that the appearance of the prints encouraged the adoption of similar stylistic elements, among them strong contour lines, hatching and cross-hatching for shading, and white areas for highlights. These features were constantly present, even though each master of grisaille developed a distinctive style: the intensely white, monumental figures of Jean II Pénicaud and the Leonardesque *sfumato* of Jean III, the crisp and heavily outlined compositions of Pierre Reymond and Martin Didier Pape (whose techniques were most akin to that of the printmakers), the nervous, calligraphic lines and diaphanous whites of Master KIP and Jean Miette, the elegant, sculptural forms of Léonard Limousin and Pierre Courteys, and the decorative, highly finished exuberance of Jean de Court.

A shift to Old Testament imagery occurred at the same time as grisaille enamel achieved popularity. This has been ascribed to the sobering influence of the Counter-Reformation and the growing power of the Inquisition, with its emphasis on a vengeful God. We must look for reasons not in the ateliers of the enamel painters, however, but in the models they chose to copy, which in this case were the popular *Bibles moralisées*. These books, originally "a form of illustrated biblical exegesis, first conceived by religious scholars in the service of the royal family of France, and for the use of the latter, during the first half of the 13th century" (Avril 1978, cat. no. IX), thanks to the printing press, were now available to all. They depicted scenes from the Bible, primarily the Old Testament, accompanied not by biblical verses but by descriptive and moralizing texts. They reflected the Protestant view—even where Protestantism was only barely tolerated—that the Old Testament was in itself as important a revelation of God as the New Testament, not just a prefiguration of it (Panofsky 1969, 10).

The chief source for Old Testament iconography was the engraved work of Bernard Salomon (c. 1508–after 1561). Born in Lyons, Salomon may have gone to Paris for his training but had returned to his native city by 1540. From about 1546 onward he worked exclusively for the printing house of Jean de Tournes, forming an atelier that was maintained not by him but by the publisher. Except for a remarkably beautiful series of engravings for an edition of Ovid's *Metamorphoses* (1557), Salomon produced very little other than illustrations for *Bibles moralisées* (figs. 27–29, 33–34, 39). His engravings for Claude Paradin's *Quadrins historiques de la Bible* (1553, expanded in 1555) and *Figures du nouveau Testament* (1556)—the same illustrations later used by de Tournes in Latin and French editions of the Bible (Brun 1930, 153–56)—were models for not only the enamel painters but for designers of tapestries and ceramics, particularly the faience of Lyons (see cat. no. 23), which rivaled Italian maiolica (Rondot 1897, 21–23, 51, 66–77; Damiron 1926, 23–26).

It is difficult to separate completely the styles of the enamel painters from those of their models. As they began to copy the engravings of Marcantonio Raimondi and other Italian masters after paintings and drawings by Raphael and his school, the artists of Limoges began to show evidence of a classical purity of form and composition. This was especially true of the work of Léonard Limousin and Pierre Courteys (cat. nos. 20–22), whose grisaille figures are endowed with the substantial presence of bas-relief sculpture.

With the creation of plates and vessels painted in grisaille enamel came the establishment of large ateliers to meet the demand of a new group of patrons, the wealthy middle class. The number of these enamel objects now extant and the repetition of the decorative schemes suggest that the enamels were painted not only on commission but also to create stock for ready sales. Occasionally a piece would be customized by the addition of a coat of arms, and certain unique objects—unique by reason of exceptional quality or unusual subject matter (such as cat. nos. 9–10)—were surely created upon request. The most spectacular example was a group of grisaille objects commissioned from the prolific Pierre Reymond by the merchant Linhard Tucher of Nuremberg (Verdier 1967, 243, fig. 24; DuBon 1980, 5, fig. 2). Although the subjects depicted on these pieces are not unique in Reymond's work, the skill of the painting suggests the hand of the master himself, and the copper forms for the ewers were crafted by the celebrated German goldsmith Wenzel Jamnitzer, who later made mounts for some of the finished vessels (see the biography of

Pierre Reymond for more information on the Tucher commission). Other examples of enamels mounted in gold and gilded silver, although far less extravagant than the Tucher group, show the esteem with which Limoges work was regarded. A container for the consecrated Host was made by the Strasbourg goldsmith Abraham Berner (Musée des Arts Décoratifs, Strasbourg; Haug 1978, cat. no. 8), its sides four enamel plaques illustrating scenes from the Passion of Christ mounted in gold, an unusual instance of painted enamels used for a liturgical object (although the sides were probably originally made as individual plaques).

For those not wealthy enough to hire the finest goldsmith in Europe to make a copper vessel, copper forms were probably created in the enamel ateliers of Limoges, which were certainly large enough to encompass a metalsmith or two. The differences in form between ewers produced at different workshops, for example, suggest that if each atelier did not have its resident smith, at least it had its own supplier.

Although these plates and vessels are referred to as "tableware," there is no evidence that they were ever used for the service of food (individual plates were not yet common). At her château at Nérac in 1555 Catherine de' Medici had a buffet group of sixty-five enamels (Havard 1896, 307), which were probably arranged on the tops and lower shelves of case furniture, particularly *crédences*, elaborately carved with many of the same decorative motifs found on the enamels. Inventories of 1556 and 1568 of the contents of Anne de Montmorency's Parisian residence in rue Sainte-Avoye (or rue du Temple) list thirty-four painted enamel ewers, ewer stands, tazzas, covered cups, salts, and spoons from Limoges, some displayed on shelves in the "Cabinet du Roi," others in the library with *objets de vertu* of silver, coral, alabaster, mother-of-pearl, Venetian glass, and Palissy and Saint-Porchaire earthenware (Mirot 1918–19, 365–69). In other words, the enamels were included among their owners' treasures, not their household items.

Among the most prized of all painted enamels, then and now, were the works of Léonard Limousin (c. 1505–1575/77). Unlike the other enamel painters, who did not stray far from their city, Limousin spent much of his career at court at Fontainebleau. There is an apocryphal story that Léonard was given his surname to distinguish him from the other celebrated "Léonard" at court, Leonardo da Vinci (Texier 1842, 275), but since Limousin was about fourteen when Leonardo died in 1519 and did not even go to court until the mid-1530s, it is unlikely that the two were competitors for the king's attention. Arriving at court during the reign of François I in the entourage of his patron, Jean de Langeac, bishop of Limoges and a royal councilor, Limousin was appointed *peintre émailleur et valet de chambre du Roi* by Henri II (r. 1547–59) in 1548 and subsequently served François II

(r. 1559–60) and Charles IX (r. 1560–74). He produced striking polychrome portraits (more than 130 are extant) of monarchs and courtiers (fig. 6), often derived from the "créons" (*crayons*, or pencil drawings) by François Clouet and his school, as well as objects for amusement, such as a backgammon board of 1537 and, in 1552, a fountain for the mistress of Henri II, Diane de Poitiers. Limousin's atelier turned out more than a thousand plaques, plates, and vessels in polychrome and grisaille.

During his early career Limousin, who may have been apprenticed to Nardon and Jean I Pénicaud, copied prints by Dürer and other German artists. Once at Fontainebleau, however, influenced by the taste of his sovereign, he began to turn more and more to the paintings and prints of Italian masters of the late Renaissance and the French and Italian mannerists, particularly those working in the royal château itself, Rosso Fiorentino, Primaticcio, and Francesco Pellegrino. There is a tradition (recorded in Guilbert 1731, 80, 87 n.) that Limousin executed enamels to be integrated into Rosso's famous decorative ensemble of the Galerie de François I at Fontainebleau, but no record or trace of these remains (although there are a number of oval, round, and rectangular stucco surrounds that are the right size to have enclosed enamels). Limousin did in fact collaborate with Niccolò dell'Abbate in 1552–53 on an altarpiece for the Sainte-Chapelle in Paris, for which Limousin executed two reredos of the Crucifixion and Resurrection. Popelin (1881, 115) records the existence of drawings after Niccolò that were pricked for transfer to an enamel by Léonard Limousin; this may have been the Sainte-Chapelle commission.

What set Limousin apart from the other enamel painters was not so much his skill, which was considerable, as his originality. He was also an engraver and painter and invented (although perhaps guided by literary conceits supplied to him) a number of his own enamel compositions, particularly a delightful series of "triumphs" in which kings, queens, courtiers, and churchmen, thinly disguised as gods, goddesses, or allegorical figures, ride in elaborate chariots. The most intriguing of them, surely, is the *Triumph of the Eucharist and of the Catholic Faith* (fig. 9), which immortalizes the virulently Catholic Guise family crushing Protestant heretics (Frick Collection, New York, inv. no. 16.4.22; Verdier 1977, 121–29).

Because of his absence from Limoges, Limousin's work was outside the mainstream of painted enamel production in style and iconography. Once at court he abandoned the fashionable grisaille being produced in his native city and returned to the polychrome technique, even varying his palette from the rich, saturated dark tones of his portraits to a nearly pastel effect in his scenes—perhaps in response to the work of the Italian painters— which he achieved by a skillful use of opaque white enamel. But while he continued to

FIGURE 9

Léonard Limousin,
France (Limoges),
c. 1505–1575/77,
*The Triumph of the
Eucharist and of the
Catholic Faith*, c. 1561,
polychrome enamel
and gold on copper,
19.2 x 25.1 cm (7 9/16 x
9 7/8 in.), The Frick
Collection, New York.

produce primarily portraits, religious scenes, and allegories, his colleagues in Limoges were
developing new iconographical programs.

One of the most prevalent themes in Limoges was the cycle of Labors or Occupations
of the Months (cat. nos. 13–17, 25, 29–40). From antiquity the four seasons and twelve
months had been symbolized in literature and art by the signs of the zodiac, pagan divini-
ties, ages of man, allegorical figures, occupations appropriate to the time of year, or a combination of two or more of these. While writings of the early Christian period mentioned
both allegories and monthly occupations (Marle 1932, vol. 1, 377), the "labors," often in
conjunction with astrological signs, began to dominate. The zodiac represented the celestial
realm; the labors or festivals, the mundane.

The twelve occupations or labors were largely that: the tasks of agriculture and animal
husbandry, the cycle of planting and harvesting, raising and slaughtering, that formed the
unvarying calendar of every peasant's days and directly or indirectly regulated the lives of
the rest of the population. Even scenes of feasting, sitting by the fire, and merrymaking
reflected the peasant's life: the forced inactivity of the winter months and the ancient, originally pagan, festivals of spring.

In France the Labors of the Months began to appear with frequency in the twelfth
century, and they soon became a regular feature of medieval liturgical manuscripts. They

embellished the calendar pages of breviaries, psalters, and books of hours, from the marginalia of the mid-fourteenth-century Belleville Breviary (Bibliothèque Nationale, Paris, Ms. Lat. 10483–10484) to the magnificent full pages of the *Très Riches Heures* of the duc de Berry (1413–16; Musée Condé, Chantilly), in which the Limbourg brothers and Jean Coulombe took obvious advantage of the theme to paint landscapes. In the early sixteenth century Jean Bourdichon represented the labors as large single figures in the *Missel de Tours* (1506/11; Bibliothèque Nationale, Paris, Ms. Lat. 886). The labors also appeared in sculpture, frescoes, mosaics, and pavements in the great Romanesque and Gothic cathedrals and baptisteries of France and Italy: Autun, Vezelay, Sens, Saint-Denis in Paris, Senlis, Chartres, Strasbourg, Amiens, Rheims, Padua, Verona, Cremona, Ferrara, Modena, Parma, Lucca, Pisa, Arezzo, and San Marco in Venice. Van Marle (1932, vol. 1, 390) proposed their first appearance outside a religious context to be on the sides of a fountain in Perugia carved by Nicola Pisano (finished in 1278); although biblical scenes are also featured among those carvings, the fountain was a secular monument.

By the fifteenth century the most frequently illustrated monthly occupations in French manuscripts were as follows: January, feasting; February, warming by the fire; March, pruning vines (fig. 10); April, gathering flowers; May, riding; June, mowing; July, reaping; August, threshing; September, treading grapes; October, sowing; November, tending swine; December, killing swine. The labors themselves varied slightly from place to place—harvest scenes appeared earlier in southern cycles, for example, reflecting the actual calendar of the region. During the sixteenth century the iconography was standardized by the appearance of two series of engravings of the Labors of the Months by Étienne Delaune, one undated but probably about 1561 (figs. 42–43; Robert-Dumesnil 1865, vol. 9, 73–78, nos. 225–36; see cat. nos. 29–40), the other engraved in 1568 (fig. 25; Robert-Dumesnil 1865, vol. 9, 58–61, nos. 185–96). These and an unidentified series used as a model as early as 1559 (see cat. nos. 13–16, 25), perhaps an adaptation of the woodcuts illustrating the *Compost et kalendrier des bergères* (figs. 24, 36; Paris: Guy Marchant, 1499), were the primary sources for the enamel painters of Limoges. They produced sets of twelve plaques or plates painted with the occupation and zodiac sign for each month (cat. nos. 29–40), as well as sets of enamels representing the four seasons, either as activities or personifications. The painted enamels and some tapestries of the same period, such as a set from Brussels, now in the Kunsthistorisches Museum, Vienna (Imperial collection, inv. no. ıx), signaled the last burst of popularity for this theme, which gradually disappeared from European art, paralleling the decreasing importance of the agrarian way of life it celebrated, especially among those who commissioned or purchased works of art.

The grotesques, rinceaux, arabesques, and strapwork that twist around the rims and undersides of enameled vessels were part of a pan-European Renaissance phenomenon. These inventive and bizarre motifs were inspired by the profusion of painted ornamentation on ancient Roman architectural remains, especially the famous Domus Aurea, the emperor Nero's "Golden House," unearthed around 1500 and visited by every artist who came to Rome. Because the complex was by then below ground level and required candles and torches for light, it was much like visiting a grotto, hence the word *grotesques* from the Italian *grotteschi*. The enormously popular decorative style, consisting of interlacings of mythical and hybrid beings, architectural and vegetal caprices, drapery and arabesques, was diffused throughout Europe in prints and pattern books, first by the Italians, particularly Zoan Andrea of Mantua, Nicoletto da Modena, Giovanni Antonio da Brescia, Enea Vico, and Giovanni da Udine, later by Antonio Fantuzzi, Pierre Milan, and Bernard Salomon recording the inventions of Rosso and his assistant at Fontainebleau, Domenico Ricoveri (see Verdier 1967, xii–xiv, for a full discussion of the decorative sources). After the style had faded in Italy, it continued throughout the sixteenth century in France, Germany, and the Netherlands (Dacos 1969, 95–97). Although national characteristics did creep in— the German and Netherlandish grotesques are robust and florid, the French sinuous and elegant—the motifs are surprisingly homogeneous (Guilmard 1880–81; Berliner 1925–26). The same odd beasts appear on the borders of French enamels, Italian maiolica, German metalwork, and Flemish tapestries.

Inevitably found in combination with the grotesques on painted enamels are the strapwork motifs that often form their surrounds. Strapwork, which resembles curled strips of leather (and is appropriately called *cuir bouilli*, boiled leather, in French), was possibly invented by Rosso for the stucco friezes in the Galerie de François I. Disseminated through the prints of René Boyvin, Fantuzzi, and Milan, Rosso's designs were popular in France, and even more so in Germany and the Netherlands, for decorative motifs for engravings, furniture, and metalwork. Strapwork is found on the rims and undersides of nearly every grisaille enamel painted in Limoges.

The enamel painters often drew from or were inspired by the *maîtres ornemanistes* of their own country, particularly Boyvin (1530–after 1576), Étienne Delaune (1518/19–1583), and Jacques Androuet du Cerceau the elder (c. 1520–c. 1584). Du Cerceau published a number of books of designs that were influential on French decorative arts of the sixteenth century (Geymüller 1887, 136–207; Lieure 1927, 98–99). For the enamel painters none was more important than the *Petits Grotesques* (fig. 11), published in Orléans in 1550 (re-engraved for an edition of 1562), with designs based partly on Vico's work and partly on his own ideas, and the "grands grotesques" (fig. 21) in the *Livre de grotesques* of 1556 (Paris: André Wechel), which presents du Cerceau's designs and other compositions taken from Fontainebleau and Catherine de' Medici's château of Monceaux-sur-Provins, these probably the inventions of Primaticcio, decorator of the former building and architect of the latter (Geymüller 1887, 192).

Delaune and Boyvin, who both served the royal court, were trained as goldsmiths and were distinguished for the purity of line in their engravings. They published hundreds of prints, both ornamentation and figural compositions, many of which were used as models at Limoges, such as Delaune's two series of the Labors of the Months mentioned above. Some of the grotesque creatures painted on the wares of certain ateliers are adapted from Delaune's engraved ornament (see DuBon 1980 for a detailed analysis of the motifs on a platter by Jean de Court). Boyvin's engravings (fig. 12) are a valuable echo, if not record, of Rosso's unexecuted decorative work, especially his designs for silver, which display combinations of grotesques and strapwork similar to those on the enamels.

In the case of the painted enamels of Limoges, unless a decorative motif is taken exactly from a printed source, it is usually futile to seek to identify the precise source of this type of ornamentation. First of all, the repertoire of forms was too widely disseminated, and the ateliers of Limoges had a good supply of patterns from all over Europe. Secondly, the enamel painters did not always slavishly imitate the work of others; they were, after all, artists in their own right, capable of creating and adapting decorative motifs to suit their unique needs.

By 1560, after decades of looking elsewhere for inspiration, the majority of the enamel painters in Limoges had abandoned Raphael for the nearby school of Fontainebleau, finally catching up with Léonard Limousin, who was working after designs by Primaticcio as early as 1545 (Gébelin 1942, 69). The elongated twisting figures, expressive refinement, and decorative virtuosity of Pierre Courteys, Jean Miette, Jean de Court, and Jean III Pénicaud from 1560 onward were derived from the mannerism of the Italians called to transform Fontainebleau from a hunting lodge to a royal palace, especially the Bolognese Primaticcio, who worked there until 1570. Although some sources claim that Rosso and Primaticcio furnished cartoons to the enamel painters (Labarte 1875, 180), this is probably only true for Léonard Limousin and perhaps Jean de Court, who came to court to serve Charles IX as *peintre du roi*. When the Italian mannerist influence reached the majority of the artists in Limoges, it was most likely third-hand, in the form of prints after French artists influenced by the Italians, such as the painters Jean Cousin *père* and Antoine Caron and the sculptors Jean Goujon and Germain Pilon. The artist most to be credited with the introduction of the mannerist style into Limoges is Bernard Salomon, whose style in his *Bible moralisée* engravings was one of exaggerated elegance and mannered form and movement, clearly influenced by Primaticcio; his compositions were well balanced, his line faultless.

FIGURE 12

René Boyvin, France, 1530–after 1576, *Two Ornamental Jars*, mid-sixteenth century, engraving, 14 x 14.6 cm (5 ½ x 5 ¾ in.), Los Angeles County Museum of Art, Mary Stansbury Ruiz Collection.

Although they continued producing grisaille enamels for several decades more, the masters of Limoges returned to a polychrome style in the early 1560s. This coincided with and was probably influenced by the first "magnificences," the lavish festivals held at court and throughout the realm by the newly widowed Catherine de' Medici on behalf of her young son, François II, to contradict rumors of ruin and promote policies of peace and moderation (Strong 1984, 99–100). The enamel painters themselves contributed to the decorations for at least one of these events—the ceremonial entry of Catherine and her second son, Charles IX, into Bordeaux in 1564 (Bourdery 1895, clxvii). Léonard Limousin took several members of his family, Jean Miette, and Jean III Pénicaud to work as painters on the elaborate ephemera erected for the occasion.

Carrying on the same festive spirit, the enamels of Pierre and Martial Courteys, Jean and Susanne de Court (the latter one of the two recorded female enamel painters in Limoges) scintillate with foil and translucent enamel, celebrating secular, mainly mythological, scenes and figures lifted from the pageantry of the age. Later generations of the families, particularly a group of Limousins, including Léonard's son and grandson, François I and II, and his nephew, Léonard II, and others—two Jeans and a Joseph—whose relationship to Léonard is less clear (Verdier 1967, xxii–xxiii), continued to produce plaques, plates, and vessels of decreasing quality to increasing public indifference. The wealthy were turning their attention to metalwork and ceramics, particularly the highly prized examples of imported oriental porcelain. Few coats of arms or devices of the monarchs or the nobility appear on enamels painted after 1600, and purely functional *objets de luxe* began to dominate the production of the ateliers—mirror backs, candlesticks, saltcellars, jewelry—heralding the gradual decline of painted enamels into the trivial, such as pilgrim badges and hat ornaments. The celebrated ceramist and eccentric Bernard Palissy (c. 1510–c. 1590), who had worked for many of the same patrons as the enamel painters, especially Catherine de' Medici and Anne de Montmorency, commented sympathetically on the declining industry in his *Discours admirable de la nature des eaux et fontaines* of 1580 (cited in Garnier 1886, 501–2):

> There are some things that are contaminated and scorned because they are too common. Have you seen what has happened to the enamelers of Limoges....Their art has become so cheap that they can barely make a living from the prices they charge for their work. I am sure I saw hat badges for three *sous* a dozen—hat badges so well made, their enamel so well fused to the copper that no painting could be as attractive. And this has happened not once but a thousand times, not just with these hat badges but with ewers, saltcellars, and all the other types of vessels and plaques they ventured to make: a situation to be greatly regretted.

A last spark was struck in the seventeenth century by the Laudin family, who turned out dozens of sets of imperial plaques (see cat. no. 17 for a discussion of this iconography) and cheap copper vessels with small, beautifully painted grisaille disks surrounded by pedestrian and often garish decorative motifs (cat. no. 44). A fine small plaque by Jacques I Laudin depicting Louis XIV as the "Roi Soleil" driving the chariot of Apollo (ex-collection earl of Rosebery; sold Sotheby Parke Bernet, Mentmore Towers, May 20 [day 3], 1977, lot 1159) may even be superior in style and composition to Léonard Limousin's triumphal groups, but the technique has lost the depth and sparkle that made the earlier enamels more than flat painted surfaces. The later artists painted on enamel rather than in enamel.

The art of enamel painting never died (and neither, apparently, did some of the families—the Nouailher are recorded from 1503 to 1804 [Havard 1896, 302]), although the center of production shifted farther north. A group working at Blois evolved into an early school of miniaturists. Jean Toutin (1578–1644) is credited with perfecting the technique of painting on gold with enamel colors, the genesis of the extravagant enamel decoration of seventeenth-, eighteenth-, and nineteenth-century boxes and watchcases.

For more than two hundred years after the demand for them had evaporated, most painted enamels must have remained—perhaps on view, perhaps in a chest or cabinet—in the households for which they were originally acquired, except for a few that were known to have been destroyed for their copper content. They were certainly not on the art market during that time; records of sales and auctions do not often mention them before the mid-nineteenth century. France had been experiencing a medieval revival since the beginning of that century, in large part due to the immensely popular novels by Victor Hugo, particularly *Notre Dame de Paris* (1831); this was soon followed by a Renaissance revival of equal romanticism. Some degree of credit must be given to Alexandre Lenoir, the founder of the Musée des Monuments Français, who assembled a striking display of the huge enamel plaques painted by Pierre Courteys for the facade of François I's Château de Madrid and the statue of Diane de Poitiers from the fountain at her château of Anet (Somers Cocks 1980, 44). A demand arose for artifacts from that period of French history. Thanks to the durability of the enamels, especially in contrast to ceramics and textiles, there was an immense cache of authentic material waiting to be acquired and a large group of French and English collectors ready to acquire it. Shipments arrived in the sale rooms of Paris from châteaux all over France.

That most of the painted enamels now extant passed through the Paris art market is attested by the fact that most of their metal frames are modern, supplied sometime after the middle of the nineteenth century, especially by the Parisian dealer-restorer Corplet or by Alfred André. The latter made "hot repairs," that is, he repainted damaged or shattered areas and fired them at a temperature low enough to fuse the enamel without disturbing the original work. Because of their susceptibility to chipping, shattering, and cracking most painted enamels were in need of repair in the nineteenth or early twentieth century, and André is conjectured to have worked on the majority of the enamels that passed through Paris between 1870 and 1910 (Marquet de Vasselot 1921, 15 and n. 2).

Should the real thing not be available in sufficient quantity to supply the demand, artisans learned to duplicate and even improve upon the sixteenth-century techniques, beginning as early as 1840 to produce new compositions, "homages," and forgeries (see a contemporary account of the revival of enameling by one of its ablest practitioners in Falize 1893–94).

In 1848 Théophile Gautier isolated himself and composed a group of poems that he later published (1852) under the title *Émaux et camées* (Enamels and cameos). The poems were examples of "pure art"—cold, delicate, "fashioned and polished like jewels set to last forever" (Snell 1982, 38). This captures precisely the attitude of those who brought about the revival of enameling: they produced objects of extraordinary technical virtuosity whose very perfection repelled. The new enamel painters cannot be blamed for this; they were part of a culture that preferred to keep its Valois past preserved under a bell jar. It prized the artifacts of that era and aped the outward forms without at all comprehending the empowering spirit.

The stunningly beautiful modern enamels were prominently featured at the many international expositions of the later nineteenth and early twentieth centuries. One talented practitioner was Théophile Soyer (fig. 13), who first exhibited his work at the Paris Salon of 1870 and went on to win a silver medal at the *Exposition universelle* of 1889. Soyer, whose wife, Lucie Dejoux, was also an enamel painter, progressed from copies of contemporary paintings through a historicizing phase to original compositions. Louis Dalpayrat (1844–1910) was one of the greatest of the historicizing painters. His work was popular in England, where he lectured at the Victoria and Albert Museum in 1885.

Large groups of Renaissance enamels were on view in every exhibition dedicated to the "applied arts" in London from the middle of the nineteenth century onward; in 1874 and 1897 special exhibitions, at the South Kensington Museum (now the Victoria and Albert Museum) and the Burlington Fine Arts Club, respectively, were devoted solely to enamels. Both Renaissance and modern enamels, the latter by such as the Apoils—husband and wife—A.-T. Gobert, Charles Lepec, and Alfred Meyer (who used the technique to paint a Sioux chief!), were prominently featured in the international expositions held in Paris in the later nineteenth century. One of our most informative sources on nineteenth-century technique, the enamel painter Claudius Popelin, not only wrote about Renaissance enamels, he taught the art and wrote a treatise—unfinished at his death—on the subject (Labarte 1875, 236; Falize 1893–94, 421).

An interesting footnote testifying to the popularity of the painted enamels of Limoges is provided by a number of nineteenth-century ceramic imitations, some of which can be quite convincing. The Sèvres manufactory began making replicas as early as the 1850s. These were invariably decorated in grisaille, making use of Renaissance motifs such as strapwork, grotesques, and portraits and scenes from classical antiquity. The shapes were usually distinctively nineteenth-century, however, and some were even mounted in silver gilt or gilt bronze, such as a garniture of two porcelain vases and a bowl made in Paris in the third quarter of the nineteenth century (sold Sotheby Parke Bernet, New York, November 4–5, 1983, lot 100). Another superb example is a ewer and stand (nonfunctional, since they are of a piece) made by the Gibus & Margaine factory of Limoges sometime between 1850 and 1870, now in the Musée Dubouché, Limoges (inv. no. 4604). The English also turned out creditable ceramic versions of Limoges enamels at the Minton factory in Stoke-on-Trent; a handsome Minton covered cup painted about 1857 by S. Lawton is in the Victoria and Albert Museum (inv. no. 4773+A-1858).

Painted enamels were themselves the subjects of paintings, such as a framed polychrome plaque (Jean de Court's *Marguerite de France as Minerva* of 1555, now in the Wallace Collection) and a grisaille ewer depicted in *Curiosités* of 1868 by Antoine Vollon (Musée d'Orsay, Paris, inv. no. RF117).

MODERN COLLECTIONS OF THE PAINTED ENAMELS OF LIMOGES

The important collections of Limoges enamels are found today in a dozen museums: the Musée du Louvre and Musée de Cluny in Paris, the Musée de la Renaissance in Écouen, and the Musée Municipal of Limoges; the British Museum, Victoria and Albert Museum, and Wallace Collection in London; the Hermitage Museum in Saint Petersburg; and, in the United States, the Frick Collection and Metropolitan Museum of Art in New York, the Walters Art Gallery in Baltimore, and the Taft Museum in Cincinnati. The sources of their holdings were the great private collections of Limoges enamels assembled in the nineteenth century—to name only a few, Debruge-Duménil, Fountaine, Seillière, Spitzer, Soltykoff, a half dozen Rothschilds, Basilewsky (from which came the core of the Hermitage collection), and Du Sommerard (the collector of many of the enamels now at Cluny and Écouen).

The Louvre was appropriately one of the earliest institutional collectors of the painted enamels. To a nucleus of pieces commissioned by the French monarchs during the Renaissance were added the Durand and Révoil collections, in 1825 and 1828, respectively, by direct order of Charles X. These were supplemented by legacies from the Sauvageot, Davillier, Gatteaux, and Leroux families.

The Victoria and Albert Museum was not far behind, buying heavily from every major sale between 1850 and 1880, and then relying on the largesse of connoisseur George Salting, who at his death in 1909 left them three cases of painted enamels from the atelier of the Pénicaud onward (Mitchell 1911, 77; Somers Cocks 1980, 45).

The perpetuation of collecting in the style of a Renaissance prince by Baron Ferdinand de Rothschild added a superb collection of painted enamels to the holdings of the British Museum as part of the Waddesdon Bequest of 1898. Sir Richard Wallace was responsible for adding Limoges enamels to the collection bequeathed to him in 1871 by his father, the marquess of Hertford; most of them were from the collection of the comte de Nieuwer-kerke, which Wallace purchased in the same year.

The most important American collections in the nineteenth and early twentieth centuries were private, those assembled by J. Pierpont Morgan, whose selection of objects was usually based on their importance as historical artifacts; Charles Phelps Taft and his wife, Anna Sinton Taft; and the connoisseur Henry Walters—the latter two collections still intact in the institutions endowed by them. Many of the enamels acquired by Henry Clay Frick from 1915 onward were from Morgan's estate, and much of the rest of Morgan's collection was eventually absorbed by a number of American museums, including the Los Angeles County Museum of Art (cat. nos. 10, 19, 23, 24, 25, 29–40). The enamels now in Los Angeles were among a large number purchased from Morgan's collection and other sources by William Randolph Hearst. A group was selected for the museum in 1948–51 from Hearst's holdings by William R. Valentiner, codirector (with James H. Breasted, Jr.) from 1946 to 1950 and adviser thereafter.

*

COLOR PLATES

THE MONVAERNI
MASTER

Plaque:
The Crucifixion
c. 1475

Cat. no. 1

THE MASTER
OF THE BALTIMORE
AND ORLÉANS
TRIPTYCHS

Plaque:
The Nativity and
Annunciation to the
Shepherds
c. 1480/90

Cat. no. 2

THE MASTER
OF THE AENEID

Plaque:
The Discovery of the
Murder of Polydorus
1525/30

Cat. no. 3

THE MASTER
OF THE AENEID

Plaque:
Naval Games in Honor
of Anchises
1525/30

Cat. no. 4

PIERRE REYMOND

Tazza:
Scene from the Book
of Proverbs
c. 1558

Cat. no. 10

PIERRE REYMOND

Four plaques:
Scenes from the Passion
of Christ
1535/40

Cat. nos. 5–8

PIERRE REYMOND

Ewer stand:
Scenes from the Book
of Genesis
c. 1560

Cat. no. 12

PIERRE COURTEYS

Plaque:
An Old Woman
Narrating the Story of
Psyche
c. 1560

Cat. no. 20

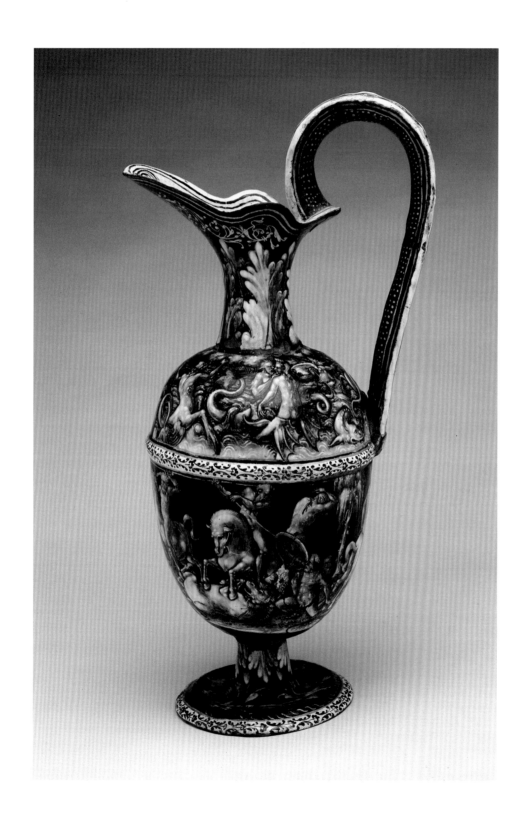

JEAN DE COURT

Oval platter:
The Rape of Europa
c. 1565/75

Cat. no. 28

MARTIAL COURTEYS

Two plates:
The Labors of the Months
(*August* and *December*)
c. 1565/75

Cat. nos. 36 and 40

MARTIAL COURTEYS

Oval platter:
The Death of Ananias
c. 1580

Cat. no. 41

ANONYMOUS
MASTER

Armorial plaques
Seventeenth century

Cat. nos. 42 and 43

ANONYMOUS
MAKER

Plaque:
Portrait of a Woman
Called the Duchesse de
Montpensier
Late nineteenth century

Cat. no. 45

A CATALOGUE OF

THE COLLECTION OF THE PAINTED ENAMELS OF LIMOGES

IN THE LOS ANGELES COUNTY MUSEUM OF ART

Active 1461–at least 1485

T HE NAME OF this anonymous master is derived from a fragment of an inscription on the sword of a figure of Saint Catherine in a triptych now in the Taft Museum, Cincinnati (inv. no. 1931.268; Taft 1958, cat. no. 176). The inscription was at first believed to be a signature (Petit 1843, cat. no. 123), then simply an undecipherable inscription (Laborde 1853, 131), later a reference to a patron—one of two late fifteenth-century bishops of Limoges named Jean Barthon de Montbas, pronounced "Monva" in local dialect (Mitchell 1910, 37–39)—and finally an anagram for the name of another enamel painter, "M. Novalher," or "Martial Nouailher," whose existence later proved to be due to the misreading of a document (Marquet de Vasselot 1921, 25–26). These varying views provoked a heated controversy, first among French experts, then with English scholars joining in, producing a lively exchange of staggeringly erudite letters in the *Burlington Magazine* of 1910–11 (see Marquet de Vasselot 1921, 19–26, for a summary of the various points of view). The matter has never been satisfactorily decided, but the fact that nearly 150 years of archival research have yielded not one mention of the name Monvaerni suggests that the inscription is not the signature of an enamel painter.

More than fifty plaques, all religious in subject, have been attributed to this master, whose blunt, realistic style is very distinctive. He is judged by most scholars to be lacking in grace, especially when compared with the elegance of the Gothic illuminators, but these critics have neglected to observe that French painting was itself becoming far more realistic in the fifteenth century, perhaps influenced by Flemish art, with which it so closely coexisted. Alfred Darcel (1883, 97) suggested that the "ugliness" of the art in this period reflected the suffering during the reigns of Charles VI (r. 1380–1422) and Charles VII (r. 1422–61).

The Monvaerni Master made the most of the small palette of colors available to the early enamel painters, creating a range of tones from a deep, barely translucent hue to a thin wash of color achieved by mixing powdered enamel with varying quantities of clear frit. His work is characterized by a far from subtle and sometimes awkward juxtaposition of these colors and by his opaque white flesh tones modeled with applications of gray and red washes.

The earliest of this artist's enamels, most of which are scenes from the Passion of Christ, demonstrate his most pronounced realism. The compositions seem to have been inspired by or even partially copied from a variety of sources: French and Flemish panel paintings and illuminated manuscripts and German prints (Marie-Madeleine Gauthier [1972, 421] wrote of possible Rhenish models), with noticeable Italianate characteristics that were present in French and Flemish art of the period. After at least twenty panels in this style, the master began to display more refinement, as evidenced by the elongation of figures, delicacy of facial features, and a more convincing landscape.

Although O. M. Dalton (1912, 63) likened the artist's use of thick layers of enamel and black outlines to a glass painter's technique, the probability that the Monvaerni Master was originally an illuminator is supported by his ability to depict perspective and his heavy reliance on painted contours rather than those created by *enlevage*. His style is very similar to that of the illuminator of a late fifteenth-century French book of hours, of which a leaf, depicting saints and angels (fig. 14), is now in the Los Angeles County Museum of Art (inv. no. M.53.9); in fact Marvin Ross attributed this leaf to him (Los Angeles 1953–54, cat. no. 68). By examining his iconographical models and a coat of arms painted on one of his plaques (Verdier 1967, xvii), it is possible to define his period of activity from 1461 until at least the middle of the 1480s. A plaque of the Adoration of the Magi in the Musée Municipal, Limoges (inv. no. 23; Limoges 1966, 68), incorporates the coat of arms of Bishop Jean I Barthon de Montbas as bishop of Nazareth, a title he received in 1484.

*

FIGURE 14

The Angelic Host,
from a book of hours,
France (use of Limoges),
late fifteenth century,
tempera and gold
on vellum, 15.2 x 11.4
cm (6 x 4½ in.),
Los Angeles County
Museum of Art, gift of
Mrs. William A. Nitze.

Color plate, page 42

THE MONVAERNI MASTER

Plaque: The Crucifixion

c. 1475
Polychrome enamel and gold on copper
20 x 22 cm (7⅞ x 8¹¹⁄₁₆ in.)
William Randolph Hearst Collection
51.13.3

DESCRIPTION

Three crosses stand on the hill of Golgotha outside the gates of Jerusalem; below the central cross are a human skull and two thigh bones, referring not only to the meaning of the word *Golgotha* as "place of the skull" but also to the ancient Christian belief that the hill was the site of the burial place of Adam. The dead Christ hangs on the central cross. The penitent thief, peaceful in death, is to Christ's right, and the unrepentant thief, still conscious, writhes on his cross. To the left of the central cross is the swooning Virgin Mary sustained by Saint John and one of the holy women. The hem of Mary's robe is decorated with gold letters in Gothic script, among which can be read MARIA GRATI...ENA. To the right are two figures on horseback: one, in fifteenth-century armor, making a gesture of devotion and another man, richly dressed in what the fifteenth century conceived of as Middle-Eastern fashion, who is indicating Christ on the cross. The walled city of Jerusalem is in the background; to the left is a garden, to the right, a rank of soldiers, only their helmets and spears visible.

LATER INSCRIPTIONS OR LABELS

On the counter-enamel and metal mount: MM 205 in black

TECHNIQUE

The ground color of the plaque is a dark, opaque enamel, but most of the ground is covered by a layer of opaque white enamel. Only the major outlines of the figures were created by *enlevage* of the white enamel, revealing the ground color beneath; all other contour lines were executed in black enamel on the fired white ground. A variety of translucent colors were applied over the white ground and black underdrawing. The darkest hues—dark blue, mulberry, and purple—are found primarily in the sky and the robes of the Virgin, Saint John, and the holy woman. Lighter, clearer tones of turquoise, mauve, emerald green, golden brown, and tan were used for the vegetation, landscape, and figures of the riders and their horses. Flesh tones were executed in opaque white thin enough to permit the ground color to show through, creating a slightly gray tone; the artist then added more opaque white for highlights, a thinned wash of black for modeling, and another of red to give color to the faces. Many of the surfaces are covered with overall decorative patterns in gold or black. There are small "beads" of red and white enamel to delineate the petals of flowers in the foreground.

The enamel surface is irregular, protruding especially where opaque white enamel has been used by itself or as a ground. The counter-enamel is an uneven, opaque mulberry-brown.

There is a great deal of crizzling in the Virgin's dark blue robe and the halos of Saint John and the holy woman. The enamel in the hat and robe of the man in Middle-Eastern costume, the trappings of his horse, and several areas of foliage have disintegrated to the point that the original color is no longer discernable.

*

The Crucifixion was one of the scenes most frequently represented by the early enamel painters of Limoges, reflecting its ubiquity in fifteenth-century illuminated manuscripts, panel paintings, and devotional woodcuts. Indeed, one of the fragments of the *Bois Protat* of 1370/80, the earliest extant woodblock, depicts a centurion and his soldiers at the foot of the cross (Blum 1978, 20–21, pl. III).

Given the overwhelming number of possible sources for any Crucifixion scene, it is not surprising that no specific model for this plaque and similar compositions has yet been identified. The iconographic and stylistic elements in this *Crucifixion* suggest that it was taken from or modeled after a slightly earlier French or Flemish composition whose artist had been influenced by Italian painting. In Italian Crucifixions, as magnificently illustrated by that scene in Duccio's *Maestà* (Opera del Duomo, Siena), completed in 1311, the two thieves flank Christ, a crowd of Jews and Romans surrounds the crosses, the swooning Virgin is tended by the holy women, and a gesturing centurion acknowledges the Son of God. Such models were not only accessible to French and Flemish artists during their travels in Italy but could also be found in the north in Italian manuscripts and panel paintings acquired by their patrons. Important examples of fourteenth-century painting and illumination, such as Jean Pucelle's *Heures de Jeanne d'Évreux*, 1325/28 (Cloisters Collection, Metropolitan Museum of Art, New York), and the *Parement de Narbonne*, about 1375 (Musée du Louvre, Paris), demonstrate that some Northern painters almost immediately abandoned the traditional hieratic Crucifixion—the cross flanked only by the Virgin and Saint John—for the more crowded, emotionally charged narrative scene derived from Italian models. By the mid-fifteenth century this format was nearly ubiquitous in French and Flemish panel painting (although less so in manuscript illumination, where the size of the composition necessarily limited the number of participants). One possible source among many

for this enamel is a woodcut of the Crucifixion from Artois (fig. 15), dated about 1467 (Bibliothèque Nationale, Paris; Estampes réserve ea. 5., incunable, no. 24; Courboin 1923, pl. 21): while the woodcut illustrates dozens of onlookers, some individual figures, groups, and details of the composition are nearly identical.

The relationship of mystery plays to the iconography of the Passion has been much debated. These *mystères sacrés* (holy mysteries), or *jeux* (performances) or *miracles*, as they were called earlier, were immensely popular. One of the most famous, *Le Mistère de la passion* (The mystery of the Passion), was written by Arnoul Gréban around 1450 and widely imitated; the title page of a printed version of about 1500 features the woodcut of a Crucifixion (London 1926, cat. no. 322). The absence of passion in the these long, stylized passion plays is reflected not only in the title woodcut, but also in many of the Crucifixion scenes depicted in Northern art. As in this enamel, pathos is evoked by the inherent tragedy of the scene, not by the manner of its representation. Jean-Joseph Marquet de Vasselot (1921, 39–40) suggested that the plays, rather than inspiring the compositions of the Passion, simply came from the same religious traditions.

Very few details of the iconography of the enamel are medieval. Even the smaller scale of the thieves in relation to Christ can be explained by the artist's grasp of one-point perspective: the central cross is obviously much closer to the picture plane. Perhaps only the anonymity of the holy woman is a vestige of medieval art. Although the woman, who wears a mulberry-colored dress, has frequently been identified as the Magdalene, she does not have the long, uncovered fair hair that had already become a convention by the early fifteenth century; also, at that time the Magdalene would usually have been depicted kneeling at the foot of the cross (as, for example, in a *Crucifixion* by Nardon Pénicaud; see fig. 7). The representation of Christ in peaceful death, the swooning Virgin, and the bloody legs of the thieves, broken to hasten their deaths (John 19:31–32), are fifteenth-century developments. The full frontality of the Christ figure, its lack of torsion, and the angle of the head could already be seen in Northern painting in the early fifteenth century; it was particularly conspicuous in the work of Jean Bourdichon in the 1480s.

Léon de Laborde (1853, 150 n. 1) claimed to read a repetition of the name "Maria" (which he said could also possibly be interpreted as "Monvaerni") in gold on the hem of the Virgin's robe. One *maria* is indeed partially preserved on the left edge of the hem, but much of the rest of the gold has been rubbed off. Under magnification, however, another part of the inscription may be deciphered as *grati...ena*; thus it appears that the gilded decoration was part of the devotional phrase, "Ave Maria, gratia plena" (Hail Mary, full of grace).

Men in armor on horseback also entered Northern iconography from fourteenth-century Italy, where both Giovanni Pisano and Ambrogio Lorenzetti had depicted mounted soldiers in scenes of Christ's Passion (Mâle 1922, 16 n. 1); in the *Crucifixion* by Giovanni's atelier on the pulpit of the cathedral of Pisa, completed in 1310, at least one of the equestrians is even wearing fairly authentic Roman armor. Figures similar to the knight in this enamel appear in French manuscripts as early as about 1465: in woodcuts of the *Neuf Preux* (Nine Worthies) from a Picard atelier (Courboin 1923, pls. 26–27), the legendary warriors wear identical armor and illustrate the same proportion of man to (rather small) horse.

The mounted civilian, rather than the knight, is probably to be identified as the Roman centurion who acknowledged Christ's divinity (Matthew 27:54; Mark 15:39). The medieval and Renaissance convention was to depict the centurion as richly attired in non-military garb, although he sometimes wears a short tunic and carries a sword; he can be distinguished from the other onlookers by his gesture toward the cross, and he is often accompanied by figures in armor making gestures of devotion like that of the knight in this enamel.

The coats of arms were originally identified as those of Guy de Montfaucon, lord of Saint-Mesmin and Roydan and a follower of Joan of Arc, and his wife, Marie de Marteau (Fillon 1882, 104–5). By extension the figure of the knight was once believed to be Guy himself. The enamel, however, was executed at least thirty years after Guy's death at the battle of Patay on June 18, 1429. Since a similar figure appears in other Crucifixions and Passion scenes by this painter, it is unlikely that the knight is intended to portray any particular donor.

Marquet de Vasselot (1921, 46–48) discarded a second theory that the quartered coat of arms referred to two Norman families, Lindebeuf and Hugleville, for a more plausible identification with the prominent Dinematin family of Limoges, which produced a dozen men active in local government during the fifteenth and sixteenth centuries, as well as Jean Dorat, the court poet of François I.

The dark hues, gray flesh tones, heavy draperies, and blunt facial features are characteristic of the distinctive style of the Monvaerni Master, as is the apparent *horror vacui*. The latter was a quality shared by most of the enamel painters of Limoges, but each had a different solution. The Monvaerni Master filled spaces in his compositions with vegetation ranging from tiny flowers to huge trees and often covered solid areas of color with elaborate patterns, as here in the asterisk-like stars in the darkened sky, the brocade pattern on Christ's loincloth and the holy woman's mantle, the regular, decorative knotholes in the wood of the crosses, and the dappling and bristles of the centurion's horse.

The Monvaerni Master has been criticized for the ungainliness and ugliness of his figures, which his detractors interpreted as the result of a lack of skill (Lavedan 1913, 76; Mitchell 1917, 219–20). Some of the faces in his work are indeed hideous, but they are usually the faces of Christ's tormentors, like the derisive unrepentant thief in this scene, who appears almost deformed. This suggests the Monvaerni Master's adherence to a common convention equating ugliness with evil; certainly the other faces in the *Crucifixion* demonstrate the artist's ability to achieve a range from the realistic (Christ) to the delicately beautiful (Saint John), not to mention the winsome personalities of the horses.

The vigor and uncompromising realism of the figures are especially akin to the work of Flemish illuminators of the later fifteenth century, such as Loyset Liédet of Brussels (active c. 1460–80); the structure of the composition, the aerial view of the landscape background, and the use of small-scale trees to border the scene are all elements introduced by the French Boucicaut Master in the early decades of the fifteenth century (Meiss 1968, 12–22).

Such a plaque may have been commissioned as a devotional object *per se* or as the central panel of a triptych. It is also possible that it was one of a group of scenes from the Passion of Christ, although the extended Passion series popular with the enamel painters of Limoges did not otherwise begin appearing until the second third of the sixteenth century. Laborde (1853, 150) mentioned a series of twelve plaques by the Monvaerni Master depicting scenes from the Passion—of which he claimed this *Crucifixion* was one—including a *Pietà* or *Descent from the Cross* in the Czartoryska collection, three others in the Bouruet collection, and a *Flagellation* on the art market. None of these can now be identified with certainty, but it is more probable that the twelve plaques were rather those framed together sometime between 1850 and 1860 by a Parisian restorer named Corplet; in 1909 they were given to the Musée du Louvre (Dreyfus 1909; Marquet de Vasselot 1910, 299–301; Marquet de Vasselot 1914, cat. nos. 466–77). This group—which is in fact not an integral Passion series, since it includes two nearly identical Processions to Calvary and one unrelated plaque of Saint Christopher—does indeed include a *Crucifixion* (see below), *Pietà*, and *Flagellation*.

At least twelve Crucifixions (four are the central panels of triptychs) are attributed to the atelier of the Monvaerni Master; they may be divided into groups on the basis of style and iconography, reflecting the artist's use of different models. The earliest type is illustrated by the Los Angeles plaque and a similar plaque in the Louvre (inv. no. 6309; Marquet de Vasselot 1914, cat. no. 467; Marquet de Vasselot 1921, cat. no. 14). The figures in the latter are smaller in proportion to the landscape; the contour lines and drapery folds are slightly more fluid; and there are differences in details—for example, another Roman soldier appears behind the two figures on horseback, and the legs of the thieves are unmarked. The nature of the stylistic variations in the Louvre plaque suggests another hand in the Monvaerni atelier, but the compositions are identical and obviously taken from the same model.

In four other *Crucifixions* in a slightly later style (the Taft triptych mentioned above; Metropolitan Museum of Art [inv. no. 17.190.1642]; ex-collection Henri Leman, Paris [Marquet de Vasselot 1921, cat. nos. 29, 30, 31, respectively]; London art market) the artist reversed the positions of the riders and added more figures, including Longinus piercing Christ's side with a spear, Stephaton offering him a vinegar-soaked sponge, and the Magdalene embracing the shaft of the cross. A simpler scene was later produced by the atelier with only the figure of Christ on a cross attended by the Virgin, Saint John, the Magdalene or a holy woman, and the centurion (Musée de Lyon [without the Magdalene]; Kunstgewerbemuseum, Berlin; Grünes Gewölbe, Dresden [Marquet de Vasselot 1921, cat. nos. 36, 37, 38, respectively]; Victoria and Albert Museum, London [inv. no. C.37-1928]).

Three triptychs believed by Marquet de Vasselot (1921, 75–79) to illustrate a distinctive late style of the Monvaerni Master or a member of his atelier demonstrate a return to the earliest iconographic model of three crosses, with the Magdalene once more at the side of the Virgin and Saint John, but with the addition of a group of soldiers, Longinus, and Stephaton (Louvre; ex-collections Addington and Spitzer; Hermitage Museum, Saint Petersburg [Marquet de Vasselot 1921, cat. nos. 47, 48, 49, respectively]), reflecting the original Italian model.

PROVENANCE

M. A. Raifé, Paris, by 1852; sale, Paris, March 16, 1867, lot 130.

Benjamin Fillon, Paris; sale, Hôtel Drouot, Paris, March 20–24, 1882, lot 261, 1,800 francs.

J. Pierpont Morgan.

Seligmann & Company, New York.

Thomas Fortune Ryan; sale, American Art Association/Anderson Galleries, New York, November 23–25, 1933, lot 383, $3,250.

William Randolph Hearst.

Donated to the Los Angeles County Museum of Art, 1951.

EXHIBITED

Victoria and Albert Museum, London, sometime between 1882 and 1917, lent by J. Pierpont Morgan.

Los Angeles County Fair Association, Pomona, 1952, lent by the Los Angeles County Museum of Art.

LITERATURE

Laborde 1852, 144.

Laborde 1853, 150 n. 1.

Noel 1882, 156.

Dreyfus 1909, 53.

Demartial 1910, 18, no. 15.

Marquet de Vasselot 1910, 306.

Marquet de Vasselot 1911, pl. V.

Mitchell 1917, 220, n. 11.

Marquet de Vasselot 1921, text vol., 44–48, 217–18, cat. 15, pl. iv.

Active c. 1475–c. 1500

T HE MASTER OF the Baltimore and Orléans Triptychs takes his name from the most famous works by his hand: two triptychs of the Annunciation flanked by David and Isaiah, one in the Walters Art Gallery, Baltimore (inv. no. 44.316; Verdier 1967, no. 17), the other in the Musée Historique, Orléans (Orléans 1828, cat. no. 275).

This artist is thought to have worked from the mid-1470s into the sixteenth century; his early work was thus contemporary with that produced in the later period of activity of the Monvaerni Master. Like the Monvaerni Master—indeed, like many of the enamel painters of Limoges—he frequently repeated his compositions. The poses of his figures are more elegant, their draperies more fluid than those of the Monvaerni Master, but they still demonstrate a lively realism, especially in their faces and expressive gestures. From the energy of his draftsmanship and the painterly quality of decorative touches on many of his works it is likely that he worked as both an enamel painter and illuminator—in fact the existence of identical scenes in a similar style in the two media suggests that he was practicing both arts simultaneously (see below). His work in enamel appears to have had an effect on his illumination: his decorative approach to the painted surface, which he treats as an arrangement of areas of color rather than forms in space, is a likely result of the enamel painting technique.

Most of the enamels attributed to this master demonstrate a style rooted in French and Flemish painting, with the increasing influence toward 1500 of German prints. Marie-Madeleine Gauthier (1972, 309–10) believed him to have been inspired by Flemish manuscripts of the time of Mary of Burgundy, about 1475–80, especially in his composition, ornamentation, and costumes. One group of works, however, is characterized by more idealized facial features and more ample drapery, perhaps reflecting a later Italian influence (Marquet de Vasselot 1921, 89).

*

Color plate, page 43

2

The Master of the Baltimore and Orléans Triptychs

Plaque: The Nativity and Annunciation to the Shepherds

c. 1480/90
Polychrome enamel and gold on copper
20.6 x 16 cm (8 ⅛ x 6 ⁵⁄₁₆ in.)
William Randolph Hearst Collection
51.13.4

DESCRIPTION

The Virgin Mary kneels in the foreground, her hands clasped in prayer, and contemplates the newborn infant Christ lying on a fold of her mantle. To her left kneels Joseph with a candle in his right hand and a staff in his left. A substantial example of Romanesque architecture, showing signs of ruin, appears behind them to the left. Within an interior space on the lower floor are an ox and ass, the latter raising his head to bray. In the upper right corner of the plaque is a landscape, where an angel with a scroll reading GLORIA IN EXCELSIS DEO (Glory to God in the highest) appears in the sky to announce the birth to two shepherds, their sheepdog, and tiny flock; one of the shepherds turns to indicate the Nativity scene. A walled city is in the distance.

TECHNIQUE

The design for the plaque was drawn in red over a white ground; covered with translucent enamel these contour lines appear to be black. The artist used an opaque gray for the hair of the Virgin, hair and beard of Joseph, his candle and staff, and the dog in the background, and opaque white enamel over a dark ground, perhaps blue or mulberry, for the flesh, which has a violet tint. The thickness of the white enamel was varied to create lighter and darker tones. Individual facial features (and the wool of the sheep) were delineated by series of black dots and lines created by *enlevage* of the white enamel. Fine decorative lines of gold were applied to Mary's halo and hair and Joseph's beard and cowl.

The surface of the enamel is fairly smooth. The counter-enamel is an uneven, opaque greenish gray.

There is a loss in the Virgin's dress and smaller losses in her mantle, permitting the underdrawing and white ground to be seen clearly. The figure of the ass is badly crizzled, the original color now lost. Less crizzling is visible in the Virgin's blue mantle and in the right side of Joseph's cloak, the latter damage possibly caused by an earlier frame.

✳

The Nativity ranked with the Annunciation, Adoration of the Magi, Crucifixion, and Pietà as one of the most popular scenes depicted by the early enamel painters of Limoges.

The Nativity had previously been depicted in European art with Mary on a bed or couch, the Christ Child lying in her arms or in the manger beside her. The concept of the Virgin kneeling in adoration of her newborn child was widely promoted by the enormously influential *Revelations* of Saint Bridget of Sweden (1303–1373), whose vision during a visit to Bethlehem in 1370 had a great impact on the iconography of the Nativity: Mary removed her mantle and allowed her golden hair to fall loose, and as she knelt to pray, her hands clasped, "the child was suddenly born, surrounded by a light so bright that it completely eclipsed Joseph's feeble candle" (Saint Bridget of Sweden, quoted in Hall 1979, 220). In Saint Bridget's vision the birth took place in a cave, and although Joseph had brought a candle, he left before the child was born. The earliest images after the vision were executed in late fourteenth-century Italy, but the artists were reluctant to exclude Joseph, so enlisted him as a candle-holder. Northern artists carried out a further revision, most retaining the by-now-traditional shed (Panofsky 1958, 125–26).

The image of the Virgin kneeling in adoration of the Child may have occurred independently in Flemish art as early as 1300 (Panofsky 1958, 378), but it first appeared in French art in the first decade of the fifteenth century. Émile Mâle (1922, 16) claimed that the new iconography surfaced in the *Très Riches Heures* of the duc de Berry (fol. 44v; Musée Condé, Chantilly), illuminated by the Limbourg brothers between 1413 and 1416; however, the Adoration of the Child, as the scene was called, appears in the *Boucicaut Hours* (fol. 73v; Musée Jacquemart-André, Paris) and other illuminated manuscripts by the Boucicaut Master and his workshop that were executed in the first decade of the fifteenth century. Regardless of the date of its first appearance the Adoration of the Child became the standard depiction of the Nativity in Northern painting, as, for example, in the Bladelin Altarpiece of about 1454 by Rogier van der Weyden (Gemäldegalerie der Staatlichen Museen, Berlin-Dahlem).

It is possible that French artists first encountered a variant of this scene in earlier Italian frescoes or panels, such as the *Nativity and Adoration of the Shepherds* painted about 1335 by Taddeo Gaddi on a cupboard panel in the sacristy of Santa Croce, Florence (Ladis 1982, 120, fig. 6b-2). This and other similar representations were no doubt inspired by a popular devotional book of the early fourteenth century, the *Meditationes vitae Christi* (Meditations on the life of Christ), long attributed to Saint Bonaventure but now thought to be the work of the Franciscan monk Johannes de Caulibus of San Gimignano, which described Mary, Joseph, and the angels kneeling to adore the child, who was often displayed on an elaborate bed. The Nativity as envisioned by Saint Bridget, however, entered the repertory of Northern art at the same time it appeared in Italy, as in the predella of Lorenzo Monaco's *Coronation of the Virgin* (Galleria degli Uffizi, Florence), painted in 1414. This would argue that the Northern artists and their patrons were directly influenced by the literary source.

Joseph's candle, which he holds in many painted enamels of the Nativity, including the earliest depictions of this scene by the Monvaerni Master (Marquet de Vasselot 1921, cat. nos. 1, 41–43), seems to derive directly from Saint Bridget's vision, but a lighted candle was also a theatrical convention in mystery plays to indicate that the action was taking place at night (Mâle 1922, 76).

The ruined architecture, representing the Old Dispensation (Judaism) that will be replaced by the New (Christianity) after the birth of the Messiah, is strengthened as a symbol by the fact that its Romanesque style had similarly been superseded in Northern Europe by the Gothic.

The inclusion of the Annunciation to the Shepherds in the upper right background of the Nativity scene is an ancient tradition derived from Byzantine art. In the strictly observed decorative schemes of Byzantine churches the Annunciation to the Shepherds and several other episodes, including the Journey and Adoration of the Magi, were natural subsidiary scenes to the Nativity, coming as they did from the same Gospel passages (Demus 1955, 30).

There are other nearly identical versions of this scene from the atelier of the Master of the Baltimore and Orléans Triptychs, and all of approximately the same size: two others catalogued by Jean-Joseph Marquet de Vasselot (1921, cat. nos. 69, 72) are in the Musée de Lyon and the British Museum, London, and a third is the central panel of a triptych formerly in the Mortimer L. Schiff collection (*Connoisseur* 140 [September 1957]: 59, no. 16). That in the British Museum is particularly fine in quality: the drawing is assured and elegant, and the rich surface is enhanced by *paillons* (foil and enamel "jewels") decorating the garments of Mary and Joseph (British Museum 1924, 93, fig. 54). A much smaller plaque taken from the same model and probably executed in the same master's atelier was sold in London in the Flannery sale in 1983

(Sotheby Parke Bernet, December 1, lot 212). A variant that includes the Archangel Michael killing the dragon is in the Walters Art Gallery (Verdier 1967, no. 22).

The Los Angeles *Nativity* was among the early painted enamels traditionally attributed to Nardon Pénicaud for lack of another known enamel painter of the period. Marquet de Vasselot (1921, 92) first recognized it as a work in the style of the artist who had executed an Annunciation triptych in the Musée Historique, Orléans. He believed that this and the similar plaques depicting the Nativity were executed by someone outside the atelier of the Master of the Baltimore and Orléans Triptychs, although profoundly influenced by him. This view has not been adopted by other scholars; the style and technique of the Nativity plaques in question are the same as those of other accepted works from the master's atelier.

The probable source for this scene may also introduce us to the enamel painter himself. A later fifteenth-century book of hours, use of Limoges, in the Art Institute of Chicago, depicts a strikingly similar scene (fig. 16) executed in the same style as the extant Nativity plaques from the atelier of the Master of the Baltimore and Orléans Triptychs. The illuminations in the manuscript, which is inscribed to Katherine Gentille, wife of Martial Dubois, a consul of Limoges, display the same feature and costume types, expressive realism of face and gesture, and extreme clarity of style manifest in the enamels. Marvin Ross (1941, 16–23) was the first to suggest that the enamels and miniatures were executed by the same master, a hypothesis that has been widely accepted. Philippe Verdier (1967, 29) pointed to the "metallic dryness" of the book of hours, which "betrays the practice and vision of an enameller." The painterly use of gold decoration on the enamels surely supports the probability that the enamel painter had been trained as an illuminator, and the stylistic similarities are conclusive.

The Monvaerni Master depicted this scene several times, as did Nardon Pénicaud, the Master of the Louis XII Triptych, and the Master of the Violet Mantles. Although these Nativities share many of the compositional elements with the work of the Master of the Baltimore and Orléans Triptychs, differences in the arrangement of the figures and the handling of many details confirm the use of several other models.

PROVENANCE

Possibly Ducatel; sale, Paris, April 21–26, 1890, lot 111, 590 francs (as Nardon Pénicaud).

Possibly Tollin; sale, Paris, May 18–19, 1897, lot 59, 1,000 francs (as Nardon Pénicaud).

Séguin; sale, Paris, 1910, lot 282, ill. p. 40 (as Nardon Pénicaud).

Seligmann & Company, New York, 1910 (as Nardon Pénicaud).

Thomas Fortune Ryan; sale, American Art Association/Anderson Galleries, New York, November 23–25, 1933, lot 382, $1,100.

William Randolph Hearst.

Donated to the Los Angeles County Museum of Art, 1951.

LITERATURE

Marquet de Vasselot 1921, text vol., 92, cat. no. 71.

Active c. 1520–c. 1540

THIS ARTIST WAS dubbed the Master of the Aeneid because of the only work that has been securely attributed to him, a large series of plaques illustrating episodes from Virgil's *Aeneid* (see below). His style is characterized by a roundness of form coupled with a sketchiness of drawing, particularly in passages of *enlevage*, a preponderance of brown and yellow tones, and a lavish use of gold surface decoration. He has been identified at various times as Couly I or Couly II Nouailher, Jean I or Jean II Pénicaud, or even Pierre Reymond. Of these masters the only stylistically plausible choice is Jean I Pénicaud, who is recorded as late as 1543, but the theory that the *Aeneid* series is the manifestation of a weaker, "old-age" style (Verdier 1967, 76) assumes too much, particularly a deterioration of style.

Only a few other enamels have been attributed to this master. Philippe Verdier (1967, 76 n. 2) mentioned three plaques representing the months of January, October, and December in the Musées du Cinquantenaire, Brussels. Roger Pinkham (1972, 370–75) reattributed to the Master of the Aeneid a number of plaques formerly or subsequently given to the atelier of Jean I Pénicaud (Marquet de Vasselot 1921, no. 175; Verdier 1967, 67; Verdier 1977, 52), including an *Agony in the Garden* (inv. no. c.2389-1910) and a *Crucifixion* (inv. no. 2820-1856) in the Victoria and Albert Museum, London, which do appear to be by the anonymous master, although Pinkham's other reattributions are less convincing.

*

Color plate, page 44

3

THE MASTER OF THE AENEID

Plaque:
The Discovery of the Murder of Polydorus
1525/30
Polychrome enamel, gold, and silver foil
on copper
22.5 x 20 cm (8⅞ x 7⅞ in.)
William Randolph Hearst Collection
51.13.1

DESCRIPTION

A three-masted galley lies at anchor at lower left. On the coast of Thrace (**THRACIA**) in the right foreground a man swings an axe to sacrifice a bull; above him a waiting priest tends the sacrificial fire burning on an altar. Two women behind them mourn over the body of Polydorus (**POLVDORVS**). To the right Aeneas (**ENEAS**) kneels before a barren bush, a branch in his right hand. In the background at left a man digs with a shovel near the mouth of a stream flowing into the sea. A large city in the distance is dominated by an unfinished tower surmounted by scaffolding on which a man is at work.

Color plate, page 45

4

THE MASTER OF THE AENEID

Plaque:
Naval Games in Honor of Anchises

1525/30
Polychrome enamel, gold, and silver foil
on copper
22.4 x 20 cm (8 ¹³⁄₁₆ x 7 ⅞ in.)
William Randolph Hearst Collection
51.13.2

DESCRIPTION

Three small boats are engaged in a race
in the sea off a rocky coast; each has a
captain (**MENETEVS**, **CILONN**, **GYAS**) and
three crewmen. Two bearded males in the
water are pushing the central boat, and a
man (**MENTES**) falls overboard from the
boat behind it (the **ICHIMERA**). On the
shore at right Aeneas (**ENEAS**), King
Acestes (**CESTES**), and a troop of halberd-
iers watch the race. In front of them
is an enclosure containing armor, an
embroidered robe, a tripod, and a chest
of gold coins. A fourth boat, the *Centaur*
(**SENTAVRV**), captained by Sergestus
(**SERGETVS**), can be seen between two
cliffs in the background. A large masted
ship lies at anchor in the distance at left.

The copper plates are covered with silver foil on which the designs were drawn in a dark russet enamel. Various intensities of golden brown, dark blue, mulberry, and deep green translucent enamel were used in the compositions; in most areas the silver shows through, intensifying the brightness of the colors. The sea was rendered in white enamel covered by a translucent light blue; currents and waves were indicated by *enlevage* of the white enamel. Flesh tones were executed in opaque white over a dark purple-gold; the artist modeled the contours by varying the thickness of the white enamel to allow darker tones to show through. Facial features were delineated by a skillful *enlevage* of the white enamel, and a thin wash of red was added for color (red was also used for the sacrificial fire). The many details of the landscape and clothing were carried out in dark enamel under the translucent colors and in gold on the surface. Flowers were formed of dots of opaque white around translucent blue enamel.

The enamels are in excellent condition, except for small chips at the corners and a few larger losses along the edges. Two holes in the upper edge of the *Polydorus* plaque—no doubt for display purposes—have been patched and refired; at least one similar hole in the upper edge of the *Naval Games* plaque has been filled.

The counter-enamel is a slightly golden *fondant*, clear on the *Polydorus* plaque and mottled with mulberry on the other.

*

The earliest known deviation of the enamel painters of Limoges from religious subject matter resulted in a remarkable series of plaques illustrating episodes from Virgil's *Aeneid*, two of which are presented here. The *Aeneid* group is by far the largest series, numerically speaking, executed in painted enamel (only a few Passion cycles reach as many as twenty-four episodes). Seventy-eight plaques have been identified since the beginning of this century (Marquet de Vasselot 1912, 6–51; Verdier 1967, 75–89; Christie's 1991, 6–7); a few of these are now lost, but most can be found in museums in Europe and America. The largest concentrations are in the Metropolitan Museum of Art, New York (fifteen; Breck 1925, 95–98); the Musée du Louvre, Paris (eleven); the Walters Art Gallery, Baltimore (seven; Verdier 1967, cat. nos. 37–43); and Alnwick Castle, Northumberland (six; Rackham 1921, 238–44).

Such a series may have been set into the paneling of a *cabinet* or study, an arrangement described in a number of sixteenth-century inventories, such as that of the belongings of Queen Catherine de' Medici (Bonnaffé 1874, 155–56). A plaque from the *Aeneid* series illustrating the episode of Aeneas and the Cumaean Sibyl, formerly in the Kofler-Truniger collection, Lucerne, and now in the Keir collection (Schnitzler 1965, cat. no. E125; Kansas City 1983, cat. no. 123), may reflect this form of display in the depiction of narrative panels on the walls of the Temple of Apollo at Cumae (Verdier 1967, 75, fig. 6).

The choice of the patron or artist to illustrate a work by Virgil was in itself not remarkable. His writings, more than those by many other classical authors, had remained in favor with religious authorities during the Middle Ages, especially because of what was later interpreted as a Messianic prophecy in his fourth *Eclogue* (40 B.C.). For Dante, who chose Virgil's shade as a guide through Hell and Purgatory, the Roman poet represented, as Dorothy L. Sayers wrote in her translation of the *Inferno* (Baltimore: Penguin, 1960, 67), "the image of Human Wisdom—the best that man can become in his own strength without the especial grace of God." In the popular imagination the gentle and virtuous Virgil was regarded as a "white," or good, magician, and the themes of the *Aeneid*—the fall of Troy, the wanderings of Prince Aeneas and his companions, and the founding of Rome—were well-known tales incorporated into chivalric literature. Raoul Lefèvre's *Recueil des histoires de Troie* (c. 1464), based on earlier writings by Benoit de Sainte-More (c. 1160) and Guido delle Colonne (1272/87), was extremely popular in the courts of Northern Europe in the second half of the fifteenth century (Scherer 1964, xiii).

The story of Polydorus is one of the tales told by Aeneas to Queen Dido of Carthage (*Aeneid*, book 3). The Trojans have fled their defeated city and landed on the plains of Thrace, a land they believe friendly to their cause, where they begin to build a new city called Aeneadae. "So that the gods may guard our undertaking, I offer sacrifices to my mother [Venus]," recounts Aeneas, "...slaughtering along that beach a gleaming white bull to the high king of heaven-dwellers."* He finds a mound densely covered with dogwood and myrtle; as he tears out branches to lay on the altar, drops of black blood trickle from the roots:

> A moan rose from the bottom of the mound, a lamentable voice returned to me: "Why are you mangling me, Aeneas? Spare my body. I am buried here....I am no stranger to you; I am Trojan....for I am Polydorus; here an iron harvest of lances covered my pierced body; for this, sharp javelins have grown above me."

The young Polydorus had been sent away from Troy by his father, King Priam, to be brought up in the peaceful atmosphere of the court of Thrace, but the monarch of that country murdered the Trojan prince for the gold he had brought with him.

In the enamel Aeneas is seen receiving this tale of treachery. When he presents

the Trojans with the evidence, they decide to desert their unfinished city, seen in the background, to leave the land thus polluted by dishonor and bloodshed; before embarking, "we give fresh funerals to Polydorus [in the form of a sacrifice]... and around us the Trojan women stand; their streaming hair is loosened as our custom bids."

In book 5 Aeneas lands his fleet at Dardanus (Drepanum in Sicily) in time to commemorate the first anniversary of his father Anchises's death and burial there. Among the ceremonies are a series of contests, the first of which is a boat race (in Virgil's time games were regarded as religious observances rather than sporting events). The four fastest ships in the fleet are chosen to compete: the *Shark, Chimaera, Centaur*, and *Scylla*, commanded by their respective captains, Menestheus, Gyas, Sergestus, and Cloanthus. In the enamel the long passage describing the exciting race is reduced to a conflation of the more dramatic incidents: the *Scylla* is pushed to ultimate victory by sea gods— here Portunus and perhaps Nereus—in answer to Cloanthus's vows; Gyas flings his pilot, Menoetes, overboard for refusing to steer by the shortest route near the dangerously rocky shore; the *Centaur* runs aground on the rocks. Aeneas and Acestes, king of Dardanus, watch from the shore, behind an enclosure where the prizes are displayed: "the sacred tripods...and armor, garments dyed in purple, talents of gold and silver."

The images depicted on these and all the other enamels in the series were taken from a single source, a fact that was discovered at the *Exposition universelle* in Paris in 1867, when Victorien Sardou, the playwright (*La Tosca*) and bibliophile, saw twelve *Aeneid* enamels on view and recognized the similarity of the compositions to the illustrations in a sixteenth-century edition of Virgil's works in his possession. The book was the *Opera Virgiliana cum decem commentis...* published by Jean Crespin in Lyons in 1529. Alfred Darcel (1868, 380–82), the organizer of the enamel exhibition, discovered that the woodcuts in Sardou's volume were originally prepared for an edition of 1502, *Publii Virgilii Maronis opera cum quinque vulgatis commentariis...*, published in Strasbourg by the master printer Johann Grüninger and illustrated with 215 woodcuts executed by an unknown printmaker on themes apparently supplied by the humanist and poet (*Das Narrenschyff* [The ship of fools]) Sebastian Brant (1457/58–1521).

An examination of the numerous editions of Virgil's works illustrated with these woodcuts—several printed from the original blocks themselves, which were passed from Strasbourg to Lyons—has led scholars to conclude that it was in fact the 1502 edition that must have served the enameler as a model (Marquet de Vasselot 1912, 15–19). Aside from significant correspondences in the details of the composition, only in that early edition are the Latin inscriptions, most of which were copied by the enameler, complete and legible. (The many discrepancies in the spelling and forms of the inscriptions were undoubtedly the result of errors in transcription; the enamel painters, as craftsmen, had not been educated to have a working knowledge of Latin.)

---

*Quotations from the *Aeneid* are from the translation by Allen Mandelbaum (Berkeley: University of California Press, 1981).

FIGURE 17

The Discovery of the Murder of Polydorus, from Virgil, *Opera virgiliana cum decem commentis...*, Lyons: Jean Crespin, 1529, woodcut, 15.2 x 17.3 cm (6 x 6 ¹³⁄₁₆ in.), The British Library, London.

FIGURE 18

Naval Games in Honor of Anchises, from Virgil, *Opera virgiliana cum decem commentis...*, Lyons: Jean Crespin, 1529, woodcut, 17.6 x 14.9 cm (6 ¹⁵⁄₁₆ x 5 ⅞ in.), The British Library, London.

The 1502 Virgil contains 143 woodcuts illustrating scenes from the *Aeneid*. Even allowing for the destruction of some of the plaques, it is unlikely that the series of enamels reproduced all of the woodcuts; someone, the patron or a scholarly advisor, probably chose the more interesting prints or the more significant episodes from Aeneas's adventures. Also, there are no extant enamels based on the woodcuts in book 10, 11, or 12, which suggests that some circumstance — the death or waning interest of either the artist or patron, or perhaps another commission — prevented the projected series from reaching a conclusion.

Despite the sixteenth-century date of the edition of Virgil's works, the printmaker's style is still largely Gothicizing, beginning with the bird's-eye view and flatness of the forms and including details of architecture and furniture, corkscrew curls and jagged drapery folds, and even the use of the uncial forms of the letters *E, D,* and *G* in the inscriptions. The castles, costumes, and marvelously detailed ships are those of fifteenth-century Northern Europe. The only concession the printmaker has made to the classical work he is illustrating is the presentation of the gods as nudes, but even those are the full-bellied, Germanic nudes of Lucas Cranach and Albrecht Dürer.

The enamel painter did not copy the book illustrations exactly; in addition to adopting a different format—many of the prints are wider than they are tall, the enamels taller than they are wide—the main figures in the enamels are relatively larger than those in the woodcuts, and the artist has omitted secondary figures, subsidiary scenes, and excessive details where the scenes would otherwise have been too crowded. He has clearly been influenced by an Italianate style; his figures are fuller and rounder, the contours and folds softened, and the uncials have been replaced by a thoroughly classical epigraphy. In the *Polydorus* plaque, after the woodcut on folio 185 of the 1502 edition (fig. 17), the painter cut off a landscape on the right and expanded the height of the whole composition (as well as providing the priest with a bishop's miter); because of the crowding of figures in the enamel it is not evident that the man with a shovel is digging a new grave for the body of Polydorus. In the *Naval Games* (fig. 18; folio 234) the painter omitted elements of the landscape at the top and left of the print.

Although in theory a copy of the 1502 Strasbourg *Aeneid* could have been available to the artist fairly soon after publication, the style and technique of the enamels demonstrate that they were not executed until considerably after the turn of the century; it was not uncommon, it should be remembered, for the enameler's graphic models to be decades old. The use of *fondant* as a counter-enamel began sometime between 1520 and 1525, probably in the atelier of Jean I Pénicaud. By 1530 the use of Italian or Italianizing models was fairly ubiquitous in the workshops

of Limoges; it is unlikely that a patron or enamel painter would have chosen so "Gothic" a model after that. These three factors can be used to date the series to a period between 1525 and 1530 (Marquet de Vasselot 1912, 17–19).

Extremely unusual is the fact that only one version of each plaque exists; no copies or variants have come to light. This and the consistency of style throughout the series suggests a single artist, rather than a workshop, working from a Grüninger *Aeneid* that had been provided by his patron. The Nouailhers, Pénicauds, and especially Pierre Reymond, all proposed as candidates for the Master of the Aeneid, maintained ateliers, however, and the size of their output is evidence that none of them could have committed himself to such a time-consuming task as the personal execution of all the extant *Aeneid* plaques, not to mention those that must have been destroyed. As Jean-Joseph Marquet de Vasselot (1912, 22) pointed out, there are many enamelers mentioned in archival documents to whom no works have yet been attributed. The Master of the Aeneid may well be one of these, perhaps a particularly promising member of the Pénicaud workshop who, in the interest of advancement and financial security, was willing to accept a commission that might well have occupied his entire professional life.

PROVENANCE

Possibly Hollingworth Magniac, Colworth, Bedfordshire; sale, London, July 2 and following days, 1892, lot 511 or 528.

Possibly J. and S. Goldschmidt, Frankfurt. Jules Porgès, Paris.

Arnold Seligmann, Rey & Company, New York.

Thomas Fortune Ryan; sale, American Art Association/Anderson Galleries, New York, November 23–25, 1933, lot 388a, $800 (cat. no. 3); lot 388b, $1,250.

William Randolph Hearst.

Donated to the Los Angeles County Museum of Art, 1951.

LITERATURE

Marquet de Vasselot 1912, cat. nos. 14, 30.
Verdier 1967, 76 n. 1.

c. 1513–after 1584

 IERRE REYMOND, the most prolific of the enamel painters, came from an ancient Limousin family. An ancestor, another Pierre, was recorded as a consul of Limoges in 1375 and 1377. That office indicated a degree of civic prominence reserved for the city's master craftsmen, and given the number of goldsmiths later in the family and the obvious metalworking skills of the sixteenth-century Reymond enamel workshop, it is likely that the medieval Reymonds were involved in metalwork-related enamel techniques such as champlevé before the destruction of the city in 1371.

Pierre was probably born in 1513, the son of James or Jacques Reymond. In 1530 he married Jeanne Martel. His atelier was located in rue des Étaux, also called rue Basse Manigne or Descendant-Manigne, where his neighbor was fellow enamel painter Jean Court *dit* Vigier, and he owned a house in rue de la Barreyette.

Reymond's earliest known signed and dated work is from the year 1533, a polychrome plaque depicting the Bad Shepherd, who neglects his sheep (formerly in the collection of Ernst and Marthe Kofler-Truniger, Lucerne; sold Sotheby's, London, December 13, 1979, lot 11; London art market, 1983 [*Antiques Collector*, June 1983, 108–9]). His early oeuvre consisted of similar small plaques of religious scenes (see cat. nos. 5–8), including a poly-chrome *Adoration of the Virgin and Child* dated 1534 (Thomas Fortune Ryan collection; sold American Art Association/Anderson Galleries, New York, November 25 [day 3], 1933, lot 378) and two triptychs for members of the Bourbon family, one in grisaille with a coat of arms reflecting a marriage that took place in 1530, now in the Hermitage Museum, Saint Petersburg (Dobroklonskaya 1969, no. 29), and another, dated 1538, formerly in the collection of Baron Gustave de Rothschild.

By 1540 Reymond was producing copper plates and vessels painted in grisaille enamel. He was instrumental in popularizing these types of enamel objects, which enjoyed an enor-mous commercial success; he may in fact have originated them. The 1540s saw the pro-duction of the finest of these pieces, when his personal participation and close supervision must have been at its height. As the demand for the grisaille pieces grew, so too did the size of his atelier. Léon de Laborde (1853, 214) speculated that Reymond would execute a group of pieces himself and then have ten copies of each reproduced by various studio painters, who were unfortunately of varying abilities. It is a fact that the quality of enamel painting in his atelier began to fluctuate widely in the 1550s and fall off a great deal in the 1560s, as assistants took over the production of the most popular forms, especially sets of calendar plates, repeating designs and motifs *ad nauseam*. It is not uncommon to be able to distinguish three different hands on these pieces: one for the main scene, a second for the decorative motifs on the rims and undersides, and a third for the inscriptions and other "customized" elements, such as coats of arms. There is evidence that in later years Reymond used a sliding scale of fees, as Peter Paul Rubens was later to do: the more prestigious the client or the more he or she was willing to pay, the greater Reymond's personal involvement in the commission. Although his signature or, more commonly, his initials appear on many pieces,* it has always been a practice in the arts for the master of a studio to sign any work executed under his or her supervision, regardless of the degree of participation. Only a small number of the later dated enamels are comparable in finesse to his early works.

Late in his career Reymond returned briefly to polychrome enamel, as evidenced by a ewer stand illustrating Moses Striking the Rock, now in the Frick Collection, New York (inv. no. 16.4.25; Verdier 1977, 140–45), and four oval plaques on a theme variously called, depending on one's point of view, *The Power of Women* (Eve, Lot's daughters, Delilah, Judith) or *The Weaknesses of Wise Men* (Adam, Lot, Samson, Holofernes), dated about 1575, in the Victoria and Albert Museum, London (inv. nos. 8410-1863, 8411-1863, 8412-1863, 1813-1863; Pinkham 1975, 1446, fig. 8).

Reymond's style was precise and sharply contoured. At his best he displayed a judicious editing of his print sources, a skillful depiction of surfaces and textures, and an impressive modeling of rounded forms with highlights and shadows. His shading was accomplished primarily with hatching and cross-hatching, a technique probably inspired by the style of the prints he used as source material. His work is also characterized by a distinctive salmon-pink flesh tone produced by a wash of particles of red enamel suspended in a clear flux.

In the hands of Reymond's less able assistants the later figural compositions became lifeless and flat, the style dry or even harsh, the contouring merely surface decoration. In contrast, the decorative motifs and grotesques that adorn the rims and undersides of

---

*Pierre Reymond shared with other Limoges artists a blithe disregard for any particular spelling of his name: extant pieces are signed "Reymon," "Remon," "Rexmon" (the substitution of *x* for *y* was common in the Limousin region), "Raymond," and "Raymon."

many of the grisaille objects display an almost uniformly high standard of elegance and skill throughout the period of production, a testimony to the specialists who executed them.

Reymond worked in other media as well. Parish records of 1582 document his illumination of registers and account books with miniatures of goldsmith's work acquired by the Confrérie du Saint-Sacrement in the parish of Saint-Pierre-du-Queyroix, Limoges, from 1550 to 1581. He designed a silver *bourdon* (staff finial) for the Confrérie and in 1556 executed a cartoon of the Last Supper for a stained-glass window in the Confrérie's chapel, the cartoon now preserved in the confraternity's register in the parish of Saint-Michel-de-Lions.

Although Reymond clearly had the ability to invent compositions, only at the very beginning of his career did he execute enamels that may have been of his own design, such as the Good Shepherd/Bad Shepherd plaques, for which no visual models have been found (see Verdier 1967, 213–14). His other early polychrome works are primarily copies of prints by Albrecht Dürer, whose stylistic influence on Reymond is still evident in the mid-1550s, as can be seen, for example, in the cartoon for the stained glass mentioned above. He also utilized Netherlandish and Italian models, especially the work of Lucas van Leyden (cat. nos. 11–12) and Marcantonio Raimondi. Later he worked mainly from French sources, including the Old Testament scenes of Bernard Salomon (cat. nos. 18–19), the Labors of the Months by Étienne Delaune (cat. no. 17), and the exquisite ornamentation of the *maîtres ornemanistes* of the school of Fontainebleau, particularly Jacques Androuet du Cerceau (cat. nos. 9–10).

Few of Reymond's patrons can be identified. Although many of the enamels display coats of arms, the bearers, presumably the commissioners, cannot usually be determined, possibly because the arms are oversimplified or inaccurate in format or color. From what little can be determined, his clientele seems to have included the highest nobility and the most distinguished and wealthiest of the middle class. One coat of arms that can be identified is the escutcheon of Pierre I Séguier (1504–1580)—*président à mortier* of the Paris *parlement* and opponent of the Inquisition—which appears on at least two sets of calendar plates dated 1566. An inventory of the *cabinets* in the Paris residence of the queen mother Catherine de' Medici records 188 "pièces d'émail de Limoges" (these are plates and vessels, as opposed to plaques, which are inventoried separately; see Bonnaffé 1874, 74, 81), and an inventory of the Parisian *hôtel* of the constable of France, Anne de Montmorency (fig. 6), on rue Sainte-Avoye (rue de Temple), itemizes ewers, basins, oval platters, tazzas, covered cups, saltcellars, spoons, and plaques (Mirot 1918–19, 367–69, 410). Although no artist is named, it is certain that some, if not most, of these objects must have been grisaille vessels commissioned from Reymond, who was the chief supplier of such work.

To judge from the number of enamels by his hand bearing German coats of arms and now displayed in German museums, Reymond received a number of commissions from Germany, especially from Nuremberg and Augsburg, the most notable being that from the wealthy Nuremberg merchant Linhard I Tucher (1487–1568). Between 1558 and 1562 the artist executed a group of beautifully painted grisaille plates and vessels, including tazzas, covered cups, and ewers, bearing the arms of Tucher and his successive wives, Magdalena Stromer and Katerina Nützel (the surviving pieces are now in the Germanisches National-museum and Tucher-Schlösschen [Stadt Nürnberg Museen], Nuremberg, and the Residenz-museum, Munich; Verdier 1967, 243, fig. 24; DuBon 1980, 5, fig. 2). The ewers are not of the usual Limousin shape: Tucher commissioned the copper vessels from the celebrated German goldsmith Wenzel Jamnitzer (1508–1585) and sent them to Limoges, by way of his commercial office in Lyons, to be decorated by Reymond. The finished ewers were given elaborate silver gilt handles, spouts, and mounts by Jamnitzer.

Reymond served as consul of Limoges in 1560 and 1567. His last known dated enamel is a plate of 1578 in the Musée du Louvre, Paris (Laborde 1853, cat. no. 479). He is not mentioned in any records after 1584 and is presumed to have died in that year or shortly afterward.

The large Reymond family was active in the arts in Limoges and elsewhere, but no relationship has yet been established between Pierre and the other members of the clan, including the brothers Jean (died 1602/3) and Joseph Reymond and Jean's son Martial (died 1599), all enamel painters. Another Martial, a goldsmith, was mentioned in 1606, and a relative of his, Joseph (who may or may not be the same Joseph mentioned above), was active as an enamel painter from at least 1599 though 1625. A Pierre Remy, who intro-duced enamel painting to Krakow, where he worked as a goldsmith from 1563 to 1574, was thought by Verdier (1967, xxiv) to be a relative, and yet another Pierre (died 1631) was a goldsmith in Limoges.

*

PIERRE REYMOND

Plaque:
Christ Washing the Feet of Peter

1535/40
Polychrome enamel and gold on copper
12.5 x 9.8 cm (4 15/16 x 3 7/8 in.)
William Randolph Hearst Collection
51.1.1 (1/4)

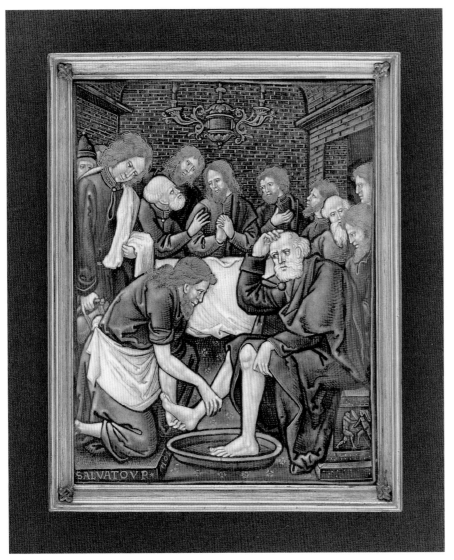

Color plate, page 46

DESCRIPTION

Christ kneels at left on a shallow plinth, his sleeves rolled up and a towel around his waist; on the edge of the plinth is the inscription SALVATOVR MO[N?]. He holds the right foot of the apostle Peter, who is seated on a stone bench at right and is scratching his head with his right hand. Peter's left foot rests in a basin of water. Behind Christ stands a younger man, probably John, holding towels and a ewer; two other men, one wearing a cap, the other with only the top of his head and part of his forehead visible, watch over John's shoulder. In the background and behind Peter are six men seated at a cloth-covered table and two men standing, most of them gesturing and talking among themselves, the two seated nearest Peter turning to watch the foot washing. The thirteen figures are in a small, brick-walled room with a doorway at right; overhead is a large metal chandelier in which two candles are burning.

LATER INSCRIPTIONS
OR LABELS

On the counter-enamel: 8/6627 in ink on a paper label; 4881 in ink on a red-edged paper label; 16 stamped on a paper label; DOUANE stamped on a paper label (French customs stamp)

PIERRE REYMOND

Plaque: The Flagellation

1535/40
Polychrome enamel and gold on copper
12.7 x 9.7 cm (5 x 3 ¹³⁄₁₆ in.)
William Randolph Hearst Collection
51.1.1 (2/4)

Color plate, page 46

DESCRIPTION

Christ is bound to a stone column in a
brick portico and is being scourged by
two men with bound bundles of birch
branches; his body is covered with the
marks of the scourges. At left a man with
a short tunic and cropped hair gestures
to Christ. Pilate and another onlooker, in
elaborate turbans, stand in the left middle ground; behind them an archway
opens up onto a view of a fortified building, trees, and a starry sky.

LATER INSCRIPTIONS
OR LABELS

On the counter-enamel: **8/6627** in ink on
a paper label; **4881** in ink on a red-edged
paper label; **17** stamped on a paper label

PIERRE REYMOND

Plaque: Christ Crowned with Thorns

1535/40
Polychrome enamel and gold on copper
12.7 x 10 cm (5 x 3 ¹⁵⁄₁₆ in.)
William Randolph Hearst Collection
51.1.1 (3/4)

Color plate, page 46

DESCRIPTION

Christ is seated on a stone plinth at right in front of a portico in a brick-walled courtyard or large hall; he wears an elaborate purple and gold-patterned cloak, and his body is covered with the marks of his flogging. Two men behind him use a forked stick and pincers to place a crown of thorns on his head; one of the men also raises a rod to strike him. In the foreground kneels a third man, hat in hand, presenting Christ with a wand. Pilate converses with a companion at the left, Pilate wearing a turban and carrying a rod, the other man wearing a peaked hat and holding a scroll.

LATER INSCRIPTIONS
OR LABELS

On the counter-enamel: **4881** in ink on a red-edged paper label; **23** stamped on a paper label; **DOUANE** stamped on a paper label (French customs stamp)

PIERRE REYMOND

Plaque: The Resurrection

1535/40
Polychrome enamel and gold on copper
12.7 x 9.9 cm (5 x 3⅞ in.)
William Randolph Hearst Collection
51.1.1 (4/4)

Color plate, page 46

DESCRIPTION

The risen Christ stands before his tomb, holding a staff with a triumphal banner flying, his head wreathed with flame. On the ground around him are four armed soldiers, two on each side, asleep or dazed. Behind the figures are a garden landscape and a sky filled with stars. A lightening of the horizon can be seen in the landscape to the left, where three women have come through an open gate.

LATER INSCRIPTIONS
OR LABELS

On the counter-enamel: **488**[**1**?] in ink on a red-edged paper label; **26** stamped on a paper label; **DOUANE** stamped on a paper label (French customs stamp)

TECHNIQUE

The ground color of these four plaques is a dark, opaque enamel, most of which is covered by a layer of opaque white. The heavy contour lines and hatching were executed primarily by *enlevage* of the white enamel, allowing the dark ground to show through. Most surfaces are covered with translucent glazes in blue, purple, turquoise, burgundy, green, golden brown, and yellowish green. Highlights were created by an additional application of opaque white before the colored glaze was laid down. Flesh tones were executed in opaque white thin enough to permit the ground color to show through, creating a slightly gray tone; the artist then added more opaque white for highlights and a thinned wash of red for a salmon-pink color. Iron red was applied to the surface for the marks of Christ's flagellation in two of the plaques and for a cross on the *Resurrection* banner. Gold was lavishly used for the hair of the figures and many decorative details, such as stars, flowers and vegetation, ceiling and floor patterns, delineation of the courses of bricks or stones, and highlights on relief sculpture and armor.

The enamel surface is relatively smooth, with protrusions where there is a considerable build-up of opaque white. The counter-enamel is a translucent reddish purple.

The enamels are in excellent condition, with only a few losses around the edges of the plaques.

*

Series of painted enamels illustrating scenes from the Passion and Resurrection of Christ were executed in Limoges from the time of the Monvaerni Master (see cat. no. 1). The earliest known group to be modeled after the work of a German artist, however, is a series of twelve splendid polychrome plaques dated to about 1500, executed after mid-fifteenth-century engravings by Martin Schongauer (Bartsch 1978–82, vol. 8, 222–33, nos. 9–20) and currently attributed to the late fifteenth-/early sixteenth-century Master of the Large Foreheads (ex-collections Ferdinand II of Portugal and Charles Mannheim; sold Christie's, London, December 11, 1978, lot 24). Although scenes from Schongauer's Passion were copied by other Limousin artists, his cycle was soon outstripped in popularity by Albrecht Dürer's Small Passion (Bartsch 1978–82, vol. 10, 111–47, nos. 16–52), a series of thirty-seven woodcuts (1511), which were later copied by Marcantonio Raimondi (Bartsch 1978–82, vol. 27, 270–306, nos. 584–620). Except for more fluidity in the drapery, the Raimondi copies are so true to the originals, it is often difficult to tell which source an enamel painter has used.

Jean I Pénicaud was the first enamel painter in Limoges to use the Dürer woodcuts as his source: two signed plaques, the *Flagellation* and *Christ Crowned with Thorns* in the Victoria and Albert Museum, London, are the earliest known copies after the prints (Marquet de Vasselot 1921, 187, nos. 154–55, pls. LXII–LXIII). Large extant groups after Dürer, all unattributed, are: thirty-six plaques in an altarpiece from Zimmerlehen, now in the Tiroler Landesmuseum Ferdinandeum, Innsbruck; twenty-six in the Museu Nacional de Soares dos Reis, Oporto, formerly (incorrectly) attributed to Jean II Pénicaud, in a style very close to the finest work of Pierre Reymond; twenty-four in a retable in the basilica of Saint-Hubert-en-Ardennes, Luxembourg, c. 1560; and twenty-four in the Wallace Collection, London (inv. no. III F 250).

The four woodcuts from Dürer's Small Passion copied by Reymond for the Los Angeles enamels are straightforward presentations of scriptural passages or, in the case of the *Resurrection*, traditional iconography (Bartsch 1978–82, vol. 10, 120, no. 25; 128, no. 33; 129, no. 34; 140, no. 45). The episode of Christ washing the apostles' feet after the Last Supper occurs only in the Gospel of John (13:4–17). Dürer chose the moment usually depicted, Peter's bewilderment that Christ should perform so humble a task:

> Jesus...rose from the supper table, took off his outer garment and, taking a towel, tied it round him. Then he poured water into a basin, and began to wash his disciples' feet and to wipe them with the towel. When he came to Simon Peter, Peter said to him, "You, Lord, washing my feet?" Jesus replied, "You do not understand now what I am doing, but one day you will." Peter said, "I will never let you wash my feet." "If I do not wash you," Jesus replied, "you have no part with me." "Then, Lord," said Simon Peter, "not my feet only; wash my hands and head as well." (John 13:4–9 ERV)

Christ uses the incident to foreshadow his betrayal by Judas ("you are clean, though not every one of you" [John 13:10 ERV]) and to demonstrate the servanthood of his followers to all men. Reymond has followed the woodcut model almost exactly;

due to the size of the copper plaque, however, he cut off the chain of the chandelier and compacted the two onlookers at the far left until they nearly disappeared. He also omitted the sponge in the basin. Dürer's monogram on the end of Peter's bench has been turned into a relief sculpture of a battle, perhaps to suggest a sarcophagus, a reminder of death to come. The inscription on Christ's plinth is probably meant to be *Salvator Mundi* (Savior of the world), one of Christ's titles (the enamel painters of Limoges were notorious for their mistakes in inscriptions, not having been trained as scholars).

Although Reymond's versions of this and the other woodcuts are far less subtle and elegant in style and technique than Dürer's work, the enamel painter occasionally enhanced his composition by small changes, as here in a few wisps of hair falling over Christ's brow in his exertion and in Peter's look of genuine befuddlement to accompany the gesture of scratching his head.

The Flagellation or Scourging of Christ is mentioned in a short phrase by all four evangelists (Matthew 27:26; Mark 15:15; Luke 23:16, 22; John 19:1). Pontius Pilate, finding no guilt in Christ under Roman law, decrees the comparatively minor punishment of flogging; his desire to release Christ is thwarted, however, by the priests and people of Jerusalem, who demand his crucifixion. One of the turbanned men can be identified as Pilate from another woodcut in the Small Passion, *Christ before Pilate* (Bartsch 1978–82, vol. 10, 126, no. 31); the man in the left foreground who seems to be directing the procedures also appears in another woodcut in the cycle as the attendant holding the basin in which Pilate washes his hands (126, no. 36); his features are negroid, and he wears a large hat of feathers.

Dürer's *Flagellation* (fig. 19) is the one scene in the Small Passion with which copyists took great liberties or which they rejected altogether in favor of another model. It was probably not regarded as a successful composition: all six figures are standing and of approximately the same scale, Christ is seen in profile, and the scourger at left would be hitting the column and not his victim. There is a series of Passion scenes after Dürer attributed to Reymond in which the enamel painter has substituted Schongauer's *Flagellation* for the Dürer version (Metropolitan Museum of Art, New York, inv. no. 45.60.26). Although Reymond followed the woodcut closely in the Los Angeles plaque, there are some differences worth noting: he added marks of the birch all over Christ's body, transformed the man at far left into a close-cropped white man, and, most unusually, dressed the scourger at left from the waist up in contemporary French clothing, including hat. The features of the latter figure are so distinctive as to suggest a portrait. Although it is possible that Reymond, in an attitude of humility and repentance, depicted himself as one of the tormentors of Christ, it is more likely that the man is someone else, perhaps a personal enemy or a Protestant heretic (compare, for example, Léonard Limousin's *Triumph of the Eucharist* (fig. 9), in which a chariot symbolizing orthodox Catholicism crushes Protestant heretics beneath its wheels [Frick Collection, New York, inv. no. 16.4.22; Verdier 1977, 121–29]).

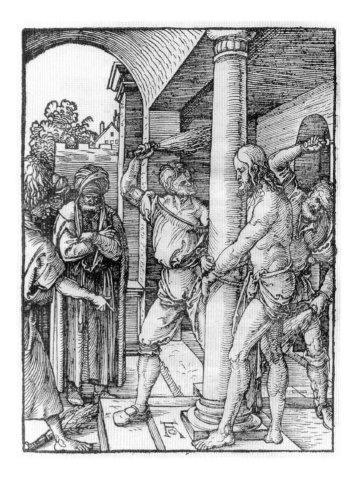

FIGURE 20

Albrecht Dürer,
Germany, 1471–1528,
*The Crowning with
Thorns*, from the Small
Passion, Nuremburg:
Holzel, 1511, woodcut,
12.6 x 9.7 cm (4 15/16 x
3 13/16 in.), Spencer
Collection, The New
York Public Library,
Astor, Lenox and
Tilden Foundations,
New York.

The scene of Christ Crowned with Thorns is sometimes confused with the Mocking of Christ, which occurred before he was delivered to Pilate. In the Mocking, Christ is also beaten and taunted, but he is often bound and blindfolded and he does not wear a crown of thorns. The Crowning (Matthew 27:27–31; Mark 15:16–20; John 19:2–3) took place after he was condemned to be crucified:

> Then the soldiers of the governor took Jesus into his residence, the Praetorium, where they collected the whole company round him. They stripped him and dressed him in a scarlet [purple, according to Mark] cloak; and plaiting a crown of thorns they placed it on his head, and a stick in his right hand. Falling on their knees before him they jeered at him: "Hail, king of the Jews!" They spat on him, and used the stick to beat him about the head. (Matthew 27:27–30 ERV)

Although the presence of Pilate is not mentioned in the scriptural passages, Dürer (fig. 20) included him as a witness, along with another man who holds a scroll and may be a military or civil official (he is not Caiaphas, Annas, or Herod, who are all depicted differently in other prints in the series). The pattern of fleurs-de-lis, the emblem of the French kings, on the ceiling of the portico serves a double purpose as an attractive surface decoration, of which the enamel painters were so fond, and as a reference to the palace of Pilate, the effective ruler of Judea, where the flogging took place.

Beside some adjustment to the architecture—the creation of brick walls and two oculi with gratings—and another battle relief added to the end of Christ's bench, Reymond's deviations from Dürer's original have to do with the relationship between Christ and the kneeling figure. Dürer depicted Christ with downcast eyes and his left index finger raised to balance his "scepter"; in the enamel Christ stares sternly into his mocker's eyes and his finger points in an accusatory gesture. This may explain why Reymond's kneeling figure, confronted with such authority, does not copy Dürer's model in sticking out his tongue to spit at or deride Christ.

There is no passage in the Gospel depicting Christ triumphant before his tomb; this image dates from the late medieval period. The arrival of a group of women at dawn to anoint the body of the dead Christ is mentioned in all the Gospels (Matthew 28:1–8; Mark 16:1–8; Luke 24:1–11; John 20:1–9); they were the first to whom the message of the Resurrection was given. Their number and identities differ from account to account, but the group always includes Mary Magdalen and Mary [Cleophas], the mother of the apostle James, and usually a third woman identified either as [Mary] Salome (Mark 16:1) or Joanna (Luke 24:10). Reymond's changes in this plaque are limited primarily to details of the soldiers' weapons and armor and to the fact that, while Dürer's guards are asleep or stupefied, several of his are wide-awake and cheerfully blasé. Small polychrome plaques signed by or attributable to Reymond are from the earliest phase of the artist's career. More than fifteen plaques on religious and social themes dealing with shepherds or peasants date from the period 1533–43, and several other enamels of religious subjects were executed in the same years, including the *Adoration of the Virgin and Child* of 1534 (see Reymond's biography). The style and technique of the Los Angeles Passion plaques would place them in the period 1535–40, since dated extant Passion scenes executed by Reymond after 1540 were all painted in grisaille, including six plaques dated 1542 in the Detroit Institute of Arts (inv. nos. 21.171–.176); a *Last Supper*, also of 1542, in the Fitzwilliam Museum, Cambridge (inv. no. M.52-1904); and a triptych dated 1543 in the Victoria and Albert Museum (inv. no. 4401-1857). The color of the counter-enamel is also consistent with that on dated small plaques of this period. The execution of the Los Angeles plaques, especially the subtlety of the modeling with highlights, is very fine, and must therefore be by the master's hand.

The four plaques were probably part of a larger group that, judging by labels on the back of the plaques, was broken up as recently as the earlier decades of this century, but it is no longer possible to identify existing single plaques or groups as part of the same series. In 1951 plaques of the same dimensions illustrating Pentecost and the Ascension, both after the Dürer Small Passion, were sold as the lot (lot 83) immediately after the Los Angeles plaques (lots 81 and 82) and were probably from the same series (see Provenance). Unfortunately, they went to a different buyer and cannot be traced.

The series containing the Los Angeles plaques was not the only polychrome Passion group executed by Reymond, although most groups documented in the nineteenth and earlier twentieth centuries are not presently identifiable and thus cannot be securely attributed. A group of twenty-four rectangular polychrome plaques modeled after the Small Passion was exhibited in 1862 at the Victoria and Albert Museum (at that time the South Kensington Museum) with a suggested attribution to Reymond (London 1862, cat. no. 1661, lent by H. G. Gordon, Esq.). Another group of nine scenes after the Small Passion, now in the Walters Art Gallery, Baltimore (inv. no. 44.364; Verdier 1967, cat. nos. 121–29), was attributed to Reymond by Émile Molinier in the sale catalogue of the collection of Dmitri Schevitch, Madrid (sold Paris, April 4–7, 1906, lot 225): they are in fact close to Reymond's style and seem to be signed with his monogram, but Philippe Verdier read the monogram as "PV" and presented several reasons for an attribution to the little-known Pierre II Veyrier. There are extant series of Passion scenes based on other print cycles by Dürer (the Large Passion or the Small Passion on Copper): a series of twelve, with four plaques of the evangelists, was commissioned by Anne de Montmorency for the altar of the chapel of his château in Écouen (now the Musée de la Renaissance)—these were ascribed to Reymond by Léon de Laborde (1853, cat. nos. 332–47) and Jean-Joseph Marquet

de Vasselot (1914, cat. no. 586), although Alfred Darcel (1891, cat. nos. 540–55) attributed them to Pierre Courteys—and a group of twelve circular plaques attributed to Reymond are in the Taft Museum, Cincinnati (inv. nos. 1931.502–.513; Taft 1958, nos. 89–100).

Other series of polychrome plaques signed by or attributed to Reymond and based on models other than Dürer's prints include five signed **P.R.**, c. 1534/40 (sold Nouveau Drouot, Paris, March 27, 1984); a series of medallions at Luton Hoo, Bedfordshire (Natanson 1954, cat. nos. 339–41); twenty-four rectangular and twelve narrow plaques sold at Christie's, London, in 1930 (July 17, lot 73); from the "school of Pierre Reymond," sixteen plaques in the Musée de Cluny, Paris (inv. nos. 4639–54; Du Sommerard 1883, 365–67), and nine plaques formerly in the collection of Thomas Fortune Ryan (sold American Art Association/Anderson Galleries, New York, November 25 [day 3], 1933, lot 395).

PROVENANCE

Aharon; sale, Parke Bernet, New York, January 4, 1951, lots 81–82.

William Randolph Hearst.

Donated to the Los Angeles County Museum of Art, 1951.

EXHIBITED

Los Angeles Museum of Contemporary Crafts, 1959.

PIERRE REYMOND

Tazza: Scene from the Book of Proverbs

1558
Grisaille enamel, flesh tones, touches of color,
and gold on copper
Height 8.9 cm (3½ in.)
Diameter of bowl 22.7 cm (8 15⁄16 in.)
Diameter of foot 12.4 cm (4⅞ in.)
William Randolph Hearst Collection
48.2.12

DESCRIPTION

In the bowl of the tazza a large pig with
a gold ring through its nose stands in the
foreground under an oak tree. In the middle ground four men in rustic dress dance
in a ring to the music of a piper seated
on a rock at the right. A town can be
seen in the central distance. In the deeper
woods at left four other pigs forage for
food. On a tablet at lower right are the
words **ORNAMENTVM AVREVM IN NARE
PORCI PROVERBIS XI** (A gold ornament
in a pig's snout, Proverbs 11). The scene is
surrounded by a band of gold arabesques
and a white rim.

The underside of the bowl is decorated with strapwork punctuated by four
oval cartouches, each containing a reclining
nude, three men and one winged woman.
Beneath each cartouche is a lion's head.
Gold arabesques surround the whole, and
there is a garland of fruit around the stem.

The stem is painted with four cherub's
heads and swags. A cartouche between
two of the heads is inscribed with the date
1558, and a coat of arms occupies the
same position on the other side of the
stem. The edge of the foot is a white border decorated with a guilloche in red.
The heads of the four pins joining the bowl
and stem are visible at the upper edge of
the stem.

The underside of the foot is scattered
with a flowerlike design in gold. A disk
bearing a five-petaled white flower with
gold fronds is inserted in the stem, presumably to hide the join of bowl and stem.

Color plate, page 47

PIERRE REYMOND

Tazza: Scene from the Book of Proverbs

c. 1558
Grisaille enamel, flesh tones, touches of color,
and gold on copper
Height 8.6 cm (3⅜ in.)
Diameter of bowl 22.7 cm (8¹⁵⁄₁₆ in.)
Diameter of foot 12.4 cm (4⅞ in.)
William Randolph Hearst Collection
48.2.13

DESCRIPTION

The scene in the bowl of the tazza is dominated by a large oak tree; in the branches is a nest containing four baby birds, the mother flying off to the right. At ground level to the left of the tree a man, staff in hand and dressed for traveling, strides off into the landscape. To the right is a complex of buildings, perhaps a prosperous farm, with sheep grazing in front. Two small children outside the gate look or gesture at the departing figure; in front of an entrance at far right is a woman holding another child by the hand. Cottages and other buildings can be seen at left and in the distance. On a tablet tied to a branch at the base of the tree trunk are the words SICVT AVIS DESERENS NIDVM SIC EST VIR DESERENS LOCVM SVVM PROVERB. XXVII (Like a bird that strays from its nest is a man straying from his home, Proverbs 27). The scene is surrounded by a band of gold arabesques and a white rim.

The decoration of the underside of the bowl is identical to that of the previous tazza (cat. no. 9), except for the reclining figures: on this piece all four are men, one falling backward on a dagger, another holding a snake in each hand.

The stem and underside of the foot are also identical to those of the other tazza, except for the omission of the date.

LATER INSCRIPTIONS
OR LABELS

Under the foot: P.M. 798. painted in red
(J. Pierpont Morgan catalogue number)

TECHNIQUE

The enamels were executed with opaque white enamel on a ground that appears black but is actually a dense translucent mulberry. A few touches of color were used: a wash of red enamel in clear flux gives a salmon tone to the flesh in both tazzas and to the birds, acorns, and roofs in the second. A drop of turquoise and white enamel suggests a jewel on the ring through the nose of the pig, and a deep blue was used in the coats of arms.

The entire design of each tazza was executed by removing areas of unfired white enamel by *enlevage* and applying additional patches of white over the fired surface where complete opacity was desired for highlights. The painter used hatching and cross-hatching to model forms.

The surfaces of the enamels are uneven, the raised sections being those with the highest concentration of opaque white. The tazzas are in excellent condition.

✳

The inscriptions identify the scenes in the bowls of the tazzas as illustrations of verses from the Old Testament book of Proverbs. The first tazza, however, seems to depict only partially the proverb, "Like a gold ring in a pig's snout is a beautiful woman without good sense" (Proverbs 11:22 ERV). The pig is there, but the foolish woman is nowhere to be seen: she has been supplanted by a group of dancing peasants, who seem to have little to do with the text. They are, however, certainly showing a lack of "good sense" by allowing their pigs to wander off while they disport themselves in the clearing. Perhaps a "beautiful woman...without good sense" proved too difficult a concept to be illustrated tastefully.

"Like a bird that strays from its nest is a man straying from his home" (Proverbs 27:8 ERV) is the text for the second tazza. Here, the traveler leaving his home, wife, and children is clearly likened to the mother bird leaving the fledglings in the nest. Interestingly, although the proverb only compares, rather than condemns, the bird and the man, a tone of censure creeps into the enamel painting, communicated through the stances and gestures of the two children at the gate.

Although the shape of the tazzas is fairly common, especially in the workshop of Pierre Reymond, the quality of the painting in the bowls is so high as to suggest the participation of the master himself. No print source has yet been identified for these two scenes, and it is possible they are Reymond's original compositions. Nor are any extant variations of the subjects or depictions of other scenes from the book of Proverbs known to me. The quality and rarity of the enamels suggest a commission

for which the subjects were designed by Reymond to the specifications of his patron, who lost no opportunity for self-aggrandizement: the coat of arms, which features acorns, is amplified by the special prominence given to an oak tree in each vignette.

There is apparently only one comparable piece extant, noted by Madeleine Marcheix (archives of the Musée Municipal, Limoges), a tazza in a private collection in Barcelona, depicting an old man holding his heart in his right hand, identified by a proverb from the Old Testament book of Ecclesiastes (10:2): **COR SAPIENTIS IN DESTERA EIVS COR STVLTI IN SINISTRA ILLIVS ECCLES. X** (A wise man's heart is at his right hand; but a fool's heart at his left [AV]). Although the decoration of the underside of the bowl and the stem is somewhat different, the tazza bears the same date—1558—and the same coat of arms, along with the monogram "PR," and its dimensions are approximately the same; it seems likely that it is in fact from the same "proverbial" group.

The reclining nudes on the underside of the tazza bowls are probably inspired by similar figures representing river gods and nymphs displayed in rectangular fields in a framework of grotesques engraved by Jacques Androuet du Cerceau in his *Grands Grotesques* of 1556, specifically, his design for the ceiling of the Galerie d'Ulysse at Fontainebleau (fig. 21). They are also clearly indebted to the painted and sculpted nudes of Michelangelo, particularly those on the ceiling of the Sistine Chapel: one of the reclining figures on each tazza is in the pose of the newly created Adam.

PROVENANCE

Roy.

Baron Roger; sale, 1841, lot 194, 401
francs (cat. no. 9).

Rattier; sale, Paris, March 21–24, 1859,
lot 150, 2,500 francs (cat. no. 9); lot 154,
2,900 francs.

De Blacas.

Charles Mannheim, Paris.

J. Pierpont Morgan (cat. no. 10).

William Randolph Hearst.

Donated to the Los Angeles County
Museum of Art, 1948.

EXHIBITED

Paris 1884, nos. 72 (cat. no. 10), 73, lent by
Charles Mannheim.

Paris 1889, nos. 1125a (cat. no. 10), 1125b,
lent by Charles Mannheim.

LITERATURE

Molinier 1898, nos. 182 (cat. no. 9), 183.

PIERRE REYMOND

Ewer stand:
Scenes from the Book of Genesis

c. 1558
Grisaille enamel, flesh tones, touches of color,
and gold on copper
Diameter 47.6 cm (18¾ in.)
William Randolph Hearst Collection
48.2.19

DESCRIPTION

The ewer stand illustrates scenes from the first four chapters of the book of Genesis: first in sequence is God's creation of Eve from a rib of the sleeping Adam; to the right, out of sequence, Eve plucks an apple with her left hand, as the serpent looks on, and with her right hand gives another apple to the seated Adam; next, God admonishes the pair not to eat the fruit of the tree of the knowledge of good and evil; they are subsequently expelled from Eden by an angel with a flaming sword; and, finally, their son Cain murders his brother Abel with an animal's jawbone. The scenes are played out against a continuous band of landscape inhabited by a number of creatures, including a lion,

heron, peacock or turkey, pig, squirrel, goat, rabbits, deer, hedgehogs or porcupines, dogs, cows, sheep, camels, elephants, and unicorns. Under the sleeping Adam is the monogram **P·R**.

On the boss is a three-quarters portrait in polychrome enamel of a man in sixteenth-century costume. This is surrounded by a border of opaque white enamel painted in red with a circle and small dots, a band of arabesques in gold, and a second white border painted with a red guilloche. The cavetto is decorated with a gold arabesque design. The rim of the stand depicts a group of grotesques that includes figures of Bacchus and Silenus in fanciful chariots, and satyrs, monks, goats, bulls, snails, griffins, harpies, phoenixes, and other creatures too bizarre to identify. The edge is covered with opaque white enamel.

On the underside of the stand four pairs of affronted winged grotesques, male and female, alternate with four female terms with outstretched arms, each hand grasping the edge of a basket of fruit, the arms and baskets forming the inner border of the decoration. The terms' draperies interlace to form another decorative motif. Outside a band of strapwork on which all the creatures stand is a gold arabesque. On the rim are scrolls of vegetation flanking four rectangular cartouches in which are painted three reclining figures and a winged grotesque. Leafy branches delicately painted in gold fill all the interstices. On the underside of the boss is a polychrome three-quarters view of a woman in sixteenth-century dress on a dark field sprinkled with gold dots and flowers.

PIERRE REYMOND

The stand was executed in white enamel on a dark translucent mulberry ground that appears black. A wash of red enamel in clear flux was used for the flesh tones; the red particles are clearly visible, giving these areas a grainy appearance. A darker red wash was used for the hair of the men (including some of the more human grotesques on the rim), the apples, and the beak of the peacock/turkey. A deep iron red can be seen in several decorative elements and in the two sacrificial fires behind Cain and Abel. Besides its use for overall ornamentation, gold was used for the angel's sword and nimbus in the Expulsion, Eve's hair, fruit on the trees, grass, and some hatching, especially on the body of Eve. The boss was executed in white, brown, golden brown, flesh tones, and gold on a dark blue ground.

The images were created primarily by *enlevage*, especially in the contour lines, hatching, and facial features, and by the addition of white enamel for highlights. There is not a great deal of hatching on this piece, which relies more on a palette of grays for shading; hatching and cross-hatching are confined largely to shadows on the ground and God's robe, with occasional use, softened with gold, on the nude bodies.

The enamel is in good condition, with slight abrasion from routine wear on the underside, firing cracks and a few chips on the white rims, and some small losses on the upper rim. The areas of opaque white give the enamel an uneven surface.

The portrait panel of the boss is not contemporary with the stand, and the side of the boss looks as if it was repainted when the filler was added, probably in the nineteenth century.

✳

Many ewer stands of this size and shape were produced in the workshop of Pierre Reymond between the years 1557 and 1566, demonstrating the popularity of this form, which was also carried out in metalwork and ceramic. The 1568 inventory of Anne de Montmorency's Paris *hôtel* lists four enamel "basins for handwashing" painted with figures (Mirot 1918–19, 209, items 1305, 1325). Curiously, although a number of ateliers turned out ewers, the stands were made in quantity only by Reymond's workshop, which suggests that the two vessels types were not usually made as a pair.

Reymond decorated round and oval ewer stands with several iconographical programs, including Moses on the Seat of Judgment (an example was sold at Sotheby's, London, on December 7, 1967 [lot 134], and again at Christie's, London, on May 3, 1977 [lot 108; ex-collection Robert Strauss]) and a varying group of scenes known as the Allegory of Redemption, Allegory of Life, or Allegory of the Old and New Testaments (examples are in the Walters Art Gallery, Baltimore, inv. no. 44.357 [Verdier 1967, cat. no. 144]; Musée d'Art et d'Histoire, Geneva; Wernher Collection, Luton Hoo, Bedfordshire [Natanson 1954, cat. no. 334]; and another was sold at Sotheby's, London, on May 16, 1968 [lot 45]), but episodes from Genesis were by far the most popular motif. By the 1530s the Counter-Reformation had become a pan-European movement, and by the middle of the century the Inquisition had been revived as a disciplinary instrument of the Catholic Church. Sin, redemption, and the judgment of God became central to religious imagery, and the Old Testament was rediscovered as a fertile source of appropriate subject matter—nothing more appropriate than the doctrine of original sin illustrated by the Fall of Man in the first chapters of the book of Genesis.

The scenes decorating the ewer stands produced by the Reymond atelier are taken from a series of six engravings of 1529 depicting the Creation and Fall of Man (figs. 22–23; Bartsch 1978–82, vol. 12, 131–36, nos. 1–6) by the Dutch artist Lucas van Leyden (1494–1533). Reymond used only five of the six scenes: the creation of Eve from a rib of the sleeping Adam (Genesis 2:21–22), God warning Adam and

Eve not to eat the fruit of the tree of the knowledge of good and evil (2:16–17), the serpent tempting Adam and Eve to eat (3:1–6), an angel driving Adam and Eve out of the Garden of Eden (3:24), and the murder of Abel by his brother, Cain (4:2–8). The enamel painter has reversed the order of the Admonishment and the Temptation, perhaps under the impression that the Admonishment represented God chastising Adam and Eve after they had disobeyed him and discovered they were naked: Adam is clutching a strategically placed branch and Eve is hiding behind him.

To judge from the extant stands that are dated, Reymond and his assistants followed the engravings very closely in a few early examples but soon began taking liberties, primarily in scenes of the Admonishment and the Temptation. Philippe Verdier (1967, 245) suggested that the prints kept in the studio for the copyists may have deteriorated and been discarded, so that the painters were forced to invent the scenes; it is also possible that they wished to vary the composition in order to distinguish one stand from another.

The fidelity of the scenes on this stand to the engravings suggests that it is one of the earlier group, as does the appearance of reclining figures in red on the underside of the rim, recalling the decoration of the underside of the Proverbs tazzas of 1558 (cat. nos. 9–10), which was inspired by Jacques Androuet du Cerceau's *Grands Grotesques* (1556). The closest extant example is that now in the Fitzwilliam Museum, Cambridge (inv. no. M.III-1961; ex-collections Rothschild, Sassoon,

Durlacher, Clarke; *Connoisseur* 101 [March 1938]: xxxv), also signed with the monogram "PR," although the two stands are probably not by the same hand. The stands share the same (erroneous) sequence of Genesis scenes and the same grotesque decoration of the underside, the latter occurring on only a few examples, including a stand formerly in the Debruge-Duménil, Soltykoff, and Seillière collections and another illustrating Moses on the Seat of Judgment, formerly in the Basilewsky collection, now in the Hermitage Museum, Saint Petersburg (inv. no. F-297; Dobroklonskaya 1969, no. 36). The front rim of the Cambridge stand has a different pattern, made up of cornucopias, putti, and acanthus arabesques, but the other variations are slight: the positioning of the sacrificial altars behind Cain and Abel and details of the landscape and animals. Also, on the Cambridge example the scenes are designated with Roman numerals and under the Expulsion is the inscription GENESE III (the Expulsion is described in Genesis 3:24). It is tempting to link these two stands in date with one inscribed 1557, now in the Cleveland Museum of Art (inv. no. 40.139), but the latter is unfortunately a nineteenth-century copy, although it may have been based on an authentic stand of that date, now lost.

In an oval stand dated 1561 in the British Museum, London (inv. no. 1913, 12–23, 33; British Museum 1924, 299), the four scenes of Adam and Eve are distributed around the oval, while the episode of Cain and Abel is painted on the boss. Usually, however, the bosses are not an integral part of the decorative program and are in fact extremely problematical. Some stands, such as the above-mentioned oval dish, have filled bosses, while others, including that made in 1558 for Linhard I Tucher (see Reymond's biography), were made with hollow bosses. The bosses were basically knobs to keep the ewers steady on their basins, and in a group such as the Tucher set, the stand may not have been intended to be displayed separately. Given the differences in style and technique (most are polychrome) of the painting on extant filled-in bosses, we may surmise that only a few bosses were original to the stands or supplied only slightly later— perhaps when a set was separated—while most are nineteenth-century inventions or replacements. The boss on the Los Angeles stand seems to be of the latter type.

The Genesis scenes by Lucas van Leyden were copied or adapted by Reymond's atelier on other types of vessels as well, including covered cups (one sold at Parke Bernet, New York, February 21, 1969, lot 60) and sets of plates illustrating individual scenes (two plates dated 1560 in the Musée du Louvre, Paris [Marquet de Vasselot 1914, nos. 590–91]). Other enamel painters illustrating these subjects chose to use as models the graphic work of Bernard Salomon; these artists included Jean de Court (three covered cups in the Musée de la Renaissance, Écouen [Du Sommerard 1883, cat. nos. 4597–99], and a ewer in the Taft Museum [inv. no. 1931.292; Taft 1958, no. 140]), Jean Court *dit* Vigier (covered cup, sold Sotheby Parke Bernet, Mentmore Towers, May 20 [day 3], 1977, lot 1145), Pierre Courteys (cat. no. 23), Jean Miette (five plates in the Musée du Louvre [inv. nos. 6192–95; Marquet de Vasselot 1914, nos. 712–16), and the later Pénicaud atelier (three plates in the British Museum [British Museum 1924, 299]).

The source of the decorative motifs on this and most painted enamels is often impossible to ascertain. The eight long-necked grotesque beasts on the underside of this ewer stand may have their origin in an engraved panel of 1528 by Lucas van Leyden (Guilmard 1880–81, plate vol., no. 162), and Philippe Verdier (1967, 248) has attributed the nearly identical grotesques on the rim of a similar ewer stand in the Walters Art Gallery (inv. no. 44.208; Verdier 1967, cat. no. 141) to the influence of engravings by the Netherlandish artists Jost Amman and Cornelis Bos. But similar decorative conceits appear in the engravings of several dozen French, Italian, German, and Netherlandish artists of the period (a representative selection may be found in Guilmard 1880–81). Only rarely is a purely decorative motif on a painted enamel lifted exactly from a print source (see cat. no. 19). While the enamel painters were clearly influenced by European ornamental styles, they must be given credit for being capable enough to invent their own variants for the objects they decorated.

PROVENANCE

Possibly Debruge-Duménil collection, Paris, by 1846; sale, Hôtel des Ventes, Paris, January 23 and following days, 1850, lot 709.

Possibly Prince Soltykoff; sale, Hôtel Drouot, Paris, April 8 and following days, 1861, lot 481.

Possibly Seillière collection, Paris.

Maurice Kann, Paris.

William Randolph Hearst.

Donated to the Los Angeles County Museum of Art, 1948.

EXHIBITED

Possibly Paris, *Exposition universelle*, 1878, lent by Seillière.

Paris 1889, no. 1108, lent by Maurice Kann.

LITERATURE

Possibly Du Sommerard 1838–46, ser. 7, pl. XXVIII.

Possibly Labarte 1847, cat. no. 709.

Color plate, page 48

PIERRE REYMOND

Ewer stand:
Scenes from the Book of Genesis

c. 1560
Grisaille enamel, flesh tones, touches of color,
and gold on copper
Diameter 46.7 cm (18 ⅜ in.)
William Randolph Hearst Collection
48.2.18

DESCRIPTION

This ewer stand illustrates the same five
scenes from the book of Genesis as the
previous example (cat. no. 11), but in their
correct chronological sequence: the Creation of Eve, Admonishment, Temptation,
Expulsion, and Cain's Murder of Abel.
There are some differences in the composition: God is crowned; the tree of the
knowledge of good and evil is between
God and Adam and Eve during his instruc-
tions to them; and there is an archway
suggesting the gate of Eden through which
the couple is expelled. The animal kingdom is represented on this ewer stand by
a snail, lion, cow, heron, dog, stags, rabbits,
sheep, and possibly a camel.

On the central boss is the profile
portrait of a woman, identified by an
inscription as SVSANNA BELLA (beautiful
Susanna), in sixteenth-century dress.
This is surrounded by a border of opaque
white enamel painted in red with a scallop
pattern, a band of arabesques in gold,
and a second white border painted with
a red guilloche. The cavetto is decorated
with a similar gold arabesque design.
The rim is a continuous band of grotesques, including harpies, monks, snails,
and other less familiar creatures, with an
opaque white edge.

On the underside two lion masks, two draped heads of Diana, and four putto heads are arranged symmetrically on a band of strapwork in which is intertwined a garland of fruit. Outside this is a delicate gold arabesque, and the rim is painted with a series of vegetal rinceaux with grotesque heads at one end. On the underside of the boss is a coat of arms on a dark field sprinkled with gold flowers.

TECHNIQUE

The ground of the ewer stand is a dark translucent mulberry that appears black. The figures and landscape were built up from successive layers of white enamel. A wash of red enamel particles in clear flux was used for the flesh tones. A darker red wash was used for the apples, and a deep iron red can be seen in the two sacrificial fires behind Cain and Abel and the angel's flaming sword. Gold was used on both surfaces for decorative foliage and arabesques, in the sacrificial fires, the angel's nimbus, and God's crown.

The front of the boss was executed in a thin, almost watery white over a dark blue ground. The coat of arms on the underside was painted with white, gold, a rich deep blue, and a spotty iron red.

The designs were created primarily by *enlevage*, especially in the contour lines, hatching, and facial features, with the addition by brush of white enamel for highlights. This stand employs more hatching and cross-hatching in the shadowed areas than did the previous example.

The enamel is slightly abraded and scratched on the underside and has some small cracks and losses on the upper rim. The surface is uneven, the raised sections being those with the highest concentration of opaque white.

✳

The primary decoration of this ewer stand, like that in the previous entry (cat. no. 11), is based on five of six engravings of 1529 by the Dutch artist Lucas van Leyden (1494–1533), illustrating the Creation and Fall of Man (figs. 22–23). This example follows the model more frequently painted in the atelier of Pierre Reymond, in that it deviates significantly from the engravings in one or two scenes. This is a characteristic of the later dated stands, which prompted Philippe Verdier (1967, 245) to suggest that the atelier's prints eventually deteriorated or were destroyed or lost, presumably leaving the painters free to invent variants. Here, God stands to the left of the tree in the scene of the Admonishment, and in the Temptation the tree is between Adam and Eve, who has her back to the viewer. Also, an arch, symbolizing the gate to Eden, is inserted behind the Expulsion, another common feature of the later stands.

Other examples that fall into this category (and with a similar head-and-strapwork underside) are in the Hermitage, Saint Petersburg (inv. no. F-288; ex-collections Pourtalès and Basilewsky; Dobroklonskaya 1969, no. 31), dated 1558; the Germanisches Museum, Nuremberg (one of the pieces made for Linhard I Tucher; see Reymond's biography), also dated 1558; and the Walters Art Gallery, Baltimore (inv. no. 44.208; Verdier 1967, no. 141), dated 1563. A similarly decorated stand with explanatory inscriptions, dated 1570, in the collection of D. C. Marjoribanks, M.P., was exhibited in 1862 at the South Kensington Museum (London 1862, cat. no. 1789). The same pattern of grotesque decorations on the underside was used on oval as well as round plates, such as *The Allegory of the Old and New Testaments* in the Wernher Collection, Luton Hoo, Bedfordshire (inv. no. E34). Heads crowned with a crescent moon are usually identified as the goddess Artemis or Diana; the motif itself, as with all images of the moon goddess created between the mid-1530s and 1560, may have originated as homage to Diane de Poitiers (1499–1566), the influential mistress of Henri II.

Although in these stands many of the enamel plaques in the central bosses are later additions (see cat. no. 11 for more information), in this example the boss filler, if not original, must have been added in the same century. The coat of arms has been identified as that of the de Mesmes or de Mèmes family, noted sixteenth-century collectors and bibliophiles. The same coat of arms appears on the underside of the boss of the above-mentioned stand in the Hermitage, but in

a completely different style, and the painting of the bust-length female figure on the front of the Hermitage boss suggests that the filler was added in a later century.

See the previous entry for additional information about the ewer stand form, iconography, and comparative examples.

PROVENANCE

William Randolph Hearst.

Donated to the Los Angeles County Museum of Art, 1948.

PIERRE REYMOND

Plate: June (Mowing)

1561
Grisaille enamel, flesh tones, touches of color,
and gold on copper
Diameter 17.9 cm (7 1/16 in.)
William Randolph Hearst Collection
48.2.5

DESCRIPTION

Three people in peasant garb are working in an enclosed field. At center is a man with a scythe, to the left and slightly behind him a woman with a pitchfork, to the right and farther back another man with a rake. The ground is covered with loose hay, some of which has been gathered into five small haystacks. Beyond the wall is a mountainous landscape with trees, shrubs, and a winding path or river.

The cavetto is decorated with a gold guilloche, and the rim is painted with four pairs of centaurs holding the handles of a strapwork container filled with fruit, alternating with four oval cartouches. The cartouche at the top of the plate contains the symbol of Virgo, at right the monogram P·R, at bottom IVN∗ (for *juin*, June), and at left 1561. The edge of the plate is painted with opaque white enamel.

At the center of the underside of the plate is the bust-length profile portrait of a woman, facing right, in sixteenth-century attire, her hair in a snood, on a dark ground dotted with gold. She is framed by a band of beading between two solid circles, which is surrounded by a band of strapwork and fruit. The curve is painted with a continuous gold vine, from which leaves sprout at regular intervals, broken by four decorated lozenges. On the rim are four pairs of griffins joined at the tail with a strapwork roundel, alternating with four oval cartouches. On the top and bottom cartouches is the date 1561, on the right and left the monograms P·R and P·R·.

PIERRE REYMOND

Plate: July (Harvesting)

1561

Grisaille enamel, flesh tones, touches of color,
and gold on copper

Diameter 17.9 cm (7 1/16 in.)

William Randolph Hearst Collection

48.2.6

DESCRIPTION

At center a man dressed as a peasant, with
a straw hat, is bending over to cut stalks of
wheat with a sickle; a bound sheaf lies in
front of him. To the left is a well-dressed
woman holding a tazza and a basket of
bread. A path behind the figures leads to a
barn and large farmhouse with a smoking
chimney. Behind the wheatfield at right is
a rolling landscape with trees and shrubs.

The rest of the plate is identical to the
June plate, except for the content of the
four oval cartouches on the rim: at top is
Taurus, at right PR, at bottom IVLIET (for
juillet, July), at left 1561.

The underside of the plate is identical
to that of the June plate, except for the
portrait and the content of the cartouches.
At center is the bust-length profile portrait
of a man, facing right, wearing an elaborate helmet with a crest. The cartouches
at left and right read 1561 and 1561*; the
top and bottom contain symmetrical
arabesques.

PIERRE REYMOND

Plate: August (Sowing)

1561
Grisaille enamel, flesh tones, touches of color,
and gold on copper
Diameter 18.1 cm (7⅛ in.)
William Randolph Hearst Collection
48.2.7

DESCRIPTION

Seated in the left foreground is a well-dressed woman similar to the one on the July plate. She holds a tazza and a large loaf of bread; on the ground in front of her are a pilgrim flask and a basket of fruit. To the right of center a peasant sows seed on a neatly furrowed field. A large barn and smaller farmhouse can be seen behind the figures. At right a path meanders through a grove of trees and a rolling plain to a walled city or castle in front of wooded hills.

The cavetto and rim are identical to those of the other plates in this group. The oval cartouches contain the symbol for Pisces at top, **P·R** at right, **AOVST** (for *août*, August) at bottom, and **1561** at left.

The decorative motifs on the underside are identical to those on the June plate, except that a guilloche replaces the beading in the portrait frame and there is no fruit in the strapwork band in this example. At the center is a bust-length profile portrait almost identical in pose and feature to the woman in the June plate, although the costume and hairdo have been slightly changed and the woman wears an elaborate, tall headdress. The oval cartouches read, clockwise from top: **1561**, **PIERE**, **1561**, and **REXMON**.

PIERRE REYMOND

Plate: November (Baking Bread)

1561
Grisaille enamel, flesh tones, and gold
on copper
Diameter 17.8 cm (7 in.)
William Randolph Hearst Collection
48.2.8

DESCRIPTION

A baker holding a long-handled bread paddle inserts a loaf (*fouace*) into a large oven, in which can be seen more than twenty other loaves. Nearly a dozen loaves lie on the floor at his feet. Behind him in the brick-walled kitchen a female cook stands kneading a loaf and watching a well-dressed woman (she of the July and August plates) touch two of the loaves lying on a wooden work surface. Behind them is a door with stone jambs and lintel.

The cavetto is decorated in gold with the leafing vine and lozenge motif seen on the underside of the other three plates; the rim is identical in design. The top cartouche contains the figure of Sagittarius, that at right the monogram P·R, at bottom NOVĒBR/E (for *novembre*, November), at left 1561.

On the underside the bust-length portrait is that of a man, facing right, in Eastern dress, including a turban, tunic, and fur- or fleece-lined coat. The other decorative motifs are identical to those on the July and August plates, except for the portrait frame, which displays the beading motif seen on the underside of the June plate. The cartouches are on the diagonal axes of this example; the inscriptions at upper right and lower left are 1561, those at upper left and lower right P·R.

TECHNIQUE

The designs on these plates were executed in opaque white enamel on a dense translucent mulberry ground that appears black. The contour lines were created by *enlevage* of a first layer of unfired white enamel. After the first application of white was fired, the highlights were built up with additional layers of white enamel. The flesh tone was achieved by mixing finely ground iron-red enamel with clear frit and applying it like a wash; the color was also used for pieces of fruit in the basket on the August plate and the loaves of bread in the November scene. A darker, almost brownish red was used for the inscriptions, contents of the wine cups (July, August), and decorative motifs on clothing (June, July) and architecture (July). Besides his use of gold for filler arabesques, dots, lines, and other ornamental motifs, the painter applied it as a border for the clothing worn by most of the figures.

The plates are in good condition, only the June plate showing some cracks and losses in the rim. There was considerable bubbling during firing in the densest areas of opaque white. Signs of wear and superficial scratches can be seen on all surfaces.

✳

These four plates are from a dispersed calendar set illustrating the traditional occupations or labors for each month (see introductory essay). The Reymond atelier turned out many of these sets over a period of years (extant dated plates range from 1548 to 1566), as did the workshops of Jean de Court (cat. no. 25), Martial Courteys (cat. nos. 29–40), and Pierre Courteys; they were obviously popular as items of display in affluent households. Most of Reymond's sets were executed in grisaille, but a few polychrome plaques are extant, including ovals for January, March, and August in the Victoria and Albert Museum, London (inv. nos. 2047-1855, 4877-1901, 4859-1901); others for February, June, July, and October in the Wernher Collection, Luton Hoo, Bedfordshire (inv. nos. 328–31), and an oval for May in the Taft Museum, Cincinnati (inv. no. 1931.281; Taft 1958, cat. no. 150). It is rare for a set to remain intact: a complete set signed by Reymond and dated 1559, formerly in the collection of Baron Lionel de Rothschild (London 1862, cat. nos. 1762–73), was sold in June 1992 (Sotheby's, Monte Carlo, June 19–20, lot 807), and another set was formerly in the collection of the Kunstgewerbemuseum in Berlin (Ilg 1884, 126). It is not now possible to make up complete sets from dispersed pieces, especially since different decorative motifs were sometimes used on the rims and undersides of the same set. At most, a few related plates may be identified.

During his career Reymond used three different series of models for the Labors of the Months. The earliest dated sets, from 1548 (Spitzer 1891, vol. 2, cat. no. 94; sold Chevallier-Mannheim, Paris, April 17–June 16, 1893, lot 510) to 1562, including the Rothschild set and the set from which these four plates came, are based on an as-yet-unidentified source. It is improbable, although not impossible, that this series was Reymond's own composition, because the scenes occur on plates by other enamel painters, for example, a complete set by Jean de Court (R. C. Pritchard collection; sold Sotheby's, London, December 8–9, 1988, lot 339). A more likely possibility would be an adaptation of a group of twelve woodcut illustrations for the *Compost et kalendrier des bergères* (fig. 24; see also fig. 36), published in Paris in 1499 by Guy Marchant. These prints served as models for other artists (see, for example, a set of fruitwood reliefs sold in London in 1979 [Sotheby Parke Bernet, December 13, lot 160]), and most of the scenes are very close in composition to the plates executed by the enamel painters. The appropriate signs of the zodiac are also incorporated in the woodcuts.

One curious feature added by the enamel painters is the well-dressed woman who appears in three of the four Los Angeles plates. She is also in the January and February plates of the Rothschild set and the set by Jean de Court mentioned above, where she appears to be the wife of the wealthy landowner, and as such may have been meant to represent Abundance, literally a Lady Bountiful. This conceit would have appealed to her real-life equivalent, who was a likely customer for just such a set of plates.

Later the Reymond atelier used two sets of engravings by Étienne Delaune (1518/19–1583), one dated 1568 (fig. 25; Robert-Dumesnil 1865, vol. 9, 58–61, nos. 185–96; see cat. no. 17), the other undated, but probably earlier, about 1561 (figs. 42–43; Robert-Dumesnil 1865, vol. 9, 73–78, nos. 225–36; see cat. nos. 29–40 for plates by Martial Courteys copied from this series).

Three of the four plates are distinguished by the incongruity of the specific labor, the name of the month inscribed on the rim cartouche below, and the sign of the zodiac in the rim cartouche above.* Mowing, the traditional labor for July, is inscribed June and assigned Virgo, the sign for August. Harvesting (August) is inscribed July and assigned Taurus (April). Sowing (October) is inscribed August and assigned Pisces (February). There are,

---

*The bread-baking scene, although traditionally assigned to December (see fig. 24), also appears on the November plate in the Rothschild set and has the correct sign of the zodiac for November, Sagittarius. December is represented in this series by the butchering of a pig, a common alternative for the twelfth month (see cat. no. 40).

however, many plates from the Reymond atelier based on the same iconographical source that share this type of error: in the Rothschild set, for example, the scenes for January and February are switched, as are the signs of the zodiac for September and October. This type of error was inevitable, given the haste with which these sets were probably turned out in order to fulfill the demand for them. Also, to judge from the painting techniques, the calendar sets were probably produced on the sixteenth-century equivalent of an assembly line. Occasionally as many as four artists may have been involved: one artist for the main scene, another for the decorative rims and undersides, a third for the sign of the zodiac, and a fourth for the inscriptions. This would certainly explain why decorative components were sometimes mismatched. This set may have been decorated by three different artists. The lack of subtle modeling and the dryness of form demonstrate that the plates are a workshop production. Indeed, in Reymond's atelier it would be very unlikely that the master or his best assistants would be engaged in the production of calendar sets.

Other plates that might be from the same set would also bear the date 1561 and would probably illustrate the occupation for the subsequent month, as these four do. One candidate is a plate for March now in the Rijksmuseum, Amsterdam. Other plates that are less likely but still possible pieces from the same set include plates probably for January, March, and April, formerly in the Spitzer collection (Spitzer 1891, vol. 2, cat. nos. 89, 92, 91); a plate for February formerly in the La Sayette and Kann collections; and a plate for May formerly in the Debruge-Duménil and Jacquiot-Godard collections.

There are other documented or extant plates by Reymond illustrating the same scenes as those depicted on the Los Angeles plates. They include the plates for July, August, October, and November (corresponding to June, July, August, and November in the present set) in the Rothschild set; a plate for July (corresponding to June in the present set), dated 1560, sold in Paris in 1975 (Ader Picard Tajan, November 14, lot 17); and plates for July, August, and September (corresponding to June, July, and August in the present set), dated 1562, in the Palais des Arts, Lyons (inv. no. L.439).

The scenes depicted on the Los Angeles plates also appear on a number of extant calendar plates by other artists (who managed to match the various elements correctly). In the complete series by Jean de Court mentioned above, the July, August, October, and December plates correspond to the June, July, August, and November plates in Los Angeles. A plate for July (corresponding to June in the present set) by Jean de Court was sold in London in 1988 (Sotheby's, December

8–9, lot 339). A plate for December by Jean Court *dit* Vigier in the Taft Museum, Cincinnati (inv. no. 1931.301), another by the same artist in the University of Michigan Museum of Art, Ann Arbor (inv. no. 1977/1.168), and a third by Jean de Court in the British Museum (inv. no. BL.1469) depict the bread-baking scene found on the Los Angeles November plate. Plates for August and October corresponding to the Los Angeles July and September plates were in the Spitzer collection (Spitzer 1891, vol. 2, cat. nos. 133–34; sold Chevallier-Mannheim, Paris, April 17–June 16, 1893, lot nos. 550, 549).

As many as three other sets of calendar plates by Pierre Reymond (also now dispersed) similar to the Los Angeles plates bear the coat of arms of Pierre I Séguier (1504–1580) (see Reymond's biography) and the date 1566 (see Verdier 1967, nos. 142–43, for two of these plates and the suggested whereabouts of others from the sets). The monthly occupations are taken from the same models as those on the Los Angeles plates, the underside rim motif on the Los Angeles plates is used for the front of the Séguier plates, and the undersides, although more elaborate, also illustrate portraits in strapwork roundels. The name of the month is not included on the Séguier sets, but the sign of the zodiac is painted in red on a roundel in the front rim. Here, too, the signs do not usually correspond to the labors depicted below them, but Verdier (1967, 251) explains the discrepancy in this instance by the suggestion that the painter was following the old calendar, in which the year began in March. Unfortunately, this explanation can only be valid when the elements are two months out of sync, as they are in only some of the Séguier plates.

The nature of the wear and scratches on these four plates suggest that they might actually have been used for food service, although probably considerably after they were made, since they, like all painted enamels from Limoges, were originally made for display purposes.

PROVENANCE

William Randolph Hearst.

Donated to the Los Angeles County Museum of Art, 1948.

17

PIERRE REYMOND

Plate: March (Pruning Vines)

c. 1570
Grisaille enamel, flesh tones, touches of color,
and gold on copper
Diameter 19.8 cm (7 13/16 in.)
William Randolph Hearst Collection
48.2.1

DESCRIPTION

On the front of the plate a man prunes vines, while a woman shoulders a bundle of the bound cuttings. Behind them are trees, and above the scene a ram reclines in a patch of clouds. A section of a building with a high podium pierced by an archway and topped by a column is in the background at left; a small stream, a shepherd with his flock, and some cottages can be seen at right. Under the right foot of the man is the number **3** in red enamel.

The cavetto is decorated with a gold guilloche, and the rim features four strapwork cartouches flanked by chimeras, with gold foliage filling any spaces in the design. The usual white edge is replaced by gold circles on the dark ground.

On the underside is a profile portrait of a bearded man, facing right, wearing a crown of laurel and a tunic with a fur or fleece collar. He is framed by an egg-and-dart border, which his head slightly overlaps, and inside which is the inscription **VESPASIANVS*IO*AMPEREVR** (Vespasian tenth emperor). Outside the border is a motif in gold of leaves shooting from a stem divided by four lozenges; the rim is decorated with four strapwork cartouches between grotesques scrolls.

TECHNIQUE

The ground is a dark mulberry that appears black, over which the designs were executed in white enamel of varying thicknesses, allowing the dark ground to show through. The artist used *enlevage* to create contour lines and hatching. Very thick opaque white was used for areas of highlighting. Gold is used for Aries's field and the man's pruning tool.

Some firing bubbles are visible on the surface, and the rim shows shatter cracks on the left, right, and upper right sections. On the underside are scratches and abrasion consistent with normal wear.

*

FIGURE 25

Étienne Delaune,
France, 1518/19–1583,
March (Pruning), from
the series *Les Douze
Mois, ou les différentes
occupations des hommes
pendant le cours de
l'année*, 1568, engrav-
ing, 7.5 x 5.4 cm (2 ¹⁵⁄₁₆
x 2 ⅛ in.), Print Collec-
tion, Miriam & Ira
D. Wallach Division
of Art, Prints and
Photographs, The New
York Public Library,
Astor, Lenox and
Tilden Foundations,
New York.

The activity depicted here (pruning of vines), the astronomical sign for the month (Aries the Ram), and the number **3** at the bottom center of the scene identify this as a March plate from a calendar set. Although the occupations depicted might change from region to region, by the fifteenth century most French illuminated manuscripts depicted pruning as the activity for March; see, for example, the Bedford Hours, c. 1423 (fig. 10; British Library, London, Add. MS. 18850); the Playfair Book of Hours, late fifteenth century (Victoria and Albert Museum, London, inv. no. L.475-1918]; and Jean Bourdichon's *Missel de Tours*, 1506/11 (Bibliothèque Nationale, Paris, MS Lat. 886).

The scene itself, including the ram in its cloud-bordered cartouche, is taken directly from an engraving by Étienne Delaune (1518/19–1583) (Robert-Dumesnil 1865, vol. 9, 58, no. 187), one of a series of the twelve months (fig. 25), the January print of which is dated 1568.

As remarked in the previous entry (cat. nos. 13–16), the Reymond workshop turned out many calendar sets after three different models: an unidentified print source (perhaps the *Compost et kalendrier des bergères* of 1499; see figs. 24, 36), Delaune's 1568 series, and another, undated, series by the same artist probably executed about 1561 (figs. 42–43). One of Reymond's sets after the 1568 engravings is nearly intact: a group of nine grisaille plates (missing May, June, and October) in the Musée du Louvre, Paris (Laborde 1853, cat. nos. 307–15; Darcel 1891, cat. nos. 481–89; Marquet de Vasselot 1914, cat. nos. 605–13).

In addition to its occurrence on the March plate in the Louvre, the vine-pruning scene on the Los Angeles plate was repeated by Reymond on a polychrome plaque in the Victoria and Albert Museum (inv. no. 4877-1901), on another in a set of six formerly in the collection of Baroness Maria de Reitzes-Marienwert (sold Parke Bernet, New York, April 30–May 2, 1948, lot 105), and on a grisaille plate from a dispersed set sold at auction in 1950 (Goldschmidt-Rothschild sale, Parke Bernet, New York, March 10, lot 63a). An oval polychrome plaque of the scene from a complete set in the Virginia Museum of Fine Arts, Richmond (inv. no. 63-37C; ex-collection Heinrich Wencke, sold Cologne, October 27–28, 1898, lot 134), once attributed to Reymond, is now believed by Philippe Verdier (1967, 253) to be by Jean de Court, and another grisaille plate of the same scene, although attributed to Reymond's atelier in an auction catalogue (Hôtel Drouot, Paris, December 2, 1974, lot 83), is also in the style of a member of the Courteys family and has a border design that was used almost exclusively by the artists of that family.

Reymond occasionally represented March with a scene of hunting, which activity was illustrated in Delaune's earlier series of engravings for April. The painter adding the inscription—who was probably not the artist of the main scene—may have captioned the plates out of sequence, a very common occurrence (see cat. nos. 13–16), or, in the case of a March hunting plate dated 1565, now in the Victoria and Albert Museum (inv. no. 2032-1855), the model used by Reymond was from the early unidentified print source, in which March was represented with a hunting scene.

The decorative motifs on the rims are found on many other plates from the Reymond workshop, including two calendar plates dated 1566, now in the Walters Art Gallery, Baltimore (inv. nos. 44.162, 44.190; Verdier 1967, nos. 142–43), from a set commissioned by Pierre I Séguier (see Reymond's biography).

The decoration on the underside of the plate—the profile image of the emperor Vespasian, actually Titus Flavius Sabinus Vespasianus (A.D. 9–79)—is an example of a type of iconography that was popular for decorative and fine arts of all descriptions during this period. Especially striking are the late fifteenth-century wooden *crédences* and cabinets carved with portraits of ancient and modern rulers; several superb examples are preserved in the furniture collection at the château of Langeais in the Loire Valley. Imperial profiles carved in relief were often used as architectural decoration for the exteriors and interiors of French châteaux. The custom had begun in Italy as a result of a renewed interest in numismatics during the Italian Renaissance; the French saw many examples in Lombardy during their campaigns in and control of that region. Cardinal Georges d'Amboise, a former governor of Lombardy, acquired three sets of Italian imperial portrait medallions in marble and bronze to decorate the courtyard and loggia of the château of Gaillon (begun 1502) in Normandy (Weiss 1953, 7, n. 3; La Coste-Messelière 1957, 65–70).

Complete groups of twelve enamel imperial portraits still extant include a set sold in New York in 1981 (Sotheby Parke Bernet, May 29–30, lot 337). A casket with imperial portraits in polychrome enamel is in the Frick Collection (inv. no. 16.4.15;

ex-collections Soltykoff, Spitzer, Gibson-Carmichael, and Morgan; Verdier 1977, 98–103); a tazza and cover with twelve imperial medallions was lent to the South Kensington Museum in 1874 by the earl of Warwick (London 1874, cat. no. 770). Two elaborately framed grisaille roundels from a dispersed series by Pierre Courteys are in the Hermitage Museum, Saint Petersburg (inv. nos. F-305, F-306; ex-collection Basilewsky; Dobroklonskaya 1969, cat. nos. 44–45). The mid- and late-seventeenth-century ateliers of the Laudin family not only turned out sets of imperial portrait plaques in a variety of sizes (for example, two incomplete sets once belonging to Gladys Marie, dowager duchess of Marlborough, sold at Sotheby Parke Bernet, London, March 10, 1983, lot 74) but used the profiles on cups and saucers with other images as unrelated as Joan of Arc and Judith with the head of Holofernes (Taft Museum, Cincinnati, inv. nos. 1931.226, 1931.311; Taft 1958, cat. nos. 169–70).

It is unusual to find imperial portraits on the underside of a set of calendar plates, although the fact there are usually twelve emperors certainly makes it an obvious choice. From evidence provided by a comparison of extant plates, at least six such sets, including that to which the Los Angeles plate belongs, were turned out by the Reymond atelier, one and possibly two with the arms of Pierre I Séguier (see Reymond's biography), one with the arms of Chaspoux de Verneuil, another with the arms of Chapuis. Albert Ilg (1884, 126), describing a set of calendar plates formerly in the Kunstgewerbemuseum, Berlin, reported that the undersides were decorated with portraits of Roman emperors; he does not mention a coat of arms however.

Plates that could have been part of a set with the Los Angeles example are those for February, July, and December, with identical borders and portraits of ANTHONIVS, identified as the twelfth emperor (possibly Antoninus Pius, who was actually the sixteenth emperor), Nerva (13), and Trajan (14), respectively (the February and December plates are from the Léon Decloux sale, Paris, April 27–28, 1891, lots 12–13, sold to Dr. Émile Allain; the July plate is in the Victoria and Albert Museum [inv. no. 789-1877]). In addition, plates for May and August sold at the Edward J. Berwind sale in 1939 (Parke Bernet, New York, November 9–11, lot 333) have grisaille scenes painted in the same style from the same Delaune series of engravings and with the same border designs; unfortunately, the undersides are not illustrated in the auction catalogue, and the description of their decoration as "antique heads in cartouches" could apply equally to the imperial profiles or to another type of decoration more common to the Reymond workshop (see, for example, cat. nos. 13–16).

The probable sources of imperial portraits for the painter of this plate and the rest of the series were Marcantonio Raimondi's engravings of the twelve Caesars (Bartsch 1978–82, vol. 27, 174–85, nos. 501–12) and Hubert Goltzius's *Vivae omnium fere imperatorum imagines...* (Antwerp, 1557). Raimondi's engravings particularly are of the same scale and overlap their round frames as the Los Angeles Vespasian does his egg-and-dart border.

These sources, however, seem to have served as inspiration rather than model: the resemblance between the engraved and the enamel portraits is usually not very striking. The engraved Vespasian (fig. 26), for example, is a jowly, clean-shaven man with a pronounced bump on the bridge of his nose. The enamel painter did not come at all close to this representation; he also added a beard and a fur-collared tunic.

Although in Raimondi's series of engravings Caligula is omitted and Nerva added at the end of the list, the numbering system on the extant enamel plates adheres to the historical sequence: Vespasian was the tenth emperor in the line beginning with Julius Caesar. It is clear from all existing examples, however, that the sequence of emperors did not follow the sequence of the months: here, for example, the tenth emperor appears on the third plate or, even going by the old calendar in which the year began in March, the first plate.

FIGURE 26

Marcantonio Raimondi,
Italy, c. 1480–c. 1534,
Vespasian, from the
series *The Twelve
Caesars*, engraving,
17.6 x 15.5 cm (6 ¹⁵⁄₁₆ x
6 ⅛ in.), Graphische
Sammlung Albertina,
Vienna.

PROVENANCE

Frédéric Spitzer, Paris; sale, Chevallier-
Mannheim, Paris, April 17–June 16, 1893,
lot 506, 1,505 francs.

William Randolph Hearst.

Donated to the Los Angeles County
Museum of Art, 1948.

LITERATURE

Spitzer 1891, vol. 2, cat. no. 90.

LE IVGEMANT DE MOISE 1573

EXODE XVIII

18

PIERRE REYMOND

Covered cup:
Scenes from the Story of Moses

1575
Grisaille enamel, flesh tones, touches of
color, and gold on copper
Cup: height 15 cm (5 ⅞ in.),
diameter of bowl 18 cm (7 ¹⁄₁₆ in.),
diameter of foot 11 cm (4 ⁵⁄₁₆ in.)
Cover: height (including knop) 7.6 cm (3 in.),
diameter 18.5 cm (7 ¼ in.)
William Randolph Hearst Collection
48.2.14

DESCRIPTION

In the bowl of the cup the horned Moses
sits on an elaborate throne raised on two
steps, on the lower of which is inscribed
LE IVGEMANT DE MOISE 1575 (The judgment of Moses 1575). A bearded older
man sits to the right of Moses and leans
his arm on the armrest of the throne. Two
women are seated on a rock in the right
foreground, with a child peering out from
under the raised left arm of the woman to
the left. The monogram **PR** is to the right
of the group. In the left foreground is a
nude child sitting beside a tablet inscribed
EXODE XVIII (Exodus 18). Groups of
men, some wearing armor, stand convers-
ing on either side of the throne. In the
background can be seen tents, two adults
and a child, trees, and paths meandering
through a landscape. A gold arabesque
and white rim surround the scene.

The underside of the bowl is decorated with strapwork with four masks bearing baskets of fruit alternating with four
smaller ram's heads; outside this is a zone
of gold arabesques surrounded by an egg-
and-dart pattern at the rim.

The baluster is decorated with four
portrait roundels of bust-length figures on
a ground dotted with gold, surrounded
by a frame of thick white enamel. The
portraits depict a woman in antique dress
facing left, a man in antique dress facing
right, a woman in contemporary dress
facing left, and a man in antique armor
facing right.

On the foot a bearded man with a staff is seated to the left of a large tent to which another man carries a basket of manna. Above the scene is inscribed **EXODE XVI AARON** (Exodus 16 Aaron). On the other side of the foot three men, one of whom holds a staff, are shown in a tent. The monogram **PR** is in the lower right corner of the tent opening. At the bottom of the scenes are bands of gold circles on black and a red guilloche on white. The underside of the foot is painted with stylized red flowers on white.

The outside of the cover illustrates the Fall of the Manna, its source identified as **EXODE XVI** (Exodus 16). A bearded man with a staff and other figures of men, women, and children observe the small white particles falling from the clouds or hold or carry vessels or baskets full of the food. The edge of the cover is made up of four zones of decoration: stylized gold flowers, an egg-and-dart motif between bands of white, a gold guilloche between bands of gold, and an opaque white rim. The knop, which is original, is painted with eight acanthus fronds.

The inside of the cover is painted at the center with a large acanthus rosette of sixteen fronds, surrounded by a band of gold guilloche. The outer band is made up of a variety of grotesque creatures.

TECHNIQUE

The tazza was painted with opaque white enamel on a dark translucent mulberry ground. The outlines and surface texturing were executed by *enlevage*, and shading was achieved by hatching or cross-hatching for shadows and the addition of white enamel for highlights. A wash of particles of red enamel in clear flux gives the flesh a salmon-pink tonality. Gold and red were reserved for decorative areas or rims and inscriptions.

The knop is attached to the lid by a screw.

The cup is in excellent condition. The arabesque on the inner edge of the bowl is somewhat rubbed. There are two small losses on the edge of the cover and another on the edge of the foot.

*

Scenes from the life of Moses are very common in extant grisaille enamels from the atelier of Pierre Reymond; dated pieces range from 1556 (a tazza formerly in the collection of Robert Napier [London 1862, cat. no. 1758]) to 1575 (this cup). Episodes from Exodus were also illustrated in polychrome enamel by Jean de Court, Pierre Courteys, and Jean Reymond. The common source was the *Quadrins historiques de la Bible* by Claude Paradin, canon of Beaujeu, first published in 1553 in Lyons by Jean de Tournes, a recounting of biblical stories in short verses (quatrains) with a simple narrative and occasionally moralistic style. The book was illustrated with engraved vignettes by Bernard Salomon (figs. 27–29, 33–34, 39). The elongated and convoluted figures in the prints, which are also particularly evident in the

FIGURE 27

Bernard Salomon,
France, c. 1508–after
1561, *Moses on the
Judgment Seat*, from
Claude Paradin,
*Quadrins historiques de
la Bible*, Lyons: Jean
de Tournes, 1558,
engraving, 5.5 x 7.7 cm
(2³⁄₁₆ x 3¹⁄₁₆ in.), Rare
Books and Manuscripts
Division, The New
York Public Library,
Astor, Lenox and
Tilden Foundations,
New York.

bowl of the enamel cup, reveal the influence of the Italian mannerist style as disseminated in France through the school of Fontainebleau and were influential in communicating this style to the enamel painters of Limoges. Marvin Ross (1939, 94) has pointed out that Reymond probably had the expanded edition of the *Quadrins* that was published in 1556, because the earlier edition did not contain all the vignettes the painter copied in his grisaille enamels.

A mixture of sacred and secular iconography, not to mention decorative motifs, is quite common in these vessels. This is sometimes due to the marriage of an unrelated cover and cup, but it is not unusual to find religious and mythological episodes combined on a cup or a cover, emphasizing the purely decorative function that enamel vessels must have assumed in a French household. This cup is unusual in that most of the subject matter is religious—even rarer, stories about the same person.

The scene inscribed LE IVGEMANT DE MOISE, literally the Judgment of Moses, but more accurately described as Moses on the Seat of Judgment or the Counsel of Jethro, is narrated, as the inscription records, in Exodus 18, particularly verses 13–23: Jethro, Moses' father-in-law, appalled that Moses was the sole judge for the whole host of Israelites, urged him to appoint judges to handle all but the most difficult cases, a suggestion that Moses followed with alacrity (and, one imagines, great relief).

The quatrain by Paradin that accompanies this scene in the *Quadrins historiques* reads:

> *Moïse entend tout Israël plaider,*
> *Dequoy Iethro, esbahi de ses peines,*
> *Lui fait creer, pour en ce lui ayder,*
> *Bons & loyaux Iuges & Capiteines.*

> (Moses hears all Israel plead their cases, whereupon Jethro, amazed at his labors, has him appoint good and loyal judges and captains to help him.)

Both the print (fig. 27; no. 145 in the *Quadrins*) and the enamel show Jethro leaning with nonchalance on his son-in-law's throne, his head turned, almost certainly in the act of whispering the type of advice that is the in-law's prerogative: "'This is not the best way to do it. You will only wear yourself out and wear out the people who are here'" (Exodus 18:17b–18a ERV). In the print Moses is shown holding a long staff, and there are no figures in the foreground. The two women and children added by Reymond are probably meant to be Moses's wife Zipporah, her handmaiden, and her two sons, Gershom and Eliezer (Exodus 18:2–5). They appear in most of the versions of this scene, although they are occasionally

placed in different areas of the foreground. Of the two groups of suppliants waiting for judgment, that on the right is the same in both print and enamel (although cut off at the edge, due to the round format of the bowl); that on the left is quite different in the poses and arrangement of the figures.

The cover depicting the Fall of the Manna was copied fairly accurately from the Salomon engraving (no. 138), with a slight rearrangement of figures. The incident is taken from Exodus 16:2–31, in which the starving Israelites in the desert are miraculously provided with a strange source of food: "When the dew was gone, there over the surface of the wilderness fine flakes appeared, fine as hoar-frost on the ground....Israel called the food manna; it was like coriander seed, but white, and it tasted like a wafer made with honey" (Exodus 16:14, 31 ERV). The quatrain reads:

> De Dieu vivant le pouvoir manifeste
> Dens les desers nourrit les bons Ébrieus,
> De l'aliment & viande céleste,
> Qui est le pain de la Manne des cieus.

> (The manifest power of the living God nourishes the good Hebrews in the desert with celestial food and meat, which is the bread of the manna of heaven.)

The figure with the staff can be identified as Moses, gesturing as he commands the Israelites to gather up the manna. This scene was regarded as a prefiguration both of Christ feeding the multitudes with loaves and fish and of the Eucharist.

FIGURE 28

Bernard Salomon, France, c. 1508–after 1561, *Aaron Conserving the Manna*, from Claude Paradin, *Quadrins historiques de la Bible*, Lyons: Jean de Tournes, 1558, engraving, 5.5 x 7.8 cm (2 3/16 x 3 1/16 in.), Rare Books and Manuscripts Division, The New York Public Library, Astor, Lenox and Tilden Foundations, New York.

The scene on the foot of the cup is a continuation of the story of the manna and is taken from the same chapter of Exodus, verses 32–36, in which Jehovah commanded Moses to preserve some of the manna as a reminder of his goodness to the Israelites: "Moses said to Aaron, 'Take a jar and fill it with an omer of manna, and store it in the presence of the Lord to be kept for future generations.' Aaron did as the Lord had commanded Moses, and stored it before the Testimony for safe keeping" (Exodus 16:33–34 ERV).

The quatrain by Paradin accompanying the Salomon engraving (fig. 28; no. 139) reads:

Aaron mit la Manne au Tabernacle,
Pour estre ainsi à l'avenir montree,
Representant comme Dieu par miracle
Nourrit les siens en deserte contree.

(Aaron puts the manna in the Tabernacle to be displayed to future generations, showing how God miraculously feeds his people in the hostile desert.)

In the print and the enamel Moses is seated at center, while Aaron carries the basket of manna into the Tabernacle. The other scene painted on the foot, of three men in the Tabernacle, does not illustrate any verse in the sixteenth chapter of Exodus, but Moses may again be identified by his staff, one of the other men is probably Aaron, and the other is possibly God himself, since they are in a holy place.

The grotesques on the underside of the lid are familiar motifs from Reymond's atelier, appearing as they do on many plates and platters (see cat. no. 19 for identical motifs).

Other covered cups with identical bowls from the Reymond workshop include one formerly in the collection of Otto B. Schuster (sold Sotheby's, London, July 16, 1931), sold in London in 1969 (Sotheby's, April 17, lot 126) and again in 1981 (Christie's, July 8, lot 289); one formerly in the collection of the earl of Rosebery (sold Sotheby Parke Bernet, Mentmore Towers, May 20 [day 3], 1977, lot 1125a; Sotheby Parke Bernet, New York, November 27, 1981, lot 56a), also with the Fall of the Manna on the cover and a similarly decorated cover interior; one dated 1572, formerly in the Pourtalès collection (cat. no. 1763; Jacquemart 1864, 388–89; sold February 6 and following days, 1865, lot 1764) and Basilewsky collection (Darcel and Basilewsky 1874, cat. no. 325); one formerly in the Debruge-Duménil collection (sold Hôtel des Ventes, Paris, January 23 and following days, 1850, lot 708); and one sold in London in 1968 (Sotheby's, May 16, lot 37). Reymond also used the scene for the bowls of low tazzas, ewers, and ewer stands.

The cover of the Los Angeles cup is not a good fit, but there is no way to determine if these two pieces were meant to go together or were assembled later. The late nineteenth-century provenance records only a cup, but it cannot be ascertained whether there was no cover with it at that time or whether the presence of a cover was assumed in this vessel form and thus not worthy of mention. The inventories

of many of the nineteenth-century collections record covers without cups, and the cover could easily have been matched at that time to a cup whose cover was missing or severely damaged. The Los Angeles cover would correspond exactly to the description of a cover (without a cup) formerly in the Basilewsky collection (Darcel and Basilewsky 1874, cat. no. 327), except for the border of grotesques on the underside of the Los Angeles example.

PROVENANCE

J. Monot; sale, Hôtel Drouot, Paris, March 8–9, 1869, lot 69, 1,700 francs (the cup).

Bolchow collection; sold, May 1, 1891, lot 5 or 9 (the cup).

William Randolph Hearst.

Donated to the Los Angeles County Museum of Art, 1948.

19

PIERRE REYMOND

Oval platter: Abram Returning the Goods of the King of Sodom

1577
Grisaille enamel, flesh tones, touches of color, and gold on copper
38.4 x 52.9 cm (15 ⅛ x 20 ¹³/₁₆ in.)
William Randolph Hearst Collection
48.2.15

DESCRIPTION

At center a man in cloak and armor points to a crowned man who kneels with his arms across his chest. His headgear, incorporating a crown, sits on the ground in front of him, and behind him are several other men coming through a doorway in a fortified wall. To the right three other men in armor gesture toward the scene. The initials ·P·R· are on the ground between the right and central figure of this group and the date 1577 between the feet of the man farthest to the right. Behind them and the man in the center are other groups of soldiers. A grove of trees is in the right background, and the rather exotic buildings and monuments of a large city are seen in the distance at center.

The cavetto is decorated with a gold arabesque pattern. The rim is painted with a frieze of grotesque creatures of various combinations of human, animal, and plant forms. At top center is a strapwork tablet with the inscription GEN/ESE·/XIIII (Genesis 14). The edge is of opaque white enamel.

On the underside of the platter a nude male with a cloak draped over his head is depicted with a club in his right hand. He stands in an elaborate architectural caprice inhabited by grotesques, birds, branches, flowers, and fruits. At the bottom is a small roundel painted with the monogram P·R. The curve of the platter is decorated with a gold arabesque between two bands of gold. The rim is painted with grotesque rinceaux, some terminating in animal heads.

LATER INSCRIPTIONS
OR LABELS

On the edge of the underside: [P.M.] 853. painted in red (J. Pierpont Morgan catalogue number)

The platter was painted with white opaque enamel over a dense mulberry ground. The contour lines and hatching were executed by *enlevage*, and more white enamel was added for highlights. The flesh tones were created by a wash of red enamels mixed with clear flux; red was also used for the inscriptions. Swords and spears were painted with gold, as were the crowns and blades of grass. On the rim a gold vegetal motif runs through the grotesques.

The platter is in excellent condition, except for scratches and abrasions on the underside caused by normal wear.

*

The scene of Abram refusing the goods of the king of Sodom, although like Moses on the Seat of Judgment (cat. no. 18) not a familiar motif outside Limoges, was very popular with the enamel painters. The little-known incident is related in Genesis 14:11–24: Abram—as Abraham is known before his covenant with God (Genesis 17:5)—discovering that his nephew Lot and all his flocks and herds had been seized in enemy raids on Sodom and Gomorrah, leads his own raiding party to win back the captives and the booty. Abram returns victorious, having recovered not only Lot and his property but the households, goods, and provisions of the kings of Sodom and Gomorrah, which had also been taken by the raiders. To reward Abram, King Bera of Sodom offers to divide the recovered property, with the hero taking the livestock and provisions, the king the people of his household. In the scene depicted on the platter, Abram refuses:

> I lift my hand and swear by the Lord, God Most High, Creator of the heavens and the earth: not a thread or a sandal-thong shall I accept of anything that is yours. You will never say, "I made Abram rich." I shall accept nothing but what the young men have eaten and the share of the men who went with me, Aner, Eschol, and Mamre; they must have their share. (Genesis 14:22–24 ERV)

The scene on the enamel was taken from a folio of Claude Paradin's *Quadrins historiques de la Bible* (Lyons: Jean de Tournes, 1553), where a print of the scene (fig. 29; no. 24) by Bernard Salomon illustrates the following quatrain by Paradin:

> *Des Sodomois le Roy, ses gens demande*
> *A Abraham, lui quittant l'autre bien:*
> *Mais Abraham, voulant bien qu'il entende*
> *Qu'il ha assez pour soy, lui rend le sien.*

(The king of Sodom asks for his people from Abraham, leaving him the other goods, but Abraham, desiring that [the king] should understand that he has enough for himself, returns to him all that is his.)

The scene is difficult to read, and there has been some confusion among those who have attempted to identify the scene from the enamel version without benefit of the print and the quatrain that accompanies it. The most common mis-identification of the episode is as Abram (kneeling) receiving the blessing of the priest-king Melchizedek (identified either as the figure in armor at center or the man standing behind the kneeling figure). To be sure, this incident is also related in the fourteenth chapter of Genesis, immediately before the conversation between Abram and Bera. But aside from the evidence of the print, in which the kneeling figure wears a crown, and of the quatrain, which clearly identifies the artist's intended subject, there is another print in the *Quadrins* that depicts Melchizedek and several attendants bringing bread and wine to Abram, which was also used as a model in Reymond's atelier (see, for example, one of four extant ewers [inv. no. 44.168] and a tazza [inv. no. 44.66] in the Walters Art Gallery, Baltimore [Verdier 1967,

cat. nos. 136, 139]). In that scene Abram
is the same figure in armor that can be
seen at center on the Los Angeles platter.
The dress of the two protagonists on the
platter is revealing in itself: a priest-king
who had not been in battle would not
be wearing armor and a helmet, nor would
a warrior just back from a raid wear civilian clothes and a crown. No other participants may be securely identified.

In Reymond's version the king retains
his crown as well as placing his crowned
hat on the ground (although other enamels
of this scene show the king bareheaded),
the background architecture is different,
and the subsidiary groups of soldiers are
more distinct, holding lances and gesturing
expressively. The man behind the kneeling
king (there is no such prominent figure in
the print) may be Melchizedek, to judge
from his resemblance to the figure in the
engraving mentioned above, and it has
been suggested that the three prominent
soldiers in the right foreground are Abram's
lieutenants, Aner, Eschol, and Mamre.

The figures of Abram and his soldiers
are perfect examples of the elongation
and unnatural, twisted poses so common
in the work of the Italian mannerists at
Fontainebleau who inspired Bernard
Salomon.

The caprice on the underside of the
platter is copied exactly from an engraving
from a series of pagan deities by Étienne
Delaune (fig. 30). In Delaune's engraving
(Robert-Dumesnil 1865, vol. 9, 108,
no. 360), however, the figure at the center
is the goddess Juno; here the male nude
may be identified by his club as Hercules
(the cloak is possibly an erroneous substitution for the hero's usual lion skin),
a figure perhaps adopted from Delaune's
Neptune from the same series of engravings (Robert-Dumesnil 1865, vol. 9,
116, no. 398). The same framework was
used for a figure of Fame on the underside of a polychrome oval platter by
Martial Reymond in the Frick Collection
(inv. no. 16.4.29; Verdier 1977, 167).
The Juno engraving was exactly reproduced in at least two enamels, although
not from the Reymond atelier: two polychrome mirror backs of about the same
date by Jean de Court (Taft Museum,
Cincinnati, inv. no. 1931-284; Taft 1958,
cat. no. 172; Victoria and Albert Museum,
inv. no. 2035- 1855).

A platter by Reymond in the Musée
du Louvre, Paris (inv. no. OA 97313; Darcel
1891, cat. no. 492; Marquet de Vasselot
1914, cat. no. 622), illustrates the Old
Testament scene, with the addition of the
inscription NŌ ACCIPIAM EX OMNIBVS
QVE TVA SVNT NE DICAS EGO DITAVI
(I will not accept anything that is yours,
nor will you say I have given...), the words
of Abram in Genesis 14:23. The underside
also depicts Hercules in the same framework, but the Hercules is drawn from a
different source: he stands facing front,
wearing his lion skin, his club in his left
hand. The decorative motifs on the rims
are identical to those on the Los Angeles

platter, but they have been moved an eighth of the way around the rim.

A similar platter of identical size, painted with the arms of Chaspoux de Verneuil and inscribed with the exact date of May 28, 1577, is now in the collection of the Hermitage Museum, Saint Petersburg (inv. no. F-1388; ex-collection Paskevitch; Dobroklonskaya 1969, cat. no. 33). The underside depicts the goddess Juno in a far more elaborate framework, which Madeleine Marcheix identified as after René Boyvin (archives of the Musée Municipal, Limoges); the rims are identical to each other and more ornate than the top rim of the Los Angeles platter.

A slightly smaller (48.5 cm in length) polychrome platter illustrating the same scene, also with Hercules in an architectural caprice with grotesques, was sold in London in 1975 (Eleanor, Lady Nathan; sold Christie's, April 7, lot 49) and again in 1980 (Sotheby Parke Bernet, July 17, lot 47).

Reymond used Delaune's deities on the undersides of plates illustrating other scenes as well. A platter in the Taft Museum, Cincinnati (inv. no. 1931-235; Taft 1958, cat. no. 144), illustrating Joseph Interpreting the Dreams of Pharaoh has a sixteenth-century lady standing in a framework created by Delaune for the goddess Bellona (Robert-Dumesnil 1865, vol. 9, 108, no. 361).

A polychrome platter depicting the same subject, attributed to Jean or Susanne de Court, with different rims and underside, was in the collection of the earl of Rosebery (sold Sotheby Parke Bernet, Mentmore Towers, May 20 [day 3], 1977, lot 1149). Another polychrome version in the Saint Louis Art Museum (inv. no. 42.63.1) is signed by Susanne de Court but is believed by Marie-Madeleine Gauthier and Philippe Verdier to be a nineteenth-century enamel (museum files). Jean de Court used the scene to decorate other vessel types as well, including a dish sold in London in 1976 (Christie's, December 13, lot 60).

PROVENANCE

Probably duke of Marlborough, Blenheim Castle; sale, London, June 14, 1883, lot 62.

Probably Frédéric Spitzer, Paris; sale, Paris, Chevallier-Mannheim, April 17–June 16, 1893, lot 500, 14,000 francs.

Probably Charles Stein, Paris; sale, Paris, June 8–10, 1899, lot 23, 13,500 francs.

J. Pierpont Morgan.

William Randolph Hearst.

Donated to the Los Angeles County Museum of Art, 1948.

EXHIBITED

Probably London 1874, no. 529, lent by the duke of Marlborough.

Probably Paris 1889, no. 1110, lent by Frédéric Spitzer.

LITERATURE

Probably Spitzer 1891, vol. 2, cat. no. 84 (date erroneously transcribed as 1557).

c. 1520–before 1591

As is the case with many other enamel painters, the exact dates of the birth and death of Pierre Courteys are not known. His career can be traced, however, through his dated works and the occurrences of his name in the civic and guild records of Limoges, where he lived in the rue Manigne. Augustus Franks (London 1862, 171) speculated that he may have been the son or grandson of Robert Courtois, a noted fifteenth-century glass painter from Mans. Léon de Laborde (1853, 251) mentioned as possible relatives two sculptors, Mathurin and Christophe Courtois, who were working under Primaticcio's direction at Fontainebleau in 1545. Members of the family were also conspicuous as notaries or judges.

Pierre Courteys's earliest signed work is a cup dated 1544 in the Städtisches Museum, Brunswick, painted with the Judgment of Paris and the Triumph of Diana; the latest known enamel by his hand is a roundel of the Allegory of Man after an engraving of about 1581, now in the Walters Art Gallery, Baltimore (inv. no. 44.358; Verdier 1967, cat. nos. 154–58). To judge by these dates, he was the first of the large Courteys (Corteys, Courtoys, Cortoys, Courteu—all of which spellings he used) and Court families to succeed as an enamel painter. He worked for both François I and Henri II and was in direct contact with the artists at Fontainebleau. He was probably the "Courtheys" praised for his skill in an ode written in 1583 by the Limousin poet Jacques Blanchon (Verdier 1967, xxv). The poem, a tribute to Courteys's relative, poet Jean Dorat, mentioned several enamel painters who served the royal court (see Jean de Court's biography).

Alfred Darcel (1883, 270–71) suggested that, based on his earliest works, Courteys was trained in the atelier of Pierre Reymond, but the similarities are not very pronounced and Courteys's hand cannot be seen in any of the enamels coming from the Reymond workshop. It is unlikely that a craftsman would have gone to a rival family for training that was available in his own. It is true that Courteys produced the same type of enamels as did Reymond—plates and platters, ewers, saltcellars, and cups—and used many of the same iconographical sources, but the same could be said of all the sixteenth-century enamel painters.

Courteys also specialized in small caskets mounted with polychrome panels depicting Old Testament scenes and in series of polychrome oval plaques, which may have been mounted in the wainscoting of a room or in the panels of a door (see cat. no. 20). He executed embossed enamels, including twelve enormous (164 x 100 cm [65 x 40 in.]) plaques representing allegories of the Planets, the Virtues, and a figure of Hercules, dated 1559, for the facade of the royal Château de Madrid in the Bois de Boulogne outside Paris (nine of the plaques are now in the Musée de la Renaissance, Écouen). Courteys was the only sixteenth-century enamel painter besides Léonard Limousin who executed a significant number of portraits, such as two now in the Walters Art Gallery (inv. nos. 44.62, 44.275; Verdier 1967, cat. nos. 146, 145) and two others formerly in the collection of the earl of Rosebery (sold Sotheby Parke Bernet, Mentmore Towers, May 20 [day 3], 1977, lots 1137–38).

Courteys took his compositions from printed and painted sources, especially the work of the Italians Raphael, Giulio Romano, and Rosso Fiorentino, and of Étienne Delaune and the *petits maîtres* of the Fontainebleau school, including Jacques Androuet du Cerceau, Théodore de Bry, and Virgil Solis (Rosso and the *maîtres* supplied the latter with cartoons), but he nevertheless achieved a distinctive personal style. He was the best draftsman of the enamel painters of Limoges. His figures are monumental, despite their small size, and his compositions have a breadth of design. Both his polychrome and grisaille work display great richness of tone and elegance of expression. He made judicious use of foil to heighten his translucent enamels; his color, while vivid, is full of subtle modulations. His flesh tones are subdued in comparison with those of other enamel painters. He handled the grisaille technique so deftly that the figures and designs have enormous sculptural presence, especially in contrast to the flatness of the less-successful atelier products of Pierre Reymond and Jean de Court. Courteys also maintained an atelier, but his smaller output and the high quality of the work suggest a much stricter control and greater degree of personal involvement on his part than that exercised by other sixteenth-century masters. On the negative side, he can sometimes be faulted with heaviness of design and execution, and, perhaps for that reason, his ornamentation is less graceful than that of Pierre Reymond. Citing these factors and Courteys's choice of the most extreme of mannerist models, Henry Havard (1896, 305) saw in Courteys's work the beginning of the decadence of enamel painting.

Courteys illuminated three books for the Confrérie du Saint-Sacrement at Saint-Pierre-du-Queyroix, Limoges (Guibert 1908, no. 149), as had Pierre Reymond, and an anonymous nineteenth-century guidebook documents the existence of a stained-glass window at Bernecy signed "Pierre Courtoys."

Courteys's three sons continued his craft: Pierre II was goldsmith and enameler to Christine de Lorraine, the wife of Ferdinando de' Medici, grand duke of Tuscany, and later became goldsmith and *valet de chambre ordinaire* to Henri IV of France; Martial (died c. 1592) was a skilled enamel painter (see cat. nos. 29–40); and Pierre III worked in Tours as goldsmith and enameler to Catherine de Bourbon, the sister of Henri IV.

*

20

PIERRE COURTEYS

Plaque: An Old Woman Narrating the Story of Psyche

c. 1560
Polychrome enamel, gold, and foil on copper
30.4 x 22.1 cm (12 x 8 11/16 in.)
William Randolph Hearst Collection
49.26.12

DESCRIPTION

A old woman holding a distaff sits on the ground at the mouth of a cave, a dog lying beside her; to the right sits a well-dressed younger woman. On the rock on which she is seated is the monogram **PC** in gold. Between the figures is a three-legged stool or table, and behind them the cave, shored up by arches of dressed stone, recedes into darkness. Another archway at the far right leads into a second cave. To the left an ass peers around the rocky outcropping at the two figures. The rock rises above the cave to a great height, capped with trees and a building with an arched gateway. To the left is a large walled city.

TECHNIQUE

The plaque was painted with translucent enamels and opaque white enamel partly over a white ground and partly over the copper plate itself (the latter in the landscape). Foil was used to heighten the colors under the garments of the two women. There is very little evidence of *enlevage*, and modeling was accomplished by using a thin coat of white over areas of bright color to produce a variety of lighter shades. The flesh tones are very pale, a thin wash of finely ground red enamel in clear flux; a blotchy, dark red wash was used for the ass. The palette is typical of Pierre Courteys—a wide range of greens, blues, and purples and a rich reddish brown heightened with gold. Gold was also used for grass, flowers, drapery folds, and highlights on the young woman's hair. The counter-enamel is clear.

There are some losses around the edge of the plaque, probably caused by the frames in which the plaque was placed. Where the artist placed translucent enamel directly over the copper, there are a few small areas of corrosion, producing a green

Color plate, page 49

that is not inharmonious with the rest of the palette. The back of the plaque reveals that the piece suffered a heavy blow that cracked, but did not break, an area of the counter-enamel. A circular pattern of shatters is visible in the same area on the front of the plaque. (This type of distress in the counter-enamel of a number of plaques [see also cat. nos. 42–43] may have occurred when the plaques were pried out of the surfaces in which they were set.)

*

The charming story of the mortal Psyche's romance with the god Cupid was first related in the second century A.D. in books 4–6 of the *Metamorphoses*, or *The Golden Ass*, by Lucius Apuleius. The narrator, who has been turned into an ass by witchcraft, overhears the tale as it is told by an old woman to distract a kidnapped bride-to-be awaiting ransom. Briefly, Psyche's beauty arouses the jealousy of Venus, who sends her son Cupid to punish the girl. The young god predictably falls in love with her himself and hides her away, visiting her only at night. When Psyche discovers his identity, the angry Cupid leaves her. She wanders in search of him, performing a series of difficult tasks set her by Venus, until the gods take pity on her and reunite her with her lover on Mount Olympus.

Apuleius crafted his tale from a far more ancient allegory that may have had oriental roots. Psyche was the personification of the human soul (literally, *psyche* in Greek). On Greek tomb monuments the soul freed by death was represented as a butterfly emerging from its cocoon, later as a human figure with wings, a motif that found its way into early Christian imagery. In the third century A.D. Plotinus wrote of "the love [*eros*] that is the soul's [*psyche*] natural companion" and of their occurrence together "in pictures and in fables" (*Enneads* VI, ix, 9, tr. Dodds). During the Renaissance the story of Cupid and Psyche—the latter sometimes supplied with butterfly wings—was perceived as an allegory of the soul's obstacle-filled journey toward either the divine or desire (Eros), the outcome of the latter being pleasure (the child Voluptas).

Apuleius's narrative became extremely popular in Italy in the later fifteenth century; it was first printed in Rome in 1469 (see Gruyer 1864, 169–70, for other Italian editions). Four different editions were published in Paris and Lyons between 1546 and 1586 (Brun 1930, 143–44). The episodes were subject matter for paintings, prints, tapestries, enamelwork, and other decorative arts. The constable of France, Anne de Montmorency (fig. 6), one of the major patrons of the Limoges enamel painters, seems to have been particularly fascinated by the story. He owned several illustrated books and manuscripts, and he commissioned a series of thirty-two stained-glass windows, in grisaille with touches of yellow, representing the entire story. Executed in 1542–44 and originally installed in the gallery of his château at Écouen, the windows are now on view at the château of Chantilly, also formerly the constable's property. Earlier sources (Gruyer 1864, 443 n. 3) attribute the windows to Bernard Palissy, but there is no proof of this; although Palissy was apprenticed to a glass painter, during the period when the windows were painted he was engrossed in his experiments with pottery and glazes at Saintes, and he is not known to have worked for Montmorency before he received a commission in 1555 for a ceramic grotto at Écouen. Given the date of the windows and the style of the glass painting it is not outside the realm of possibility that Courteys himself painted the windows.

In depicting either a group of episodes or the single scene illustrating the marriage banquet of Cupid and Psyche, the enamel painters of Limoges used as their primary iconographical source the same model as Montmorency's glass painter: a series of thirty-two engravings by the Master of the Die and Agostino Veneziano (figs. 31–32; Bartsch 1978–82, vol. 29, 195–226, nos. 39–70). The designs for the engravings have been attributed to the Flemish artist Michiel Coxie (1497–1592), who, according to tradition, took them in turn from compositions by Raphael, supposedly paintings for the decoration of his own house in the Borgonuovo in Rome (Vasari 1906, vol. 5, 435–36, 436 n. 1; Verdier 1967, 264). There is also a view that these engravings record Raphael's unexecuted plans for the decoration of the nine lunettes of the loggia in the Villa Farnesina, Rome, whose ceiling arcades are painted with several of the celestial episodes of the tale of Cupid and Psyche (Hoogewerff 1945, 9–15; Fischel 1948, 167). Whatever their original form or destined location, the scenes by Raphael have completely vanished; the latest mention of them is in 1758, when an English painter, Charles Jatris, found eight of them in Florence (Gruyer 1864, 442 n. 1).

Each print incorporates an eight-line Italian verse describing the scene depicted. The poems render the gist of Apuleius's narrative in colloquial Italian, but the author has not been identified. French verses for each scene also exist: a manuscript in the *cabinet des livres* collected by Montmorency at Chantilly provides the French text of "trente huitains pour la tapisserie faicte de la fable de Cupido et Psyché" (thirty octaves for the tapestry of the tale of Cupid and Psyche), which correspond to the inscriptions on thirty of the windows from Écouen (and which further suggest a tapestry series commissioned by the constable, now not identifiable); the manuscript must therefore have been written before 1542. These French texts are attributed to three fairly eminent poets: Claude Chappuys for the first ten, La Maison-Neuve for the next ten, and Saint-Gelais (Melin) for the last ten (Magne 1885, 130–31). Another set of French verses were published in *L'Amour de Cupido et de Psiché mère de Volupté... nouvellement historiée et exposée tant en vers italiens que françois* (Paris: Jeanne de Marnef, 1546; 2d ed. Paris: Étienne Groulleau, 1557); these were perhaps a translation by the poet Jean Maugin, "le petit angevin," of the Italian verses (Brun 1930, 143–44). (It was not unusual for books published in France to have a text in both French and Italian, thanks to the influence of an Italian queen, Catherine de' Medici, and the many Italian artists who had come over the Alps.)

According to Philippe Verdier (1967, 264 n. 2), there were two sets of plates for the engravings: the originals and a set retouched by Francesco Villamena, the latter of which Verdier claimed were used by Pierre Courteys as his models. Jacques Androuet du Cerceau also executed copies of the engravings (Geymüller 1887, 322), reversed from the original prints and retaining the Italian verses. The fable and the engravings were immensely popular with the enamel painters: series or individual episodes were painted by Jean de Court, Susanne de Court, Jean Court *dit* Vigier, Joseph Limousin, Jean Miette, Jean III Pénicaud, Pierre Pénicaud, and Pierre Reymond. Léonard Limousin, perhaps the first to copy the engravings, painted one series of grisaille plaques in 1535 and a polychrome series in 1543; they reproduce not only the images from the prints but the Italian verses as well. Courteys himself used the fable to decorate tazzas, calendar plates, caskets, ewer stands, and oval platters (one in the Fitzwilliam Museum, Cambridge [inv. no. M.116-1961], is dated 1560).

In this oval plaque the metamorphosed narrator overhears the tale of Cupid and Psyche told to the abducted bride-to-be by her guardian. Courteys took this scene from the first engraving of the series (fig. 31; Bartsch 1978–82, vol. 29, 195, no. 39), by the Master of the Die, which is accompanied by the following verse:

> *Narra Apuleó, che (mentr'egli cangiato*
> *In Asino, serviva à gentiladre)*
> *Vna sposa rubbaro il destinato*
> *Di dele nozze le rapaci squadre,*
> *Cui (per farle scordare un sogno ingrato)*
> *Dona conforto una canuta madre,*
> *Che l'havea in guardia, & con grata favella*
> *Le racconta di Psiche la novella.*

(Apuleius tells that while he, transformed into an ass, was serving a gang of thieves, the unscrupulous group kidnapped a bride on the day appointed for her wedding. An aged woman who was guarding her comforted her to make her forget her unhappiness, and in a kind voice told her the story of Psyche.)

Courteys made few changes in the engraved composition when he adapted it to the enamel plaque, but because the oval format provided a great deal more space, he added a fantastic rocky landscape behind the figures and a view of a city in the left background. This was a formula he often followed on his oval plaques, confining the nominal subject to the lower half of the composition so that the rest of the enamel was free for his landscape caprices, as in five beautiful polychrome plaques, four illustrating occupations of the months of April, August, September, and December, formerly in the collection of the earl of Rosebery (sold Sotheby Parke Bernet, Mentmore Towers, May 20 [day 3], 1977, lot 1141; Sotheby's, New York, November 27, 1981, lot 57), and a

FIGURE 31

Master of the Die, Italy, active middle of the sixteenth century, after Michiel Coxie, Flanders, 1497–1592, *An Old Woman Narrating the Story of Psyche*, from the series *The Fable of Psyche*, engraving, 19.4 x 22.8 cm (7 5/8 x 9 in.), Print Collection, Miriam & Ira D. Wallach Division of Art, Prints and Photographs, The New York Public Library, Astor, Lenox and Tilden Foundations, New York.

fifth, for May, in the Hermitage Museum, Saint Petersburg (inv. no. F301; Dobroklonskaya 1969, cat. no. 43).

With no identifying inscription, and separated from any other scenes in the Psyche series, the subject of this plaque was misidentified as "Youth and Fate" (1868 sale; see Provenance)—undoubtedly the distaff-bearing woman was mistaken for Clotho, one of the Three Fates—and "A young woman consulting a sorceress at the entrance to a cave" (Paul sale, 1882; see Provenance). A nineteenth-century enamel after the engraving (sold Sotheby's, New York, February 19, 1983, lot 62) reproduces the verses, but the auction catalogue wrongly identifies their source as Dante's *Divina Commedia*.

The scene was also used by Courteys on the first of a series of calendar plates, now in the Victoria and Albert Museum, London (inv. no. 2446-1910; see cat. nos. 21–22 for two plates in the same series in the Los Angeles County Museum of Art). The corresponding plaque from Limousin's 1543 series is in the British Museum (inv. no. 1913, 12-20, 49), and a grisaille plaque of the same subject attributed to Martin Didier Pape is in Lyons (Lyons 1887, cat. no. 212).

Only two other oval polychrome plaques by Pierre Courteys depicting episodes from the story of Psyche are documented: *Psyche Discovering the Identity of Cupid*, in the Walters Art Gallery, Baltimore (inv. no. 44.41; Verdier 1967, cat. no. 147), from the thirteenth engraving in the series, by Agostino Veneziano, and *Psyche Searching for Cupid*, which title could be given to one of several prints in the series, recorded in the mid-nineteenth century in the collection of Louis Fould (sold Paris, 1860, lot 2001). An enamel described as a "scene taken from the *Golden Ass* by Apuleius" by "Pierre Courtois" was on view in an exhibition in Beauvais in 1869 (no. 1545), lent by Charles Mannheim, and an oval plaque from the collection of Charles Stein with a "subject taken from Psyche" and signed "PC" was exhibited at the Union Centrale des Beaux-Arts, Paris, in 1880. Unfortunately, there is no way to identify either of these plaques (which may be the same plaque) as one of the three known ovals.

PROVENANCE

Sale, Paris, April 17, 1868, lot 24.

Johannes Paul; sale, Cologne, October 16–24, 1882, lot 637.

Henry Oppenheimer, F.S.A.; sale, Christie's, London, July 15, 1936, lot 108, £231.

William Randolph Hearst.

Donated to the Los Angeles County Museum of Art, 1949.

PIERRE COURTEYS

Plate: The Adoration of Psyche

1560
Grisaille enamel, flesh tones, and gold
on copper
Diameter 21.4 cm (8⁷⁄₁₆ in.)
William Randolph Hearst Collection
48.2.4

DESCRIPTION

Psyche stands to the left of center; behind her, to the left, are her two sisters. In front of her is a group of men, women, and children; prominent among them are a kneeling elderly man and two children carrying a large urn. Classical architecture can be seen behind the figures. In the upper right Venus and Cupid look down on the scene from a surround of clouds.

The cavetto of the plate is ornamented with a guilloche motif painted in gold. The rim displays two grotesque ram's heads and two satyr's heads separated by S-scroll strapwork linked by swags of fruit. The edge is of white opaque enamel.

On the underside a central medallion represents Pisces the Fish against a gold-dotted ground. This is framed by an acanthus-leaf border and surrounded by strapwork containing four oval medallions. The top medallion contains the signature PC, the bottom the date 1560. Around the rim runs a wreath of laurel leaves and berries, bound at the top and bottom with fillets.

PIERRE COURTEYS

*Plate: Psyche Carried by Zephyr
to Cupid's Palace*

1560
Grisaille enamel, flesh tones, and gold
on copper
Diameter 21.4 cm (8 7/16 in.)
William Randolph Hearst Collection
48.2.3

DESCRIPTION

Three scenes are depicted on this plate: at left Psyche sits dozing, at upper center she is carried off, still sleeping, by the cloud-shaped west wind, Zephyr, and at right she is greeted by three women outside a magnificent portico. At far right is a lion-legged tripod table on which is a ewer and basin. A fountain plays in the background.

The cavetto and rim are painted with motifs identical to those on the previous plate (cat. no. 21), although here all four heads on the rim are ram's heads. The underside is also identical to that of its companion plate, except for the central roundel, which depicts Taurus the Bull surrounded by a torsade of white enamel.

TECHNIQUE

The apparent black ground color of both plates is actually a very dense translucent mulberry. The designs were executed in a thin layer of opaque white that allows much of the dark ground to come through, producing a rich dark gray. Heavy contour lines were created in the unfired white layer by *enlevage*; after that was fired, successive applications of white enamel created highlights. The flesh tones were produced by a wash, a mixture of red enamel in clear flux. In addition, subtle contouring of the flesh was accomplished with fine red lines visible only under magnification. Gold was used for inscriptions, overall decorative patterns, drapery borders, foliage, and the nimbus and breath of Zephyr.

The plates are in good condition, the *Zephyr* plate having firing cracks or a shatter pattern in the lower right zone and the corresponding area of the underside.

*

Zephir le gonfia come uela in naue
La uefte, et ponla mun pian dietro al monte
Onde, dormito un fonno affai foaue.
A un palagio ne mien preffo a una fonte

Cui mentre mira, & gran merauiglia haue.
S'ode dir da non uiste uoci, & pronte,
Cio tutto e tuo, noi tue, che guardi omai.
Lauati, e corca, e pofcia a cena andrai.

Ant. Sal. txt.

FIGURE 32

Master of the Die,
Italy, active middle of
the sixteenth century,
after Michiel Coxie,
Flanders, 1497–1592,
*Psyche Carried by
Zephyr to Cupid's
Palace*, from the series
The Fable of Psyche,
engraving, 19.4 x 22.8
cm (7⅝ x 9 in.), Print
Collection, Miriam &
Ira D. Wallach Division
of Art, Prints and
Photographs, The New
York Public Library,
Astor, Lenox and
Tilden Foundations,
New York.

For the story of Cupid and Psyche and the source of these episodes, see the previous entry (cat. no. 20).

These plates illustrate the second and sixth scenes from the series of engravings executed by the Master of the Die and Agostino Veneziano; these engravings are by the former. In the second episode (Bartsch 1978–82, vol. 29, 196, no. 40) Psyche stands modestly before an admiring crowd that calls her a second Venus and pays her homage worthy of a goddess. From the clouds a jealous Venus indicates to her son Cupid her empty temple and the individual at whom her wrath is directed; the group of Venus and Cupid is reminiscent of the same figures frescoed on the vault of the Loggia di Psiche at the Villa Farnesina in Rome, the decorative program executed by Raphael and his school.

The Italian verse on the engraving reads:

*Dun Ré, & d'una Regina tré Donzelle
Nacquero già di gran bellezza ornate,
Ma le due prim (anco, che fusser belle)
Pur come mortal donne, eran lodate.
La piu gioven si vaga fer le stelle
Che l'adoran per vener le brigate,
La quale sdegnata lei mostra ad Amore,
Per che facci vendetta del suo honore.*

(Three maidens of great beauty were born to a king and queen. The elder two, who were very beautiful, were praised as mortal women. The youngest is so incredibly ravishing that the multitudes worship her as Venus, who, indignant, points her out to Cupid so that he may defend Venus's honor.)

The second print (and plate) is a conflation of three separate incidents (fig. 32; Bartsch 1978–82, vol. 29, 200, no. 44): Zephyr, the west wind, at the behest of Cupid, gently lifts the sleeping Psyche and carries her to a valley. When she wakes she beholds a magnificent palace where she is greeted by beautiful nymphs. The verse accompanying the print describes the events:

*Zephir le gonfia, come vela in nave,
La veste, et ponla in un pian dietro al monte
À un palagio ne men presso à una fonte
Cui mentre mira, & gran meraviglia have,
S'ode dir da non viste voci, & pronte,
Cio tutto è tuo, noi tue, che guardi omai:
Lavati, e cerca, e poscia à cena andrai.*

(The west wind fills her garments like a ship's sail and sets her on a plain behind the mountain, where, having slept very sweetly, she is led to a palace near a fountain. While she gazes with great wonder at it, she hears the voices of invisible beings nearby: "Everything here is yours, we are yours, whom you now see. Bathe and explore and come to dine.")

The plates are typical of Courteys's grisaille style. The color ranges from a heavy white impasto to a deep black with only a few intermediate tones, producing figures that are more sculptural than painterly. There is some outlining, but the artist prefers to use the effects of chiaroscuro to separate one figure from another. The draperies are unusually elaborate for this medium and, owing to the thickness of the white enamel with which they are painted, add to the substance of the figures.

The signs of the zodiac for February (Pisces) and April (Taurus) on the undersides of the plates demonstrate that they were part of a now-dispersed calendar series. There are two other plates extant, signed with the monogram of Pierre Courteys and dated 1560, that reproduce the first and fifth engravings in the Cupid and Psyche series, *An Old Woman Narrating the Story of Psyche* (fig. 31; see cat. no. 20) and *Psyche in the Mountains* (Bartsch 1978–82, vol. 29, 199, no. 43), and display the signs of the zodiac for January and March, respectively; the rims of the plates are identical to those of the Los Angeles plates. In 1853 Léon de Laborde (1853, 256 n. 1) described a set of such plates, signed "PC" and dated 1560, in the collection of Sir Andrew Fountaine, but only one of the dispersed plates can be securely traced to his collection. This is the January plate, which is in the Victoria and Albert Museum, London (inv. no. 2446-1910; ex-collections Fountaine [cat. no. 119] and Salting). The March plate is in the Walters Art Gallery, Baltimore (inv. no. 44.344; Verdier 1967, cat. no. 147); like the Los Angeles plates it was once in the Harding collection (see Provenance).

A signed and dated (1560) plate described only as the "Vision of Psyche," in the collection of the earl of Warwick, was on display in an exhibition at the South Kensington Museum in 1874 (London 1874, cat. no. 645). Without any explanatory text, the hovering figure of the woman in the clouds in *Psyche Carried by Zephyr* might well be misconstrued as the vision of the woman seated on the ground at left. And the fact that the plate was exhibited with the *Adoration of Psyche* from the same collection, suggests that the "Vision of Psyche" and *Psyche Carried by Zephyr* are in fact the same plate.

Courteys executed at least two oval polychrome plaques (see cat. no. 20) after the same set of engravings, which suggests that he might either have completed or at least planned an entire polychrome series. A casket in the Musée du Louvre, Paris, with five plaques from the Psyche series, including *Psyche Carried by Zephyr* on the lid, is attributed to Courteys's atelier (Laborde 1853, cat. nos. 352–56 [as a follower of Pierre Reymond]; Darcel 1891, cat. nos. 501–5; Marquet de Vasselot 1914, cat. no. 664). Two signed grisaille plates with the occupations for March and April that were sold at auction in 1967 (Sotheby's, London, December 7, lot 162) would seem to indicate that the artist also executed another calendar set with nearly identical undersides to the Psyche set, but with the standard scenes of the Labors of the Months on the front.

The Louvre has two other versions of *Psyche Carried by Zephyr*: a grisaille plaque from Léonard Limousin's 1535 series (Laborde 1853, cat. no. 239; Darcel 1891, cat. no. 248; Marquet de Vasselot 1914, cat. no. 530) and a tazza attributed to Limousin's atelier (Laborde 1853, cat. no. 263; Darcel 1891, cat. no. 378; Marquet de Vasselot 1914, cat. no. 567).

Pierre Reymond executed a number of grisaille plates and vessels painted with episodes from the story of Psyche, including at least one series of plates. While nine plates are documented, the present whereabouts of only two are known to me: a plate illustrating the episode in which Psyche is ferried to the Underworld by Charon (Bartsch 1978–82, vol. 29, 219, no. 63), in the Wallace Collection, London (inv. no. III F 281; erroneously identified as Psyche's Return from the Underworld), and another depicting the Toilette of Psyche, from the tenth engraving in the series (Bartsch 1978–82, vol. 29, 204, no. 48), in the Metropolitan Museum of Art, New York (inv. no. 04.6.8).

PROVENANCE

Possibly Sir Andrew Fountaine, Narford Hall, Norfolk.

Earl of Warwick; sale, London, July 17, 1896, lot 1, £29 (cat. no. 22); lot 2, £32.

Sir James Knowles; sale, London, May 25, 1908, lot 164 (both plates).

G. R. Harding, London.

William Randolph Hearst.

Donated to the Los Angeles County Museum of Art, 1948.

EXHIBITED

London 1874, nos. 645 (cat. no. 22), 648, lent by the earl of Warwick.

LITERATURE

Verdier 1967, 273–74.

23

PIERRE COURTEYS

Plate: The Temptation of Adam and Eve

c. 1560
Grisaille enamel, flesh tones, and gold
on copper
Diameter 21.5 cm (8 7/16 in.)
William Randolph Hearst Collection
48.2.9

DESCRIPTION

Around the Tree of the Knowledge of
Good and Evil at center is twined a serpent,
represented with the body of a winged
woman and the tail of a snake. It looks
out from a fork in the branches at Eve,
who stands to the right, holding an apple
with her left hand, and with her right giving an apple to Adam, seated on a bank
to the left of the tree. Both figures are
nude. Behind them is the Garden of Eden
with trees, mountains, and a lake; a deer,
lion, and a creature that resembles a small,
humpless camel or an unnaturally long-
necked goat wander or rest in the landscape. At the bottom of the scene is the
inscription **GENESE.III** (Genesis 3).

The cavetto of the plate is ornamented
with a guilloche motif painted in gold.
The rim displays four satyr's heads separated by S-scroll strapwork linked by swags
of fruit, with an edge of opaque white
enamel.

The underside of the plate is decorated
with a roundel inscribed **P CORTEYS MAF**,
the latter probably for *m'a fait* (made me).
This is surrounded by strapwork and
interlaced vegetal swags with two grotesque
heads and two lion's heads opposed. The
rest of the surface, including the rim, is
painted with gold arabesques.

LATER INSCRIPTIONS OR LABELS

On the underside rim: **P.M. 908.** painted
in red (J. Pierpont Morgan catalogue
number)

TECHNIQUE

The ground color is a dense mulberry that
appears black. The design was built up
with opaque white enamel; thick contour
lines were created by *enlevage* and highlight by the addition of layers of white
enamel. Flesh tones were used for the figures of Adam, Eve, and the serpent and
the four faces on the rim; the wash of red
enamel in clear flux is extremely blotchy,
probably due to the coarse grind of the
red particles. There is no gold on the plate
except for the arabesques on the rims and
cavetto.

The plate is in excellent condition
apart from the gold on the underside rim,
which is badly rubbed.

✱

PIERRE COURTEYS

147

FIGURE 33

Bernard Salomon,
France, c. 1508–after
1561, *The Temptation*,
from Claude Paradin,
*Quadrins historiques de
la Bible*, Lyons: Jean
de Tournes, 1558,
engraving, 5.6 x 7.7 cm
(2 3/16 x 3 1/16 in.), Rare
Books and Manuscripts
Division, The New
York Public Library,
Astor, Lenox and
Tilden Foundations,
New York.

The Temptation of Adam and Eve was (and still is) the most easily recognizable of the Old Testament scenes illustrated by the enamel painters of Limoges. The familiar story is related, as the inscription indicates, in the third chapter of Genesis:

> The serpent, which was the most cunning of all the creatures the Lord God had made, asked the woman, "Is it true that God has forbidden you to eat from any tree in the garden?" She replied, "We may eat the fruit of any tree in the garden, except for the tree in the middle of the garden. God has forbidden us to eat the fruit of that tree or even to touch it; if we do, we shall die." "Of course you will not die," said the serpent; "for God knows that, as soon as you eat it, your eyes will be opened and you will be like God himself, knowing both good and evil." The woman looked at the tree: the fruit would be good to eat; it was pleasing to the eye and desirable for the knowledge it would give. So she took some and ate it; she also gave some to her husband, and he ate it. (Genesis 3:1–6 ERV)

Courteys's source for the scene was an engraving by Bernard Salomon (fig. 33) in Claude Paradin's *Quadrins historiques de la Bible*, first published in 1553 in Lyons by Jean de Tournes. Like Pierre Reymond, who used the *Quadrins* prints extensively as models for his own work (cat. nos. 18–19), Courteys preserved the mannerist-influenced elongation and torsion of the Salomon figures. In fact, Courteys chose to be a far more accurate copyist than Reymond, even to the depiction of the same animals inhabiting the Garden of Eden (here it is clear that the puzzling animal on the plate is in fact a camel).

The quatrain under the print reads:

Le faus Serpent, à tromper entendu,
Vint finement, à Eve se renger,
Et tourna tant, que du Fruit defendu
Elle, & Adam, se prindrent à manger.

(The treacherous serpent, intent on deceit, came slyly up to Eve, and so beguiled her that she, and Adam, took the forbidden fruit to eat.)

The plate is a workshop production; the evidence lies in the awkward draftsmanship, emphasis on surface pattern, use of hatching for modeling (there is no hatching in Courteys's finest enamels, which he presumably executed himself), and badly applied flesh tones.

To judge from the serial nature of the decoration of small plates—signs of the zodiac (cat. nos. 13–17, 21–22, 25, 29–40), Roman emperors (cat. no. 17), Labors of the Months (cat. nos. 13–17, 25, 29–40), episodes from long narratives like that of Cupid and Psyche (cat. nos. 20–22)— the enamel painters created them not as isolated objects but as parts of a set. This plate is probably from a series of scenes illustrating the Creation and Fall of Man (for other examples of this theme see cat. nos. 11–12) or a wider selection of episodes from the book of Genesis. A plate of the same diameter in the British Museum, London, depicting the Sacrifice of Isaac has identical rims and underside and is signed by Courteys in the same way; it is no doubt part of the same series. Both plates were in the collection of Ralph Bernal in the mid-nineteenth century (sold Christie's, London, March 5–April 30, 1855, lots 1480 [*Sacrifice of Isaac*], 1483).

A polychrome plaque depicting the Temptation attributed to Courteys is in the Musée Municipal, Limoges (inv. no. 168; Limoges 1966, 71), with two other related plaques of scenes from Genesis, and a polychrome plaque in the Musée du Louvre, Paris (Laborde 1853, cat. no. 375; Darcel 1891, cat. no. 516; Marquet de Vasselot 1914, cat. no. 647), depicting the Sacrifice of Isaac, signed "P. Corteys. M. F.," may be from the same series.

Courteys also used the Dutch artist Lucas van Leyden's engraving of the Temptation (fig. 23; see cat. no. 11) as a source: an oval platter signed and dated 1550 (thus predating the publication of the Salomon prints) depicting scenes from the story of Adam and Eve is in the Victoria and Albert Museum, London (inv. no. 476-1873). Jean de Court used the Salomon print as his source for the bowl of a covered cup now in the Toledo Museum of Art (inv. no. 69.292), as did Jean Court *dit* Vigier for the cover of a cup from the collection of the earl of Rosebery (sold Sotheby Parke Bernet, Mentmore Towers, May 20 [day 3], 1977, lot 1145; the auction catalogue erroneously identifies the source as Lucas van Leyden). Pierre Reymond, better known for his Genesis scenes based on engravings by Lucas van Leyden (figs. 22–23; see cat. nos. 11–12), used the Salomon Adam and Eve as a vignette on an oval platter depicting an Allegory of Redemption of 1566, now in the Walters Art Gallery, Baltimore (inv. no. 44.357;

Verdier 1967, cat. no. 144), and on a ewer stand illustrating an Allegory of the Old and New Testament, 1560/70, in the Wernher Collection at Luton Hoo, Bedfordshire (Natanson 1954, cat. no. 334). Although the composition of the Walters Allegory platter was based on a French engraving after Lucas Cranach, Reymond replaced the individual figures and figure groups with a selection of the more familiar models he had used on other enamels.

The Salomon scene was also painted on a maiolica *crespina*, a shallow fluted bowl, made in Faenza or Urbino about 1560/70 (sold Sotheby's, London, October 9, 1984, lot 6, and Christie's, London, June 29, 1987, lot 124, the source identified as an engraving by Jean Mignon after Luca Penni). Another example, attributed to Rimini, is illustrated by Jeanne Giacomotti (1974, cat. no. 910). A later sixteenth-century shallow faience bowl made in Lyons, painted with the same scene, is now in the Musée de Cluny, Paris (Damiron 1926, pl. x, no. 40).

PROVENANCE

Ralph Bernal; sale, Christie's, London, March 5–April 30, 1855, lot 1483, £21.

Wright.

Possibly Baron Salomon de Rothschild, Paris.

Charles Mannheim, Paris.

J. Pierpont Morgan.

William Randolph Hearst.

Donated to the Los Angeles County Museum of Art, 1948.

EXHIBITED

Paris 1884, no. 82, lent by Charles Mannheim.

Possibly Paris 1867, no. 3033, lent by Baron Salomon de Rothschild.

Los Angeles County Fair Association, Pomona, 1952, lent by the Los Angeles County Museum of Art.

LITERATURE

Bohn 1857, cat. no. 1483.

Molinier 1898, cat. no. 189.

Active second half of the sixteenth century

*J*EAN MIETTE (also Myette or Miète) was active in the second half of the sixteenth century; he is mentioned a very few times in Limousin documents, in 1563 and 1565 (Guibert 1908, no. 842). He was probably apprenticed to Léonard Limousin, who took him, along with Jean III Pénicaud and several members of the Limousin family, to Bordeaux in 1564, where they executed decorations for the ceremonial entry of Charles IX and his mother, Catherine de' Medici, into the city (Bourdery 1895, clxvii).

Works by Miette have been identified only recently, thanks to the discovery by Hugh Tait of the initials "I.M." on a tazza in the British Museum, London (inv. no. 55, 6-2, 19), and Philippe Verdier's subsequent attribution to him of three plates in the Walters Art Gallery, Baltimore (inv. nos. 44.45, 44.56, 44.166; Verdier 1967, cat. nos. 116, 115, 117).

The artist's full-bodied and elongated figure style demonstrates the influence of Limousin and the Italian mannerists working at the French court.

*

24

JEAN MIETTE

Plate: The Sacrifice of Isaac

1560/70
Grisaille enamel, flesh tones, touches
of color, and gold on copper
Diameter 24.4 cm (9 ⅝ in.)
William Randolph Hearst Collection
48.2.10

DESCRIPTION

The young Isaac kneels at center, his hands bound, his head bowed, on a low altar covered with kindling; a bundle of wood for the fire is in the foreground. Isaac's father, Abraham, holds the boy's shoulder with his left hand and raises a sword in an arc above his head with his right. He looks up to see an angel in the clouds catching the sword blade before it can descend. To the right is a lobed urn in which burns the sacrificial fire for the altar; beyond, in the middle ground, are an attendant and several grazing animals. A ram caught in a thicket can be seen to the left. Above Abraham's head is the inscription **G · XXII**, for *Genesis 22.*

Color plate, page 50

The cavetto is covered with delicate gold arabesques, and the rim with thicker white vegetal scrollwork and rosettes interspersed with four grotesque masks alternating with four urns. At the edge of the rim is a band of opaque white.

On the underside of the plate a large putto climbs in the rinceaux issuing from an elaborate two-handled urn, lobed like the urn on the front; the interstices are filled with stylized leaves. The rim is circled by a white laurel wreath and stylized leaves.

LATER INSCRIPTIONS
OR LABELS

On the underside rim: P.M. 766. painted in red (J. Pierpont Morgan catalogue number)

TECHNIQUE

The plate has a ground of dark blue translucent enamel. The opaque white enamel in which the design was executed was thinned to create a deep gray as the ground showed through. The contours and the large areas of hatching and cross-hatching were created by *enlevage*; highlights were formed by additional applications of white enamel. The flesh color was achieved by painting a wash of red enamel in clear flux over areas of thick white. The painter also used red enamel for the fire in the brazier and for pieces of fruit on the rim. The handle of Abraham's sword, Isaac's hair, the fire, foliage, and drapery edges, as well as decorative motifs such as the arabesque "echoes" on the rim and the overall pattern of stylized leaves on the underside, are in gold.

The plate is in good condition. The underside shows normal abrasion from resting on that surface. A firing fault or bubble can be seen below the putto's right foot.

✳

The episode depicted on this plate is one of the most dramatic in the Old Testament. To test the faith of Abraham, God orders him to sacrifice his only son, Isaac, the child of his old age, born through divine intervention to the long-barren Sarah. Without protest the devout patriarch takes the boy into the mountains:

> Abraham took the wood for the sacrifice and put it on his son Isaac's shoulder, while he himself carried the fire and the knife. As the two of them went on together, Isaac spoke. "Father!...Here are the fire and the wood, but where is the sheep for a sacrifice?" Abraham answered, "God will provide himself with a sheep for a sacrifice, my son." The two of them went on together until they came to the place of which God had spoken. There Abraham built an altar and arranged the wood. He bound his son Isaac and laid him on the altar on top of the wood. He reached out for the knife to slay his son, but the angel of the Lord called to him from heaven, "Abraham, Abraham:... do not raise your hand against the boy; do not touch him. Now I know that you are a godfearing man. You have not withheld from me your son, your only son." Abraham looked round, and there in a thicket he saw a ram caught by his horns. He went, seized the ram, and offered it as a sacrifice instead of his son. (Genesis 22:6–13 ERV)

The scene of the interrupted sacrifice
was a popular Old Testament scene among
the enamel painters, partly for its inherent
drama and partly for its religious significance as a prefiguration of the Crucifixion,
the ultimate sacrifice of a son by his father.

Most enamel painters, including this
artist, used as their model engravings by
Bernard Salomon for the *Quadrins historiques de la Bible*, a presentation in poetry
of biblical vignettes, first published by Jean
de Tournes in Lyons in 1553. The print
depicting the Sacrifice of Isaac (fig. 34) is
effective for its pathos and drama, particularly in the submissive figure of the boy
and the striking gesture of the angel grab-
bing the blade of Abraham's sword on its
upswing. If a little less compact in composition, the enamel is nevertheless close to
its source, including the retention of the
figure of the angel emerging from a bank
of clouds and Abraham's billowing cloak.
On the right of the print, however, are
two retainers with a donkey mentioned in
the biblical account (Genesis 22:3–5); in
the enamel these have metamorphosed
into a shepherd with his flock.

Claude Paradin's quatrain that accompanies this engraving (no. 35) is as follows:

> *Abraham veut son cher fils immoler,*
> *Pour accomplir ce que Dieu lui ordonne:*
> *Mais sur le poinct qu'il le veut decoler,*
> *L'Ange de Dieu ne le lui abandonne.*

(Abraham is ready to sacrifice his beloved
son in order to carry out God's command
to him: but just as he is about to behead
him, the angel of God does not abandon
him.)

In the sale catalogue of the Charles Mannheim collection (Molinier 1898, cat. no. 186) this plate is attributed to the atelier of Pierre Reymond. It is not, however, in Reymond's style but has much more in common, stylistically and technically, with the small group of objects that have been assigned to the recently identified Jean Miette. The existence of a number of plates of approximately the same diameter illustrating scenes from the early chapters of Genesis and painted in a similar style on a dark blue ground suggests that Miette executed a series: extant plates include *The Creation of the Birds, Fish, and Beasts* and *The Sacrifice of Cain and Abel* in the Walters Art Gallery, Baltimore (inv. nos. 44.56, 44.45; Verdier 1967, cat. nos. 115–16); *The Creation of Eve* sold in New York in 1982 (Sotheby Parke Bernet, December 3–4, lot 64); *Adam and Eve after the Expulsion* sold in Paris in 1976 (Ader Picard Tajan, June 23, lot 95); and five in the Musée du Louvre, Paris: *The Creation of Adam, God's Admonition to Adam and Eve, The Temptation, Adam and Eve after the Fall,* and *The Murder of Abel* (inv. nos. 6192-95, MR.2438; Marquet de Vasselot 1914, cat. nos. 712–16). These plates have in common with the Los Angeles plate their style of painting and crosshatching, the modeling of drapery and limbs, especially the delicate hands, a use of heavy white scrollwork, and laurel wreaths on the underside rims. The scrollwork borders of these other plates are simpler, however, and do not incorporate rosettes, masks, or urns in their patterns; the undersides feature antique busts in a frame of scrollwork. Moreover, they are painted in a thinner

white enamel with nervous lines of *enlevage*, and the figures are almost awkwardly elongated, with sketchy faces and small heads. The Los Angeles plate displays a larger scale, a more skillful grisaille technique, and more substantial and better proportioned figures, suggesting that it is the work of the same enamel painter later in his career. The figure of Abraham is particularly reminiscent of many of the prophets and apostles on the screen of twenty-one polychrome plaques by Léonard Limousin in the Walters Art Gallery (inv. no. 44.366; Verdier 1967, cat. nos. 83–103), suggesting that even if Miette was not in fact Limousin's apprentice, he learned from his experience with the master.

There is a polychrome plaque depicting the Kiss of Judas in the collection of the British Museum, London (inv. no. 1959, 2-6, 5), that may be by the same hand. Especially striking are the similarities in the delineation of the faces and the use of flesh tones.

The Salomon model was used for the decoration of ceramics as well as enamel. A maiolica plate of about 1580 from the Patanazzi workshop of Urbino (sold Christie's, London, June 29, 1987, lot 120) and a faience pilgrim bottle of Lyonnais manufacture (Damiron 1926, pl. 1, no. 4) present the identical composition (both painters have eliminated the secondary scene of Abraham's retainers).

The composition is repeated in a number of extant enamels by Pierre Courteys, who relied heavily on the work of Salomon for his models (see cat. no. 23); they include three signed pieces: a grisaille plate (British Museum; ex-collection Bernal [no. 1480]); a polychrome plaque (Musée du Louvre; Laborde 1853, cat. no. 375; Darcel 1891, cat. no. 516; Marquet de Vasselot 1914, cat. no. 647); a polychrome plaque on a casket with other scenes from Genesis (Victoria and Albert Museum, London [inv. no. C.2444-1910]). Grisaille tazzas depicting the Sacrifice of Isaac are also attributed to Pierre Reymond (Walters Art Gallery [inv. no. 44.67; Verdier 1967, cat. no. 140], and another signed example, ex-collection Gérard Loew, sold Hôtel Drouot, Paris, May 6, 1983, lot 124) and Couly Nouailher (signed; ex-collection Shuvalov; Hermitage Museum, Saint Petersburg, inv. no. F-2653; Dobroklonskaya 1969, cat. no. 25).

FIGURE 35

Marcantonio Raimondi,
Italy, c. 1480–c. 1534,
Ornamental Panel,
engraving, 21 x 13.9 cm
(8 ¼ x 5 ½ in.),
Graphische Sammlung
Albertina, Vienna.

The motif on the underside, of a putto
climbing in vines, may have been adapted
from an ornamental panel engraved by
Marcantonio Raimondi (fig. 35; Bartsch
1978–82, vol. 27, 240, no. 557), which
depicts a grotesque creature, half-putto,
half-plant, in the same pose in a curl of
acanthus.

PROVENANCE

Charles Mannheim, Paris.

J. Pierpont Morgan.

William Randolph Hearst.

Donated to the Los Angeles County
Museum of Art, 1948.

LITERATURE

Molinier 1898, cat. no. 186.

Active 1555–85

AFTER MORE THAN a century of confusion most scholars now agree that
Jean de Court, Jean Court, Jean Courteys, Jean Courtois, I. Curtius,
Master I.C., and Master I.D.C. are one and the same. Certainly this artist was not unique
in Limoges in using a variety of spellings and forms of his name on his painted enamels.
He seems to have signed his name in full only once, on a polychrome portrait plaque
of 1555 depicting Marguerite of France as the goddess Minerva (Wallace Collection, London,
inv. no. III F 253). The signatures most frequently found on his enamels are the monograms
"IC" and "IDC."

Since de Court is usually regarded as two or three different painters by the earlier
historians of enamel painting, it is difficult to sort out the factual details of his life. Léon
de Laborde (1853, 263) stated that he was the son of the glass painter Robert Courtois of
Mans, but this claim was made by others for Pierre Courteys (see Courteys's biography).
De Court's period of activity is usually given as about 1555 to about 1585, but the artist who
painted the Wallace *Minerva* of 1555 had surely been working in the medium for some
years. Indeed, a contract of 1532 with a glass painter named Jehan Courtois for a window
in the church in La Ferté-Bernard suggests that he may have started in this medium (Ardant
1860, 147). He seldom dated his work, the *Minerva* plaque being the earliest known dated
enamel, and there are others from 1568. Some pieces may be dated approximately by their
iconography, since many models and subjects had a finite period of popularity and were
employed on dated pieces by other enamel painters.

Although not all scholars are in agreement, it is thought that this artist is the same
Jean de Court who was painter to Charles Bourbon, prince de la Roche-sur-Yon, in 1553
and to the widowed Mary, Queen of Scots, from 1562 to 1567 and who succeeded François
Clouet (died 1572) as the highly regarded (and highly paid) *peintre du roi* to Charles IX
(r. 1560–74). Jacques Blanchon mentioned him in an ode of 1583 to the celebrated poet
Jean Dorat, himself from Limoges and related to the Courteys/Court families (cited in
Verdier 1967, xxv):

La surartiste excellence　　　　　　(The outstanding artistic excellence

de l'estimable de Court　　　　　　of the estimable de Court

que tout l'univers appelle　　　　　whom everyone calls

l'admirable esprit d'Apelle　　　　　the admirable spirit of Apelles

vue en la royale court.　　　　　　seen at the royal court.)

This verse, which is certainly about the Jean de Court who was painter to the king, goes on to speak of the enamel painters Jean Court *dit* Vigier and another Courteys, probably Pierre, thus reinforcing the idea that the court artist and the enamel painter were the same man. The coat of arms on at least one of his works, a platter illustrating the Wedding Banquet of Cupid and Psyche, now in the Walters Art Gallery, Baltimore (inv. no. 44.201; Verdier 1967, cat. no. 170), suggests that he was sufficiently well known to have a German clientele.

De Court's style was less sculptural than that of Pierre Courteys; he excelled at a skillful decoration of surfaces with complicated, crowded compositions and exuberant ornamentation, producing enamels reminiscent of the *mille-fleurs* tapestries hanging in châteaux and *hôtels* throughout France. In his best polychrome enamels, lavish with bright translucent hues over foil and with gold details, the effect can be stunning. When handled by his less skillful atelier assistants, however, the enamels, particularly the grisailles, are flat and busy, but even on these pieces the striking decorative motifs on the rims and secondary surfaces are usually well executed, suggesting a division of labor like that in the atelier of Pierre Reymond. Nineteenth-century critics faulted him for parading his knowledge of anatomy by exaggerating the musculature of his nudes and for his overly red flesh tones (Darcel 1865–66, 57), but others felt his works—a balance of design, imagination, and color—were the most sumptuous of all the Limousin production (Lavedan 1913, 123).

De Court's atelier produced both plaques and the same range of vessel and plate types available from the other Limousin painters. Especially striking are the polychrome and grisaille ewers (cat. no. 26), for the graceful shape of the copper vessels, the variety of decoration, and the skill with which the source material was adapted to the zoned ewer format. Although de Court's output was not as extensive as Reymond's, his oeuvre was more iconographically repetitive, a fact that may be attributed to his frequent absences from Limoges in the service of the court, leaving his atelier to turn out copies of already successful designs. His models were primarily the works of the French *maîtres ornemanistes*, with an occasional nod to the compositions of the Italian mannerists active at Fontainebleau.

One of the two documented female enamel painters, Susanne de Court (also Court, De Cour, Decourt), praised for her draftsmanship and color, was probably a member of the same family, either by blood or marriage, although her relationship to Jean is not known. A theory (Verdier 1967, xxv; 1977, 188) that Jean was the younger brother of enamel painter Jean Court *dit* Vigier seems to be without foundation.

*

25

JEAN DE COURT

Plate: June (Sheepshearing)

c. 1560
Grisaille enamel, flesh tones, touches of
color, and gold on copper
Diameter 19.8 cm (7 ¹³/₁₆ in.)
William Randolph Hearst Collection
48.2.2

DESCRIPTION

A woman and man are seated on a grassy bank at center shearing a ewe and a ram. On the ground in front of them is a full basket of fleece, below which is the monogram ·I·C·. To the left a shepherd leans on his staff, watching the shearing; two sheep stand behind him. A thatched-roof stone barn with an overhanging second story is immediately behind the figures, and the inscription ·IVING· (for *juin*, June) is painted in gold under the two windows farthest to the right. A wooded yard enclosed by a wattle fence can be seen to the right; beyond is a rolling landscape with a house, a distant tower, and hills. Above the scene is a half-roundel of clouds containing the sign of Cancer the Crab.

The cavetto of the plate is ornamented with a guilloche motif painted in gold. The rim displays a grotesque head (at the top), two lion's heads, and a coat of arms (at the bottom) separated by S-scroll strapwork linked by swags of fruit. The edge is of opaque white enamel.

On the underside a rosette is surrounded by an interlace of strapwork incorporating two male and two female terms. Arabesques in gold cover the rest of the surface, and the rim is painted with a wreath of laurel leaves in gold with two fillets.

LATER INSCRIPTIONS
OR LABELS

On the underside rim: **P.M. 982.** painted in red (J. Pierpont Morgan catalogue number)

The ground of the plate is not black but a dense, translucent mulberry. The design was created in opaque white enamel by *enlevage* and the addition of layers of white for highlights. The unusually dark flesh tones were produced by the usual procedure of painting with a wash of red enamel suspended in clear flux. The lightest wash was used for the flesh of the figures, including the faces of the grotesques on the rim; a darker shade colors the hair of the figures and fruit on the rim, and a very dark flesh tone, almost red, appears with blue and gold on the coat of arms. The surround of the sign of the zodiac and the cavetto and overall rim decoration were executed in gold.

The gold is rubbed and faded, the underside of the plate is somewhat abraded and scratched, and the densest areas of opaque white enamel show bubbling and losses.

*

This plate depicting the occupation for the month of June is from a dispersed set of calendar plates by Jean de Court, no doubt similar to a complete set by the artist sold at auction in 1977 and again in 1988 (ex-collections Prince Soltykoff[?] and Joseph Desloge; sold Christie's, London, July 18, 1977, lot 81; ex-collection R. C. Pritchard; sold Sotheby's, London, December 8, 1988, lot 339). Since this set has three different rim motifs and four different undersides (including the same rim and underside designs as those on the Los Angeles plate), it is tempting to suggest that it was assembled later from individual plates. The similarity of style, technique, and scale in the main compositions of the auctioned set and the identical handling of such areas as the cavetto motifs, signs of the zodiac, and inscriptions seem to indicate, however, that the plates were made as a set and that variation in decorative detail was a desirable feature.

The June plate in the auctioned set has an identical scene of sheepshearing, although it is supplied with a rim more commonly found on de Court's tableware, whereas the Los Angeles plate (like four others in the complete set) is decorated with a rim motif similar to one used by Pierre Courteys (see, for example, the rims of cat. nos. 21–22). The plates for April, July, August, and September in the set have the same rim as the Los Angeles June plate (without the coat of arms), and those for January, August, and December have the same underside.

The source for the activity depicted on the June plates, and indeed on the complete set, is the same as that used by Pierre Reymond on calendar plates dating from 1548 to 1562 (see cat. nos. 13–16),

an as-yet-unidentified source perhaps adapted from the twelve woodcut illustrations for the *Compost et kalendrier des bergères* (fig. 36; see also fig. 24), published in Paris in 1499 by Guy Marchant. This and the artist's use of a rim similar to those on Pierre Courteys's grisaille Psyche plates of 1560 (cat. nos. 21–22) suggest a similar date.

Another June sheepshearing plate signed with the monogram "IC," but described, possibly erroneously, with three rather than four terms on the underside, was in the Frédéric Spitzer sale (Chevallier-Mannheim, Paris, April 17–June 16, 1893, lot 568). Other plates by de Court using the same set of prints as models are March and December plates in the Victoria and Albert Museum, London (inv. nos. C.2430-1910, C.2433-1910), but the absence of a coat of arms on the rim indicates that these cannot be part of the set that once included the Los Angeles plate. Jean Court *dit* Vigier used the same model for a plate now in the Musée du Louvre, Paris (Laborde 1853, cat. no. 409; Darcel 1891, cat. no. 574; Marquet de Vasselot 1914, cat. no. 695).

According to Léon de Laborde (1853, 263 n. 2), Sir Andrew Fountaine had in his collection at Narford Hall in Norfolk two complete series of calendar plates after a set of engravings dated 1568 by Étienne Delaune (see fig. 25; Robert-Dumesnil 1865, vol. 9, 58–61, nos. 185–96), one series signed with the monogram "IC."

PROVENANCE

Possibly Frédéric Spitzer, Paris; sale, Chevallier-Mannheim, Paris, April 17– June 16, 1893, lot 568, 1,500 francs.

Charles Mannheim, Paris.

J. Pierpont Morgan.

William Randolph Hearst.

Donated to the Los Angeles County Museum of Art, 1948.

LITERATURE

Possibly Molinier 1891, 315.

Possibly Spitzer 1891, vol. 2, cat. no. 153.

Molinier 1898, cat. no. 190.

Color plate, page 51

26

JEAN DE COURT

Ewer

c. 1560/70
Grisaille enamel, flesh tones, touches of
color, and gold on copper
Height 29.3 cm (11 ½ in.)
Gift of Varya and Hans Cohn
AC1992.152.116

DESCRIPTION

The ewer is divided into four zones of
decoration. The neck is painted with an
elaborate gold arabesque and overlapping
acanthus leaves. On the shoulder is a
frieze of grotesque sea creatures separated
from the body by a white torus painted
with stylized sprigs and flowers. The main
scene, on the body, is a battle between
nude men on horseback. One rider carries
a standard, the others wield swords; several
men and horses are wounded, a few have
fallen. Under this scene is a decorative
zone of gold patterns. The stem is decorated with overlapping acanthus leaves,
and the foot with grotesques. The edge of
the foot is decorated in a manner similar

to the torus. The inner rim of the ewer
and the outer edge of the handle are
painted with arabesque patterns in black
on a white ground; the underside of the
handle is painted with gold dots.

TECHNIQUE

The ewer is covered with a ground color
of deep mulberry that appears black,
over which the designs were built up in
layers of opaque white. Contour lines,
shading, and textures were executed by
enlevage, and highlights were created by
the addition of layers of white enamel.
The vivid flesh tones and a darker reddish
tone used for some of the grotesque creatures were rendered by washes of varying
amounts of red enamel mixed with clear
flux. Opaque iron-red enamel was used
for blood on the wounded warriors. Gold
was applied to many areas of the ewer in
arabesques and other decorative motifs
and was also used for swords, reins, grass,
and branches in the scenes.

The ewer has a loss on one figure in
the cavalry skirmish, some small losses at
the top of the stem and on the edge of
the foot, and there is a large chip on the
upper shoulder near the handle. The handle has been broken and either reattached
at its lower join or replaced. The outer
surface of the handle and the inner rim
of the ewer have been repainted in cold
enamel, and other cold repairs are visible
on the edge of the foot and the torus.

✻

FIGURES 37–38

Jacques Androuet du
Cerceau, France,
c. 1520–c. 1584, *Cavalry
Combats*, c. 1543/45,
engravings, 7.9 x 24.5
cm (3⅛ x 9⅝ in.) and
8 x 24.9 cm (3⅛ x 9¹³⁄₁₆
in.), Bibliothèque
Nationale, Paris.

The ewer form was produced by a number of workshops in Limoges, particularly
those of the Reymond and Courteys families. In surviving examples the shape of
the body may vary from a rounded to an
inverted conical form, but all are ultimately
based on a classical prototype, such as
Syrian or Italian mold-blown glass ewers
of the first century A.D.

The marine scene on the shoulder
of this ewer was taken from a design for
a tazza by Jacques Androuet du Cerceau
dating about 1550–60 (Bibliothèque
Nationale, Paris, Ed. 2.f. pet. fol. E2;
Kjellberg 1979, 58). The engraving has at
its center the smashed chariot of the sun;
from it the figure of Phaeton plunges into
a sea filled with grotesque creatures. The
enamel painter omitted the episode of
Phaeton completely and used only seven
of the nine figures or figure groups of the
sea creatures, changing their sequence to
suit his design. The lower zone is derived
from a series of six *combats de cavalerie*

engraved by du Cerceau (figs. 37–38;
Bibliothèque Nationale, Paris, Ed. 2.b.
pet. fol. E1); Heinrich von Geymüller
(1887, 323) said these engravings were after
Bramante (although he does not identify
a specific work or works) and dates them
to about 1543–45. The enamel painter
appropriated all the figures from one of
the battle scenes (fig. 37; L.P. 51, 3) and
extracted the second group from the left
from another (fig. 38; L.P. 51, 4) to fill
the register.

On many of these ewers the monogram signature of the artist appears on the inner rim below the handle join; unfortunately, since that area has been repainted here, no trace of a monogram can be seen. This ewer was attributed to Jean III Pénicaud (active c. 1571–1606) when it was in the Spitzer collection (see Provenance and Literature), and there are indeed stylistic similarities to the work of that enamel painter, particularly the skillfully rendered and dramatic chiaroscuro and the hard contour lines. But these qualities are also characteristic of the work of Jean de Court, and the ewer has other stylistic and iconographic features that correspond more closely to those of the latter artist's grisaille pieces: distinctive, and at times almost ruddy, flesh tones; a particular method of rendering human and animal musculature; the manner of *enlevage*, visible especially on the bodies of the horses; and a softer, subtler modeling within the contour lines.

The iconography of this ewer supports an attribution to de Court. Two other ewers by him illustrate the same combination of scenes: one is in the Musée du Louvre, Paris (Marquet de Vasselot 1914, cat. no. 711); the other was purchased by Baron Seillière from the collection of Prince Soltykoff (sold Hôtel Drouot, Paris, April 8–May 1, 1861, lot 474).

Only one other ewer illustrating a marine subject has been attributed to Pénicaud, and according to one description (London 1862, cat. no. 1736) the subject represented was Neptune and Amphitrite, taken from a engraving by Agostino Veneziano after Raphael. There are, by contrast, at least five other ewers signed by de Court that reproduce or adapt the marine scene engraved by du Cerceau: these include examples formerly in the collections of the earl of Rosebery (sold Sotheby Parke Bernet, Mentmore Towers, May 20 [day 3], 1977, lot 1153) and Robert Brummer (Kjellberg 1979, 54–55, 58–61); one in the British Museum, London (inv. no. 85, 4-20, 18; Norwich 1985, cat. no. 33), and another in the Taft Museum, Cincinnati (inv. no. 1931.292; Taft 1958, cat. no. 140), the latter probably

from the Soltykoff collection (see above sale, lot 519 *bis*). All are within a few centimeters of the height of this ewer and are of the same rounded form as all the ewers produced by de Court's workshop. In addition, the style of painting is similar in all these ewers, as is the use of salmon red in the flesh tints.

Several of the same grotesque figures appear in a tazza cover by de Court in the Musée de la Renaissance at Écouen (inv. no. CL.887b); other covers at Écouen by the same artist display grotesques rendered in a very similar style to those on this ewer (inv. nos. CL.887a, CL.888). The grotesques on the foot of the ewer—fabulous creatures with the head of a bird, the breasts of a woman, and the tail of a serpent, based on the ornamental engravings of Étienne Delaune—appear on the decorative borders and reverses of nearly all the plates and platters from de Court's workshop (see cat. nos. 27–28).

None of the du Cerceau cavalry battles appears on any extant enamel by Pénicaud, to my knowledge, but similar scenes after du Cerceau are found on the bodies of five ewers signed by or securely attributed to de Court, including another in the Louvre (Laborde 1853, cat. no. 405; Darcel 1891, cat. no. 570; Marquet de Vasselot 1914, cat. no. 672), one formerly in the Brummer collection (Kjellberg 1979, 54–57), and one formerly in the Bernal and Addington collections (Bohn 1857, cat. no. 156, pl. opp. 163).

It is tempting to conclude that the Soltykoff/Seillière ewer mentioned above may have come into the Spitzer collection with a cold repair obscuring the monogram "IC" and can thus be identified as the Los Angeles ewer. Unfortunately, the Soltykoff ewer seems from its description to have been more rounded and less graceful in shape. The existence of other ewers signed by de Court with the same decorative scheme nevertheless encourages a change of attribution. His workshop was known for its repetition, not just of decorative motifs, but of objects themselves, a situation possibly prompted, as Philippe Verdier has suggested (1977, 188), because he was often away at court. The quality of the decoration of this ewer suggests that it was executed by the master himself. Its fluidity of style and compositional organization would place it among the best of his signed grisaille enamels, far above the comparatively flattened, crowded figure compositions turned out by his workshop.

PROVENANCE

Frédéric Spitzer, Paris; sale, Chevallier-Mannheim, Paris, April 17–June 16, 1893, lot 445.

French and Company, New York.

Varya and Hans Cohn, Los Angeles, 1946.

Donated to the Los Angeles County Museum of Art, 1992.

EXHIBITED

Los Angeles County Museum of Art, 1983–92, lent by Hans Cohn.

LITERATURE

Spitzer 1891, vol. 2, cat. no. 29.

Cohn 1991, 276–79.

27

JEAN DE COURT

Oval platter:
Destruction of the Hosts of Pharaoh

c. 1560/70
Grisaille enamel, flesh tones, and gold
on copper
40.2 x 52.7 cm (15 ¹³⁄₁₆ x 20 ¾ in.)
William Randolph Hearst Collection
48.2.16

DESCRIPTION

Moses, to the left of center, raises his staff as a wall of water rises and curls, crashing down on the pharaoh of Egypt, in his two-horse chariot at right, and dozens of horses and riders. In the background at right can be seen grandiose buildings representing Egypt. Behind Moses the host of the Israelites, many hundreds strong, turn away to continue their journey along a road leading into the left background. Above the wall of water can be seen a swanlike pillar of cloud that guided the Israelites in the wilderness.

The cavetto is painted with gold arabesques. On the rim are four pairs of grotesque beasts confronting equally grotesque terms. At the top is a winged lion's head, at the bottom a blank roundel frame in a wreath of laurel, at the sides profile tondi of a man and woman in classical attire, framed by a band of white. Gold arabesques and foliage cover the surface of the rim; the edge is of opaque white enamel.

The underside of the platter is decorated with a complex intertwining oval of strapwork, beading, and drapery, incorporating two terms and two grotesque heads. On the strapwork near the center is the monogram ·I·C·. The rest of the surface is decorated with gold arabesques, and the rim is painted with a gold laurel wreath with fillets and berries.

TECHNIQUE

Over a dense mulberry ground that appears black, the artist applied opaque white enamel in which he traced the contours of the elaborate design by *enlevage*. Additional layers of opaque white enamel were used to form the highlights that model the forms, and there is considerable hatching in the areas of shadow. The rich flesh tones, produced in the traditional manner of red enamel mixed with clear flux, were used for skin and hair on the figures on both sides of the platter and the upper rim. Gold was used for overall decorative motifs, as well as for drapery borders, foliage, hair, clouds, and rays of light coming from heaven.

The platter is in good condition. There are some firing bubbles in the opaque white on the upper surface and some discoloration of the copper under the white edge, perhaps due to corrosion. The underside has some scratches and normal abrasion. Much of the gold on the rims is rubbed.

✱

The scene, often mistitled *The Crossing of the Red Sea* or *The Passage of the Red Sea*, actually represents the Destruction of Pharaoh's Host and is adapted from Bernard Salomon's illustrations for Claude Paradin's *Quadrins historiques de la Bible*, first published in 1553 by Jean de Tournes of Lyons. The print from which the enamel is derived (fig. 39), entitled *Dieu marche devant les Israëlites* (God goes before the Israelites; no. 131), actually depicts both that scene—the Israelites led by a pillar of cloud (Exodus 13:27)—and a later incident (Exodus 14:27) in which Moses raises his hand and the waters of the parted Red Sea fall back on the pursuing Egyptians. In the engraving the group of figures incorporating Moses is depicted in the middle distance, whereas Jean de Court, probably for dramatic emphasis, has placed it in the foreground, making it the focus of the scene. Thus the quatrain accompanying the Salomon print deals with only part of the scene depicted on the platter:

Dieu va devant en Colonne de nue,
Pour des Ebrieus le chemin adresser,
Si à propos qu'ils n'en perdent la vuë:
Car point errer il ne les veut laisser.

(God goes in front as a pillar of cloud to direct the path of the Hebrews, so that they will not lose sight of him, for he does not wish to let them go astray.)

Moses's action illustrated in this scene is referred to in a later quatrain, when the Israelites rejoice in their victory over Pharaoh.

This crowded figural composition is typical of the designs popular in de Court's atelier. Thanks to the overwhelming *horror vacui* the painter has not achieved a three-dimensional quality; the flatness is compounded by the less-than-successful perspective on the Egyptian side, where soldiers in the distance are larger than others closer to the viewer, and by the recession of the Israelites, whose many hundred heads have become just another pattern. But there is much to impress, especially the bravura passages of fluid drapery in the left foreground figures and the calligraphic exuberance of the roiling waters on the right. The draftsmanship and modeling of form are particularly striking in individual figures of drowning soldiers and horses.

Ironically, the rim is less successful, possibly because it is decorated with isolated three-dimensional figures, rather than the continuous, intertwining decorative patterns so effective as a frame for the more three-dimensional scenes painted by Pierre Reymond and Pierre Courteys. The grotesque figures are adapted from the work of Étienne Delaune, especially his gods and goddesses in architectural caprices (fig. 30; see cat. no. 19), and the *Petites Grotesques* of Jacques Androuet du Cerceau (fig. 11; see DuBon 1980, 6–15, for an excellent analysis of similar rim ornamentation on a polychrome platter in the Philadelphia Museum of Art [inv. 1979-19-1]). David DuBon's suggestion (1980, 15) that this type of profile portrait on the rim represents donors is unlikely. Profiles of figures in classical dress were frequently used by the enamel painters of Limoges (see cat. nos. 16–18, 28); they were a popular decorative motif.

The elaborate motif on the underside was frequently used in the atelier of Jean de Court for round and oval platters illustrating both sacred and secular themes. Philippe Verdier has suggested (archives of the Taft Museum, Cincinnati) that it is after a pattern by Agnolo Bronzino in the Palazzo Vecchio, Florence, which was engraved by Hieronymus Cock.

Léon de Laborde (1853, 265 n. 1) singles out for praise an oval platter in the collection of Baron Achille Seillière that may be this example (see Provenance).

Other extant oval platters of this scene from de Court's atelier include an example in the Metropolitan Museum of Art, New York (inv. no. 1975.1.1232), and another at the Hermitage Museum, Saint Petersburg (inv. no. F-820; Dobroklonskaya 1969, cat. no. 48). He also used the theme for polychrome platters, such as those in the Robert Lehman Collection at the Metropolitan Museum (Szabó 1975, cat. no. 170), Spencer Museum of Art, University of Kansas, Lawrence (inv. no. 55-69), the Waddesdon Bequest at the British Museum, London (Read 1902, cat. no. 33), and the de Young Museum, San Francisco (inv. no. 48.2), as well as large oval plaques in the Musée du Louvre, Paris (Laborde 1853, cat. no. 392), and the Musée Municipal, Limoges (inv. no. 47; Limoges 1966, 71).

Other objects by Jean de Court illustrating this episode include plaques, ewers, tazzas, and covered cups, such as an interesting example of the latter form, in which the scene is split between the bowl of the cup (drowning of Pharaoh's host) and the exterior of the lid (the Israelites led by the pillar of cloud), formerly in the Spitzer collection (Spitzer 1891, vol. 2, cat. no. 145; sold Chevallier-Mannheim, Paris, April 17–June 16, 1893, lot 560). The scene was also depicted by Jean II Pénicaud, Pierre Reymond, Pierre Courteys, and Susanne de Court.

PROVENANCE

Possibly Baron Achille Seillière; sale, Paris, March 5–10, 1890, lot 215, 24,500 francs.

William Randolph Hearst.

Donated to the Los Angeles County Museum of Art, 1948.

EXHIBITED

Possibly London 1874.

Possibly Paris 1884.

LITERATURE

Possibly Laborde 1853, 265 n. 1.

Possibly Ardant 1860, 152.

Possibly Verdier 1967, 338.

Verdier 1977, 160 n. 3.

Color plate, page 52

28

JEAN DE COURT

Oval platter: The Rape of Europa

c. 1565/75

Grisaille enamel, flesh tones, touches of
color, and gold on copper

40.6 x 54.3 cm (16 x 21⅜ in.)

William Randolph Hearst Collection

48.2.17

DESCRIPTION

At center Europa climbs on the back of
a large white bull to put a garland on his
head. Three maidens, two of whom hold
other garlands, sit on the ground to the
left. In front of a small herd of cattle (five
in the foreground and six more wandering
through the landscape) at right sits a herdsman playing a pan-pipe, his companion
listening as he leans on his staff. A dog lies
by a tree stump in the foreground. A wood-
land containing several varieties of trees
and bushes recedes to the right. In the left
background is a turbulent sea, in which
Neptune rides in a shell-chariot drawn by
two seahorses, followed by the bull carrying Europa. Three ships can be seen at
center, and a city is visible on the far shore.

The cavetto, rims, and underside are
identical to those of the previous platter,
except some details of the upper rim: at
the bottom is a grotesque head in a strapwork surround, at the sides are profile
tondi of a woman, at left, and a man in
classical attire. The underside is also
signed with the monogram ·I·C· on the
central strapwork.

TECHNIQUE

The dense translucent mulberry ground
appears black. The complex design was
executed in a layer of thin opaque white
enamel by *enlevage*, with the addition
of thicker white for highlights. The artist
created shadowed areas with a distinctive
bunching of hatched lines. Flesh tones,
a wash of ground red enamel in clear flux,
were used for the figures, human and
grotesque, on both sides of the platter.
Gold was used for drapery borders, hair,
foliage, and the chariot reins and trident
of Neptune, as well as overall decorative
patterns. A tiny touch of red enamel was
reserved for the petals of the flowers being
woven into crowns by Europa and her
handmaidens.

Aside from the usual abrasions and
scratches, there are firing bubbles in the
opaque white enamel, cracks and losses on
the cavetto and rim at upper left and a
corresponding shatter pattern on the upper
right of the underside. Four large gouges
along the axes of the underside suggest
that the piece rested on saggers during a
firing, or perhaps when it was refired to
repair the shattered area. Spots of green
under the opaque white edge also suggest
some corrosion in the copper that might
have been caused during a refiring.

*

JEAN DE COURT

FIGURE 40

Marcantonio Raimondi,
Italy, c. 1480–c. 1534,
Quos Ego (detail),
engraving, 43.2 x 33.6
cm (17 x 13 ¼ in.),
Los Angeles County
Museum of Art, collec-
tion of Mary Stansbury
Ruiz.

FIGURE 41

Antonio Montauti,
Italy, active 1707–40,
*The Triumph of
Neptune and Europa*
(detail), c. 1735/40,
bronze, ebonized wood,
101 x 105.1 cm (39 ¾ x
41 ⅜ in.), Los Angeles
County Museum
of Art, purchased with
funds provided by
Anna Bing Arnold.

The story of the abduction of Europa, the daughter of King Agenor of Tyre, by Zeus in the shape of a white bull was Greek in origin, but its popularity as a subject for Renaissance and Baroque artists was promoted by its inclusion among the *Metamorphoses* of Ovid (at the end of book 2). Several dozen illustrated editions were available in Latin or French in sixteenth-century France (Brun 1930, 274–77), including an edition of 1557 with prints by Bernard Salomon, published by Jean de Tournes of Lyons, the same team who produced Claude Paradin's *Quadrins historiques de la Bible*, which was so popular with the enamel painters of Limoges (see cat. nos. 18–19, 23–24, 27). Jean de Court reproduced Salomon's *Europa* on a small oval plaque now at Waddesdon Manor (Waddesdon 1977, cat. no. 12), but for the Los Angeles platter he chose another model, possibly a pastiche of print sources and original material. The figure of Neptune or Poseidon is adapted almost exactly from the famous *Quos Ego* engraving (fig. 40) by Marcantonio Raimondi (Bartsch 1978–82, vol. 27, 49, no. 352), thought to be after a lost original by Raphael, even to the overlapping of the farther sea-horse's head over the nearer (the other two sea-horses were omitted in the enamel). This episode from book 1 of the *Aeneid*, in which Neptune threatens the unruly winds, was used by other enamel painters, the most spectacular being a panel of ten plaques by Jean II Pénicaud, now in the British Museum, London, as part of the Waddesdon Bequest (Read 1902, cat. no. 21; Tait 1981, 43–45).

The two figures at the right have sometimes been identified as Mercury and Argus or as Pan and a herdsman, but both are clearly depicted as rustic humans in tunics and leggings, with no attributes of the pertinent god or demigods.

Neptune, seen in the background with the fleeing bull, is not a participant in either the original myth or Ovid's narrative, but his inclusion seems to have had some significance in the sixteenth, seventeenth, and eighteenth centuries, since this is not the only instance of his appearance in the Rape of Europa. Neptune in his chariot and Europa and the bull appear on a presentation dish of 1670 given by Pope Clement IX to marque Dom Luis Manuel de Tavora (sold Christie's, Geneva, November 15, 1984, lot 607); on a dish of 1674 by a Flemish goldsmith active in Genoa, Carol Bolcool, now in the Nationalmuseum, Stockholm (Hernmarck 1977, fig. 660); and in a bronze relief of 1735/40 by Antonio Montauti (fig. 41), now in the Los Angeles County Museum of Art (inv. no. M.83.52). A polychrome ewer stand by an unidentified enamel painter, formerly in the collection of Isabel Hafen (sold Christie's, Geneva, November 16, 1978, lot 263), is decorated with two cartouches depicting the Rape of Europa and Neptune in his chariot. In Greek mythology Neptune has connections to Europa and to bulls: he is variously reported to be the grandfather of Europa (Graves 1955, 191, section 56.b) and the father of her son Euphemus, a legendary swimmer (Graves 1966, 369 n. 1); Neptune was the creator of the great white bull that fathered the Minotaur, and Ovid mentions his seduction of the nymph Canace while in the form of a bull (in the story of Arachne,

at the beginning of book 6 of the *Metamorphoses*), but such connections were obscure variations of ancient myths. The significance of this combination in Renaissance and Baroque art can only be guessed at: Neptune may have been meant to symbolize Water and Europa Earth, usurping the role of Cybele, who appears, for example, with Neptune on a ewer stand of 1568 by Pierre Courteys in the Musée du Louvre (Darcel 1891, cat. no. 513; Marquet de Vasselot 1914, cat. no. 656). In fact, in the influential early novel *Hypnerotomachia Polifili* by Francesco Colonna (Venice: Aldus Manutius, 1499) the episode of Europa and the Bull represents Earth as one of four theogamies meant to symbolize the Four Elements (Wind 1968, 168 n. 62). There is also the possibility that the iconography commemorated a dynastic marriage, battle, or treaty.

The scene is another example of de Court's love of surface decoration, in which the crowding together of compositional elements creates the impression of pattern rather than three-dimensionality. Individual figures and passages of drapery, musculature, foliage, and water, however, are striking in their mastery of technique and invention. Even an element as secondary as the palm tree at center, for example, is a masterpiece of *enlevage* and highlighting. For comments on the designs of the rims and underside see the previous entry (cat. no. 27).

A nearly identical grisaille platter was sold in Geneva in 1976 (Christie's, November 10, lot 290). Very few other depictions of the subject are known on enamels, and they are based on other models, such as an unattributed smaller polychrome oval platter sold in London in 1967 (Sotheby, December 7, lot 149), in which the handmaidens of Europa in the foreground watch in dismay as she is carried off into the distance by the bull.

PROVENANCE

Possibly Debruge-Duménil; sale, Hôtel des Ventes, Paris, January 23 and following days, 1850, lot 747.

Earl of Warwick; sale, London, July 17, 1896, lot 11, £367.10.

William Randolph Hearst.

Donated to the Los Angeles County Museum of Art, 1948.

EXHIBITED

London 1874, no. 767, lent by the earl of Warwick.

LITERATURE

Possibly Labarte 1847, cat. no. 747.

Possibly Ardant 1860, 150.

Died 1592

MARTIAL COURTEYS was the second of three sons of Pierre Courteys, all of whom went on to become enamel painters and goldsmiths. Although his work is better known than that of his brothers, far less is known of the details of his life. He was mentioned as a *peintre-imagier* when he executed drawings in 1579 and 1580 in the books of the Confrérie du Saint-Sacrement in the parish of Saint-Pierre-du-Queyroix, Limoges, as had Pierre Reymond and Pierre Courteys before him.

Courteys's few extant enamels are important objects of high quality. He inherited his father's skill as a draftsman, although he did not create figures of such monumentality; stylistically his work has more in common with that of Jean de Court, with densely painted, busy surfaces. In his grisaille pieces he avoided the pitfalls of de Court's *horror vacui*, however, by a skillful modeling with a range of tones to achieve depth and sculptural presence. In his polychrome enamels he made even more lavish use of foil and gold highlighting than did his father, and his colors are jewel-bright. Although these decorative aspects sometimes overwhelm compositional focus and depth, the polychrome objects are striking. Especially noteworthy are a group of oval platters depicting mythological or religious scenes, with the decorative rims and undersides as spectacularly colored as the main scenes (cat. no. 41).

The small number of enamels that may be attributed to Courteys suggests that he did not maintain a large atelier but chose to execute most of the works himself, thereby accounting for their consistently high quality.

*

MARTIAL COURTEYS

Twelve plates:
The Labors of the Months

c. 1565/75
Grisaille enamel, flesh tones, touches of
color, and gold on copper
William Randolph Hearst Collection
48.2.11

29

January: Feasting

Diameter 20.3 cm (8 in.)

DESCRIPTION

A well-dressed couple is seated at an
elaborately carved, cloth-covered table,
their backs to an enormous hearth in an
arcaded hall. To the left of the table are
four mummers, including a dwarf, the
nearest carrying a flaming torch. Two ser-
vants carry food from the center background. In the frieze of the room is the
monogram MC.

The cavetto is painted in gold with
dots and arabesques. The rim of the plate
is decorated with strapwork and drapery
incorporating the head of Janus in a cartouche at the top, the legend ·IANVIER·
(January) in a cartouche at the bottom,
and figures of a man and a woman holding torches, bound cords of wood, and
baskets of food. The edge of the plate is
painted with a band of opaque white
enamel.

On the underside a large strapwork
surround with a cherub's head at the top
and a ram's head at the bottom frames
a figure of Aquarius walking to the right
holding a jar from which water streams.
The rim is made up of a band of framed
ovals joined together, with lozenges
between.

LATER INSCRIPTIONS
OR LABELS

On the underside: P.M. 988. painted in red
(J. Pierpont Morgan catalogue number)

30

*February: Chopping Wood and Warming
by the Fire*

Diameter 20.2 cm (7 15/16 in.)

DESCRIPTION

At right a woodcutter lays down his axe to
carry part of a load of wood into a vaulted
room with a large hearth. Before the fire
sit a man and woman and two small children. Another bound cord of wood is at
center. Outside are the base of a colonnade,
a pyramid, and a triumphal arch, with
more buildings in the right background.

The cavetto and edge are identical to
those of the January plate. The strapwork-
and-drapery rim contains a cartouche
framing the monogram ·M·C· at the top
and another with ·FEVRIER· (February)
at the bottom. Other motifs include
flaming braziers, crabs and fish, tridents,
traps, and warming pans.

The underside is identical to January's,
except for the sign of the zodiac, Pisces,
depicted as two rather fuzzy fish—one horizontal, one vertical, joined at the tail—
floating above a cloud.

LATER INSCRIPTIONS
OR LABELS

On the underside: P.M. 909. painted in red
(J. Pierpont Morgan catalogue number)

31

March: Pruning Vines

Diameter 20.3 cm (8 in.)

DESCRIPTION

Two men at left are pruning bare vines, another at right binds the cuttings. Beyond a knoll topped with a living and a dead tree are a shepherd and his flock in the middle ground at right and, in the distance, the tents of two armies outside a large city in flames. A cavalry engagement is in progress; one soldier has fallen.

The cavetto and edge are identical to those of the January plate. The strapwork-and-drapery rim contains a cartouche framing the monogram ·M·C· at the top and another with ·MARS· (March) at the bottom. Other motifs include fasces, helmets, cuirasses, swords, shields, bows and quivers of arrows, torches, and mortar shells.

The underside is identical to January's, except for the sign of the zodiac, Aries the Ram, seen reclining on the clouds.

LATER INSCRIPTIONS
OR LABELS

On the underside: P.M. 987. painted in red (J. Pierpont Morgan catalogue number)

32

April: Hunting

Diameter 20.3 cm (8 in.)

DESCRIPTION

A hunter on horseback, armed with a
bow, and his huntsman, blowing his horn,
are at left. One small hounds nips at his
master's heels, two more precede the
horse, another pair stop to drink from a
stream, and at right three more are about
to bring down a stag who has run into a
net tied between two trees. Behind a
grassy rise in the foreground are two tiny
rabbits (or one very long rabbit) going
into and emerging from a hole. In the
background is a wooded landscape with a
farmhouse and a castle visible through
the trees.

   The cavetto and edge are identical to
those of the January plate. The strapwork-
and-drapery rim contains a cartouche
framing the monogram ·M·C· at the top
and another with ·AVRIL· (April) at the
bottom. Other motifs include spears,
horns, swords, nets, gloves, and crouching
hounds.

   The underside is identical to January's,
except for the sign of the zodiac, Taurus
the Bull, seen half-length lying on a watery
surface.

LATER INSCRIPTIONS
OR LABELS

On the underside: P.M. 773. painted in red
(J. Pierpont Morgan catalogue number)

33

May: Making Music

Diameter 20.2 cm (7 ¹⁵⁄₁₆ in.)

DESCRIPTION

At center and right two women, two
children, and a man in antique dress and
crowned with laurel sing from partbooks,
while a second man, similarly dressed and
crowned, holds a lute and indulgently pats
one of the children on the head. At the
left two women weave chains of flowers;
a basket of blossoms and a pair of scissors
lie on the ground in front of them. Behind
is the lavish garden of a château, partly
seen at right, with exotic trees, parterres,
a pergola, and a fantastic fountain with six
streams of water jetting from an enormous
rocky crag. A mill with a waterwheel can
be seen along a stream in the left background, and other buildings and hills are
visible in the distance.

The cavetto and edge are identical to
those of the January plate. The strapwork-
and-drapery rim contains a cartouche
framing the monogram ·M·C· at the top
and another with ·MAY· at the bottom.
Other motifs include sackbuts, musical
partbooks, lutes, gambas and bows, lyres,
and cornettos.

The underside is identical to January's,
except for the sign of the zodiac, Gemini
the Twins, seen cavorting on the grass.

LATER INSCRIPTIONS
OR LABELS

On the underside: **P.M. 951.** painted in red
(J. Pierpont Morgan catalogue number)

34

June: Sheepshearing

Diameter 20.2 cm (7 $^{15}\!/_{16}$ in.)

DESCRIPTION

Two women shear two rams, while a shepherd with a staff directs them. A small flock of ewes and rams grazes behind the figures. In the yard of a large barn, a woman draws water from a well, doves land on the roof of their cote, and a rooster climbs a ladder to an ingenious henhouse, a conical structure on the top of a wooden post. Beyond the barnyard a stream meanders through a hilly landscape, and the buildings of a city are visible in the distance.

The cavetto and edge are identical to those of the January plate. The strapwork-and-drapery rim contains a cartouche framing the monogram ·M·C· at the top and another with ·IVIN· (June) at the bottom. Other motifs include water jugs, shears and fleece, fruit, and butter churns.

The underside is identical to January's, except for the sign of the zodiac, a lobster-like creature who represents Cancer the Crab, hovering above the ground.

LATER INSCRIPTIONS
OR LABELS

On the underside: **P.M. 983.** painted in red (J. Pierpont Morgan catalogue number)

35

July: Mowing

Diameter 20.2 cm (7 ¹⁵/₁₆ in.)

DESCRIPTION

In the foreground a man cuts grass with
a scythe, and a woman rakes the cuttings.
A water flask and cloak or sack lie on the
ground. Behind them another worker
takes a drink from his flask. A cloak has
been left hanging on a tree at right; beyond
this tree and the others at the edge of the
field is a river on which a figure is boating.
A farmhouse can be seen on the opposite
bank.

    The cavetto and edge are identical to
those of the January plate. The strapwork-
and-drapery rim contains a cartouche
framing the monogram ·M·C· at the top
and another with ·IVILLET· (July) at the
bottom. Other motifs include scythes,
bound bundles of grass, water flasks, and
fruit.

    The underside is identical to January's,
except for the sign of the zodiac, Leo the
Lion, crouching on the ground.

LATER INSCRIPTIONS
OR LABELS

On the underside: **P.M. 986.** painted in red
(J. Pierpont Morgan catalogue number)

Color plate, page 53

36

August: Harvesting

Diameter 20.2 cm (7 15/16 in.)

DESCRIPTION

At left a man cuts stalks of tall wheat with
a sickle; a second man farther out in the
field seems to be performing the same
task. Behind them a kneeling man binds
the sheaves. A fourth man at right carries
two sheaves away from the field, while a
dog barks at him. In a barn in the background at right another man can be seen
working, perhaps winnowing the wheat.
In the distance is a walled town at the foot
of a hill.

The cavetto and edge are identical to
those of the January plate. The strapwork-
and-drapery rim contains a cartouche
framing the monogram ·M·C· at the top
and another with AOVST (August) at the
bottom. Other motifs include water flasks,
flails, bound sheaves, sickles, and fruit.

The underside is identical to January's,
except for the sign of the zodiac, Virgo the
Virgin, presented as a rather muscular
winged woman, in a hat worn at a rakish
angle, reclining on the ground.

LATER INSCRIPTIONS
OR LABELS

On the underside: P.M. 957. painted in red
(J. Pierpont Morgan catalogue number)

37

September: Sowing

Diameter 20.1 cm (7 15/16 in.)

DESCRIPTION

In the foreground a man follows behind
a harrow, scattering seed he has taken
from a sack at left. Birds fly down to peck
at the seed. Behind the sower a second
man guides a plow pulled by two oxen.
A river borders the fields; a bridge spans
its width and leads to a large city in a
wooded landscape.

The cavetto and edge are identical to
those of the January plate. The strapwork-
and-drapery rim contains a cartouche
framing the monogram ·M·C· at the top
and another with ·SEPTEMBRE· at the
bottom. Other motifs include fruit, plow-
shares, sacks of seed, plows, and harrows.

The underside is identical to January's,
except for the sign of the zodiac, Libra the
Balance.

LATER INSCRIPTIONS
OR LABELS

On the underside: P.M. 778. painted in red
(J. Pierpont Morgan catalogue number)

38

October: Wine Making

Diameter 20.2 cm (7 15/16 in.)

DESCRIPTION

In the left foreground a grape picker
dumps the contents of his pannier into
a large wooden vat, in which another
worker is crushing grapes. A third man,
kneeling at right, tastes wine from another
vat, and behind him a woman pours the
liquid into a wooden cask. Sealed casks
can be seen under a thatched lean-to, with
birds roosting in the roof above. Behind
a picket fence at left are vines still laden
with bunches of grapes.

The cavetto and edge are identical to
those of the January plate. The strapwork-
and-drapery rim contains a cartouche
framing the monogram ·M·C· at the top
and another with ·OCTOBRE· at the bottom. Other motifs include grapes and
grape leaves, squash, ewers, and baskets.

The underside is identical to January's,
except for the sign of the zodiac, Scorpio
the Scorpion, against a black background.

LATER INSCRIPTIONS
OR LABELS

On the underside: P.M. 774. painted in red
(J. Pierpont Morgan catalogue number)

39

November: Feeding Hogs

Diameter 20.2 cm (7 $^{15}/_{16}$ in.)

DESCRIPTION

In the center a man is about to strike the
branches of a tree with a rod to knock
down acorns to feed a waiting herd of
swine. In his other hand he holds a shovel.
At right is a sleeping woman leaning on a
tree stump. A flock of sheep grazes in the
left middle ground, watched over by a
seated shepherd. A large palm tree is at
right, and in the distance is a city.

The cavetto and edge are identical to
those of the January plate. The strapwork-
and-drapery rim contains a cartouche
framing the monogram ·M·C· at the top
and another with ·NOVEMBRE· at the
bottom. Other motifs include oak leaves
and acorns, bucrania, and hoes.

The underside is identical to January's,
except for the sign of the zodiac, Sagittarius the Archer, with bow and arrow drawn
and ready.

LATER INSCRIPTIONS
OR LABELS

On the underside: P.M. 955. painted in red
(J. Pierpont Morgan catalogue number)

Color plate, page 53

40

December: Roasting Pigs

Diameter 20.2 cm (7 ^{15}/16 in.)

DESCRIPTION

Outside a country inn a bearded man tends a roaring fire in which two pigs are being roasted. An ax and a pan of live coals are in the foreground. A woman kneels at left, her hands in a basin of blood from the slaughtered animals; a second woman stands in the inn doorway, above which is a crescent and the words **A BON LOO**. Fields can be seen beyond a fence at right.

The cavetto and edge are identical to those of the January plate. The strapwork-and-drapery rim contains a cartouche framing the monogram **·M·C·** at the top and another with **·DECEMBRE·** at the bottom. Other motifs include brooms, sausages, bread paddles, and loaves of bread.

The underside is identical to January's, except for the rim design, which is made up of alternating ovals and rectangles created by an interlace, and for the sign of the zodiac, Capricorn, here depicted as half goat, half serpent, above the clouds.

LATER INSCRIPTIONS
OR LABELS

On the underside: **P.M. 958.** painted in red (J. Pierpont Morgan catalogue number)

The ground color of the plates is a dense translucent mulberry, which appears black. The contours were traced by *enlevage* in a thin layer of unfired opaque white enamel; additional applications of white provide areas of highlights. The modeling of the figures was accomplished primarily with white enamel and a range of gray tones rather than hatching. The flesh tones, paler than those used by other ateliers, were produced by the same process of mixing ground red enamel with a clear flux; the wash was reserved primarily for figures and foodstuffs (fruit, bread, sausages) and, on the undersides, for the heads and the signs of the zodiac (except for May, September, and November). Seven of the plates have touches of deeper flesh tones or red for fires (January, February, March, December), dogs' collars (April), flowers and a music book (May), wine (October), and blood (December); all of the underside rims have a wash of translucent blue. Gold was used for the cavetto designs, inscriptions, zodiac symbols, and for decorative borders on clothing, fires, foliage, instrument strings, ribbons, straps, leashes, tools and weapons, and August's fields of ripe wheat.

The plates are in good condition, except for the large number of firing bubbles in the areas of white, which give some of the plates a pitted surface.

*

These twelve calendar plates comprise the only complete set by Martial Courteys known to be extant. Their iconographical source is Étienne Delaune's undated series of the Labors of the Months (Robert-Dumesnil 1865, vol. 9, 73–78, nos. 225–36), in which the engravings are provided with borders incorporating objects and figures pertinent to each month's occupation among decorative elements, strapwork, and drapery. In a cartouche at the top of each print, except January (fig. 42), is the sign of the zodiac and its symbol, and in a cartouche at the bottom is a two-line Latin verse referring to the month's activities.

The December print (fig. 43) may provide a clue to the approximate date of these engravings. Earlier series of labors in manuscripts and prints usually depicted the slaughter of pigs for November and the baking of bread for December (see fig. 24). Later series, perhaps reflecting the economic emphasis of central France, gave both months over to pigs—November to their fattening, December to their slaughter—as does Delaune's series of engravings of 1568 (Robert-Dumesnil 1865, vol. 9, 58–61, nos. 185–96; see cat. no. 17). The inclusion of the activities of bread baking and pig roasting in one print, as happens in the undated Delaune series, suggests a transitional iconography engraved before the dated set. Since a set of anonymous prints used by Pierre Reymond were still the model of choice in 1561 (see cat. nos. 13–16), it is probable that Delaune's earlier series was not available until that year, and in fact the date of 1561 has been widely accepted for the engravings.

The scenes depicted by Delaune provide an invaluable glimpse into the customs of sixteenth-century France, from the scene for February, when the entire household, regardless of rank, clustered around the kitchen hearth for warmth, to the hunting vignettes for April, the less attractive practice of driving quarry into a previously strung net, where it could be easily butchered. The labors depicted are those of the peasants, from entertaining and paying tribute to their patrons (January) to the backbreaking tasks of planting and harvesting. Some scenes, such as the May musicale and the scene of war (the realm of the god Mars) in the background of the March plate, harken back to far more ancient sources and celebrations.

Courteys imaginatively adapted the prints, using the border designs for the upper rims and placing the signs of the zodiac on the undersides, while retaining the cartouches for his monogram and the names of the months. He chose to alter or omit certain elements within the scenes themselves, usually subsidiary or background scenes or figures that would have crowded the composition or made it impossible to fit into a circular format. For January he omitted a cat at lower right and the entire vignette on the left of the engraving, in which a woman breaks the ice on a stream in a landscape (fig. 42).

FIGURE 42

Étienne Delaune,
France, 1518/19–1583,
*January (Ice Fishing
and Feasting)*, from
the series *Les Douze
Mois de l'année*, c. 1561,
engraving, 17.2 x 23.5
cm (6 ¾ x 9 ¼ in.),
Print Collection, Miriam
& Ira D. Wallach
Division of Art, Prints
and Photographs,
The New York Public
Library, Astor, Lenox
and Tilden Founda-
tions, New York.

FIGURE 43

Étienne Delaune,
France, 1518/19–1583,
*December (Roasting Pigs
and Baking Bread)*,
from the series *Les
Douze Mois de l'année*,
c. 1561, engraving, 17.2
x 23.5 cm (6 ¾ x 9 ¼
in.), Print Collection,
Miriam & Ira D. Wallach
Division of Art, Prints
and Photographs,
The New York Public
Library, Astor, Lenox
and Tilden Founda-
tions, New York.

In the sky above this scene is the figure of the Water-Bearer, the only instance in the series in which Delaune did not put the sign of the zodiac in the upper border cartouche, reserving that space instead for the two-faced Janus, god of beginnings, from whose name *January* is derived. Courteys retained Janus and placed Aquarius on the underside of the plate.

On the February plate Courteys omitted the exterior scene and dog engraved by Delaune, on the March plate a boy and dog guarding a flock of geese, at right, and, in the distance, a cottage and a well. He left out an additional group of huntsmen at the left of Delaune's engraving for April, a group of four women playing instruments in an arbor on the right for May, and scenes on both sides of the sheepshearing for June. On the July plate Courteys omitted a group of bathers on the right of Delaune's engraving, although one bather's cloak hanging on a branch and their boating companion were retained. Delaune's scene for August was compressed by Courteys, and one figure, a woman carrying sheaves to the barn, was omitted on the plate; the September scene was also compressed, with only a tree at the center missing. Two men working in the background of the engraving have disappeared on the October plate, as have more of the herd of swine and a landscape on the left of the November scene. Finally, Courteys has eliminated the scene on the right of the December print in which a man and woman prepare and bake bread (fig. 43). It is also interesting to note that Courteys added the as-yet-undeciphered inscription on the inn's sign.

Courteys's elimination of the bread-baking scene from the December plate (although a reference is made to it by the prominently placed paddles on the rim), suggests that the calendar set was executed when this scene was no longer widely used, that is, beginning about 1565.

The consistent style and quality of the painting indicate that each plate in the series was executed in its entirety—upper surface, underside, and rims—by the same artist. This must have been Courteys himself, since the work is on a par with all the finest pieces signed by or attributed to him, if not superior to many of them. His range of tones from white to darkest gray are effectively used to create modeling of great subtlety, an effect that is lost on many of his brilliantly colored enamels.

In the Cooper-Hewitt Museum, New York, are January and June plates from a similar series (inv. nos. 1978-168-65, 1978-168-66), and a February plate from the same set is in the Musée du Louvre, Paris (Laborde 1853, cat. no. 383; Darcel 1891, cat. no. 537; Marquet de Vasselot 1914, cat. no. 648). Although these comparative examples are clearly by another hand—or hands, since the undersides are more broadly, less skillfully done—they reflect almost exactly Courteys's editing of the engraved scenes and his choice of rim decorations. Thus they must either have been executed by assistants in Courteys's atelier, or by another enamel painter working from the original set. The February plate is attributed to Pierre Courteys in the Louvre catalogues because it is related to a July plate signed by that artist, also in the Louvre (Laborde 1853, cat. no. 384; Darcel 1891, cat. no. 538; Marquet de Vasselot 1914, cat. no. 649); the painting techniques and styles are not similar, however, and the rims and undersides are very different.

Although he should not be given credit for the February plate mentioned above, Pierre Courteys used the early series of Delaune's engravings for at least two calendar sets, in which he also eliminated subsidiary scenes and utilized the border motifs. A signed January plate in

the Musée des Beaux-Arts, Lyons, and an August plate in the British Museum, London (inv. no. 1913, 12-20, 54), are probably from the same set, while the Louvre's July plate mentioned above has a different rim design and is no doubt from another series.

A plate for January in the Wernher Collection, Luton Hoo, Bedfordshire (inv. no. 338), and a May plate in the Wallace Collection, London (inv. no. III F 278), both attributed to Pierre Reymond, are taken from the earlier Delaune series and may be from the same dispersed set. Also modeled on these engravings is a seventeenth-century set of twelve oval polychrome plaques attributed to Jacques I Laudin (sold Sotheby's, London, December 7, 1967, lot 145).

PROVENANCE

Earl of Warwick; sale, London, July 17, 1896, lot 22, £388.12.

Charles Mannheim, Paris.

J. Pierpont Morgan.

William Randolph Hearst.

Donated to the Los Angeles County Museum of Art, 1948.

EXHIBITED

London 1874, cat. nos. 747–58, lent by the earl of Warwick.

LITERATURE

La Gazette de France, December 21, 1896.

Molinier 1898, cat. nos. 191–202.

Color plates, page 54

41

MARTIAL COURTEYS

Oval platter: The Death of Ananias

c. 1580
Polychrome enamel, gold, and foil
on copper
40.6 x 54.9 cm (16 x 21⅝ in.)
Gift of Varya and Hans Cohn
AC1992.152.117

DESCRIPTION

In the center of the scene Ananias falls
stricken; four people near him react to his
plight. Behind them eleven apostles are
standing on a raised dais in front of a curtain draped between two columns; the
two in front are gesturing as if they are
orating. Two more of the eleven, at right,
are distributing alms to five kneeling or
standing supplicants. At left other figures
are carrying sacks or counting money.
To either side of the curtain are glimpses
of architecture. At bottom center is an
inscription in gold, **ACTES CHAP V.** (Acts,
chapter 5).

The cavetto is painted with a gold
arabesque, and the rim is a band of nudes,
masks, cherub's heads, grotesques, drapery,
and strapwork in colors and flesh tones.

On the underside four female terms
are joined at the center of the platter by
their headdresses and at their bases by
an elaborate panel of strapwork in opaque
white. Above the strapwork are masks,
vases, lion's and goat's heads, stags, and
vegetal motifs in flesh tones and brilliant
colors. The rim motif is a laurel wreath
painted in gold.

The overall ground color on the top of the platter is a very dark mulberry that appears black; on the underside the ground is a deep blue. The central scene was painted in brilliant hues—primarily blues, purples, greens, and gold—of translucent enamel over opaque white. The outlines of the design were indicated in the white enamel by *enlevage*, and highlights were created by the application of additional layers of white. Flesh tones were rendered by a wash of red enamel mixed with clear flux over white. On the rims and underside the figures were built up first in white enamel and then covered with translucent colors or a flesh-tone wash. Much gold was used for decorative motifs on the rims and underside and in the main scene for ribbons and highlights on clothing, fabric, hair, and beards.

Besides small chips on the white rim and routine wear on the underside, there is a loss in the skirt of the tunic of Ananias, small losses along the outer edge of the cavetto and several large losses on the curved surface of the underside. One of the translucent enamel colors, possibly a dark blue, has crizzled; this is most noticeable in the robes of the man at left at the front of the dais and one of the kneeling supplicants at right, as well as in the headdresses of the female terms on the underside.

*

This platter depicts a scene taken, as the inscription attests, from the New Testament book of the Acts of the Apostles (5:1–5). In the period following the resurrection of Jesus, the Christians in Jerusalem agreed that all possessions would be held in common: whoever sold any type of property was to turn the whole amount over to the community so that the needs of all could be met. A man named Ananias sold a piece of land but brought only part of his profit to the apostles. The apostle Peter confronted him with his sin—lying not to men but to God—and Ananias promptly fell dead (his wife, Sapphira, suffered the same fate three hours later, when she also lied about the amount in question).

On the platter the apostles are shown at center on a raised platform, preaching, blessing, receiving the donations of the congregation, and distributing them to the needy. Peter and another bearded apostle raise their hands in judgmental gestures, as Ananias falls to the ground and the onlookers draw back in horror, for "all who heard were awestruck" (Acts 5:5b ERV).

The composition was taken from Raphael's celebrated series of cartoons, painted in 1515–16, for tapestries illustrating the acts of the apostles to be hung in the Sistine Chapel (the seven surviving cartoons are now in the British royal collection, on loan to the Victoria and Albert Museum, London; some of the tapestries, woven in Brussels, are in the Musei Vaticani, Rome).

Martial Courteys worked from a print of the cartoon, the work of Raphael being widely accessible in engravings by Marcantonio Raimondi and Agostino Veneziano (see, for example, cat. nos. 20–22). This particular scene was engraved by Veneziano (fig. 44; Bartsch 1978–82, vol. 26, 60, no. 42), but the compositions in the tapestry cartoons were in fact reproduced by many engravers, so that it is now impossible to determine what version Courteys used as a model (curiously, no other cartoons from the series seem to have been reproduced in painted enamel). Courteys's enamel, while respecting the classical harmony and dramatic action of Raphael's composition, varies considerably in the use of color—since he was working from a black-and-white print, he was free to choose his own palette—and the treatment of the background, not to mention the obvious fact that the composition is reversed from that of the original cartoon, just as his printed model must have been. Courteys also chose to omit the figure of a woman rushing up the stairway at the right, perhaps Sapphira attempting to flee her fate.

Agostino Veneziano,
Italy, 1490–1540, after
Raphael, Italy, 1483–
1520, *The Death of
Ananias*, from the series
The Acts of the Apostles,
engraving, 26.6 x 35.1
cm (10 ½ x 13 ¹³⁄₁₆ in.),
Graphische Sammlung
Albertina, Vienna.

A variant of this platter exists, also
attributed to Courteys: the main scene is
smaller in scale, and the inscription, also
ACTES CHAP V., is on the bottom step of
the dais on which the apostles stand. The
platter was published when it was owned
by Baroness James de Rothschild (Jones
1912, 190, pl. xcviii); it is now in the collection of Olivier Ziegel, Paris.

The borders and undersides of this
and the Ziegel platters display a rich
variety of grotesques derived from the
engravings of Étienne Delaune and Jacques
Androuet du Cerceau (figs. 11, 21, 30;
DuBon 1980, figs. 4, 7, 9–10, 13–14),
executed in brilliant polychrome enamel.
Other oval platters signed by Courteys
are decorated with identical motifs; it
seems to have been the stock back and
border treatment used by the workshop
and is used on many signed oval platters,
including one representing Apollo and
the Muses in the Wallace Collection,
London (Baldry 1904, 278–79), and two
others, in the National Gallery of Art,
Washington (London 1897, cat. no. 143,
pls. XXXI–XXXII), and in the Waddesdon
Bequest at the British Museum, London
(Read 1902, cat. no. 31, pl. IX), both illustrating a scene from the Apocalypse.

PROVENANCE

Possibly Vial collection.

Sale, Paris, March 15, 1824, lot 20.

Stettiner collection; sale, Paris, 1889.

Martin Heckscher, Vienna; sale, Christie's,
London, May 4–6, 1898, lot 74.

Lord Duveen.

Edward J. Berwind; sale, Parke-Bernet,
New York, November 9–11, 1939, lot 335.

Rosenberg and Stiebel, New York.

Varya and Hans Cohn, Los Angeles, 1945.

Donated to the Los Angeles County
Museum of Art, 1992.

EXHIBITED

Los Angeles County Museum of Art,
1983–92, lent by Hans Cohn.

LITERATURE

Demartial 1914, cat. no. 27.

Cohn 1991, 280–81.

Color plate, page 55

42

Anonymous Master

Armorial plaque

Seventeenth century
Polychrome enamel and gold on copper
22.9 x 19.5 cm (9 x 7¹¹⁄₁₆ in.)
William Randolph Hearst Collection
51.13.5

DESCRIPTION

A coat of arms parted palewise: on the left the mast of a ship, with rigging, sail, crow's nest, torch, and pennant, a star above the rigging; on the right two sacks tied with long ribbons, one cut off by the pale. The coat of arms is framed by two branches bound at top and bottom, and the design is on a field of gold arabesques.

LATER INSCRIPTIONS
OR LABELS

On the counter-enamel: **S.B. LOT. NO. 770/ART. NO. 89** printed and written on a paper sticker

Color plate, page 55

43

ANONYMOUS MASTER

Armorial plaque

Seventeenth century
Polychrome enamel and gold on copper
22.7 x 19.2 cm (8 ¹⁵⁄₁₆ x 7 ⁹⁄₁₆ in.)
William Randolph Hearst Collection
51.13.6

DESCRIPTION

A coat of arms parted palewise: on the
left the mast of a ship, with rigging, sail,
crow's nest, torch, and pennant, a star
above the rigging; on the right three white
horizontal stripes and a fleur-de-lis below.
The coat of arms is framed by two branches
bound at top and bottom, and the design
is on a field of gold arabesques.

LATER INSCRIPTIONS
OR LABELS

On the counter-enamel: **S.B. LOT NO.
770/ART. NO. 90** printed and written on
a paper sticker; **1952** stamped on a paper
sticker

TECHNIQUE

The ground of these two panels is white, on which the designs were drawn in a dark color. Translucent enamel—deep blue, purple, or tan—was then applied over the underdrawing, much of which is still visible. There is no *enlevage*; details were painted in greenish black enamel. The blue branches and red ribbons have additional underlayers of opaque white; the red enamel is so opaque itself, however, that the white does not brighten its hue at all. The gold ornamentation is quite thick, flat, and bright. The counter-enamel is clear.

The plaques have some firing cracks. The enamel on the four corners of both plaques is extremely damaged and repainted, suggesting that the plaques were once in octagonal frames that badly abraded the corners.

∗

Although many enamels are decorated with coats of arms, rarely is a heraldic device or insignia the primary subject of a panel. The most notable exception is a group of panels representing a pair of wings and a scroll bearing the words *sub umbra tuarum* (under your shadow) or *sub umbra alarum* (under the shadow of [your] wings), phrases that occur in several verses in the book of Psalms (17:8 and 91:1, for example). Three extant examples are in the Musée Municipal, Limoges (inv. no. 7; Limoges 1966, 69), the Musée du Louvre, Paris (Darcel 1891, cat. no. 956; Marquet de Vasselot 1914, cat. no. 554), and the Walters Art Gallery, Baltimore (inv. no. 44.284; Verdier 1967, cat. no. 81). Philippe Verdier suggested that the panels, which are all on brilliant blue grounds, are related in technique and drawing to the work of both Léonard Limousin and Pierre Reymond, particularly a group of anonymous pieces produced around 1530.

In palette the Los Angeles plaques are also somewhat similar to the early polychrome works of Pierre Reymond (see, for example, cat. nos. 5–8). There are, however, more persuasive reasons for assigning these plaques to a date early in the next century. Several are features that speak of haste, lack of skill, and the decline in quality and technical practices that characterized the end of the period of production. Translucent enamel has bled outside the contour lines and into another color in a number of area on both plaques, a sign that the painter was not allowing one color to set before the next was applied. The application of thick opaque white enamel over fired translucent enamel to serve as a ground for another color was

the shortcut of a painter who could not be bothered to plan ahead and was not used in the work of any enamel painter discussed in this volume. The abandonment of *enlevage* for painted contour lines is also a time- and effort-saving departure from the exacting technique that made the enamels unique. Some of the colors have an opacity that was common in the polychrome decoration of the Laudin school; the copper is also thinner than that used for fifteenth- and sixteenth-century enamels but quite similar to the thickness of vessels from the Laudin workshops (see cat. no. 44). Finally, the nature of the damage to the corners of both plaques, indicating that the framing element was octagonal, is another factor: the early seventeenth century saw a huge production of octagonally framed plaques and mirror backs, whereas the shape was rare before 1600.

Most coats of arms on painted enamels from Limoges are unidentifiable due to inaccuracies or oversimplification in their representation. To the painters such armorials must have been primarily a decorative or customizing device, and accuracy was not a concern. Also, the colors available to the enamel painters could not always encompass a rendering of a blazon with any precision. Apart from the identification of coats of arms of individuals who were known to have been patrons of the enamel painters—Anne de Montmorency, Pierre Séguier, Linhard Tucher—some identifications are tentative. In the case of these two plaques, there is a possibility that the coats of arms represent corporate bodies of some kind. The best-known occurrence of this type of ship on a French coat of arms is on that of the city of Paris, which dates back at least to the early thirteenth century. The ship and other elements on the armorials were used by several of the six major Parisian *corporations de marchands*, the merchant guilds. Both the *épiciers* (grocers) and the *bonnetiers* (hosiers) displayed this type of ship, the latter also including a five-pointed star; the *drapiers* (drapers) used three bags of cloth reminiscent of the tied sacks in one of the Los Angeles plaques; and the *orfèvres* (goldsmiths) prominently displayed the fleur-de-lis (which, it must be said, is extremely common in French heraldry, being a royal and national device). It may be that the enamel painter was commissioned to execute a series of plaques representing the six major Parisian *corporations*, which, judging by the damage to the corners, were perhaps inserted into the wainscoting of a *cabinet* of a city or guild official.

PROVENANCE

William Randolph Hearst Collection.

Donated to the Los Angeles County Museum of Art, 1951.

c. 1627–1695

HE LAUDIN FAMILY presents a problem of sorting out relationships, with
the added complication that the monograms "IL" and "NL," used as signatures
on most enamels from their ateliers in faubourg Manigne and faubourg Boucherie, may
refer to, in one case, Jacques I, Jacques II, or Joseph (or the shadowy Jean, who might not
have existed at all) or, in the other case, Noël I, Noël II, Nicolas I, or Nicolas II.

Jacques I was the son of Noël I (1586–1681), the founder of the enamel-painting
dynasty. The family's work arrived late on the scene in Limoges, perhaps after the families
to which the industry was limited by royal patent had thinned out, so that new talent was
welcome. Noël's father, Pierre, had been an armorer, and since parade armor was sometimes
decorated with enamel, it is possible that members of the family may already have been
working in the medium.

Noël's children Valérie (c. 1622–c. 1680), Jacques I, and Nicolas I (c. 1628–1698)
were all enamel painters, as were several members of the next three generations of the family.
Jacques is the best known, famed for beautifully painted grisaille enamels that are reminiscent of the best work of the previous century. Almost all enamels signed with the monogram
"IL" are routinely attributed to him, but it is more likely that polychrome plaques bearing
that signature are the work of his nephew, Jacques II (1663–1729). Jacques II also executed
a number of fine grisaille enamels, but his father, Nicolas I, specialized in polychrome
work (including many plaques of religious subjects for the Jesuit order), and it is likely that
Jacques II would have been trained to carry on in his father's technique. Beyond these
general clues, it is necessary to fall back on details of style and subject matter in order to
attribute each work to a specific member of the family.

Jacques I's workshop was best known for portrait plaques, two-handled cups, series
of medallions of the Twelve Caesars (see cat. no. 17 for a discussion of this iconography and
some examples by the Laudin atelier), and candlesticks that were often decorated with such
imperial portraits. In his grisailles he achieved enormous subtlety in shading, relying on
modulations of gray tones more than on hatching in *enlevage*, a technique he reserved for

the deepest shadows. The decorative elements that surround the grisaille scenes on the bowls and candlesticks seem to have been assigned to far more pedestrian painters, who used gold on a dark ground or a newly developed palette of bright colors on a matte white ground to execute repetitious floral patterns and arabesques. The fine grisaille elements seem jarringly archaic in the midst of such decoration, whose more "modern" appearance is due to the fact that the newer technique of painting on enamel rather than in enamel was used on an endless succession of small boxes in the eighteenth and nineteenth centuries.

*

44

JACQUES I LAUDIN

Bowl

Second half of the seventeenth century
Grisaille enamel, polychrome enamel,
and gold on copper
Height 4.4 cm (1 ¾ in.);
diameter 14.4 cm (5 ⅝ in.)
Gift of Varya and Hans Cohn
AC1992.151.118

DESCRIPTION

The bowl is round, with six embossed lobes creating contiguous concave areas in the interior (corresponding to convex areas on the exterior). Two thin, lobe-shaped handles are applied vertically to the exterior. The bowl sits directly on its base.

At the center of the interior of the bowl is a grisaille roundel depicting a half-figure of a man in contemporary clothes and a battered hat. On his right hand is a thick glove on which perches a hooded falcon; in his left hand he holds a staff from which dangles, over his left shoulder, a dead bird. The roundel is framed with decorative motifs in gold. The interiors of the lobes are painted with brightly colored flowers and foliage on a white ground. Small triangular areas between the lobes are decorated with gold triangles on a dark ground.

On the base of the bowl is a country scene in polychrome enamel, with a cottage amid trees on the left and a large tree on the right. The exterior rim of the bowl is decorated with arabesques, scrolls, and flowers, three large and two small per lobe, in colors and gold on a dark ground. The small areas between the lobes are decorated with black triangles on a white ground. There is a line of white enamel around the upper rim.

TECHNIQUE

The bowl is covered overall with a dense mulberry ground that appears black. In the interior of the bowl the roundel was executed in built-up layers of white enamel in which contour lines were drawn by *enlevage*. Shadows and highlights were created by a skillful modulation of tones from white to gray, with some hatching by *enlevage* in the darker areas. Gold was used for the falconer's buttons, hat brim, hair, belt, and staff, and various details of the two birds. In the lobes of the interior of the bowl opaque white enamel was laid over the dark ground and painted in "enamel colors" with floral motifs. The rest of the decoration of the bowl was executed in gold on the dark ground.

There are many small firing bubbles in the white enamel, both in the grisaille roundel and in the white ground of the lobes. There are some losses and chips on the edge of the bowl and normal wear and scratches on the base. The copper handles have lost almost all their enamel covering and are twisted out of shape.

*

This bowl is an excellent document of a period of transition in the history of enamel painting. It reflects the decline in popularity of enamels in the seventeenth century, when the ateliers of Limoges turned out objects that were smaller and less well crafted. It also marks a change from traditional methods of painting with enamel, as embodied by the grisaille roundel inside the bowl in a technique unchanged since the 1530s, to a new process of painting *on* enamel with a more varied palette, as in the interior of the lobes. Although these pigments are called "enamel colors" and contain metallic oxides as does enamel, other ingredients that make it possible to achieve a much broader spectrum of colors cannot withstand the amount of heat required to fuse true enamels. A surface thus decorated has a matte quality rather than the glazed appearance usual in earlier painted enamels from Limoges. These *petit-feu* (low-temperature) colors were widely used on earthenware, porcelain, glass, and metal from the late seventeenth century onward.

Two-handled bowls were produced in quantity in Limoges almost exclusively in the atelier of Jacques I Laudin in faubourg Manigne (a few are attributed to Jacques II). This bowl, like nearly all examples of the vessel type, displays a central figurative scene in grisaille surrounded by decorative designs—here, a common motif of flowers and foliage. Although the decoration tends to be fussy and repetitive, the quality of the painting itself is often extremely high, especially in the grisaille roundels.

Extant bowls from the Laudin atelier are most often lobed hexagons, with a rare pentagonal example, such as one sold in London in 1977 (Christie's, July 18, lot 60). A number of others are either circular or, as in the Los Angeles example, circular with embossed lobes. The central scene usually depicts religious or mythological episodes or figures; the choice of a genre subject—here a falconer with his bird and its kill—is unusual for this period. Only one similar subject is known to me: a hexagonal lobed bowl signed "IL" illustrating a man leaning on a club in a landscape (sold Christie's, London, December 15, 1975, lot 36). There are also a few bowls that are painted with coats of arms (sold Christie's, London, July 18, 1977, lot 64; sold Sotheby's, London, November 4, 1983, lot 17). Most of the extant bowls are decorated with rustic landscapes in polychrome enamel on the underside; a very few others are footed.

Only two of the extant bowls, the Los Angeles example and another formerly the property of Mrs. O. J. Fortescue (sold Christie's, London, December 19, 1977, lot 83), do not bear the familiar "IL" monogram. Given this fact and the rarity of the subject type, it is possible that the Los Angeles bowl may be a nineteenth-century reinterpretation of a common seventeenth-century type. Such objects were rarely forged, however (and not very intelligently—one nineteenth-century example is rather ridiculously signed with the monogram of Pierre Reymond, whose atelier never produced such an object), because they represented the nadir of Renaissance enamel painting and were not of interest to nineteenth-century collectors. In technique, pose, subtle modeling, and clarity of form the figure of the falconer in the Los Angeles bowl is on a par with major works definitely attributable to Jacques I, such as a plaque depicting Louis XIV driving the chariot of Apollo (ex-collection earl of Rosebery; sold Sotheby Parke Bernet, Mentmore Towers, May 20 [day 3], 1977, lot 1159) and a depiction of Apollo and Daphne in the Walters Art Gallery, Baltimore (inv. no. 44.280; Verdier 1967, cat. no. 209).

PROVENANCE

Oscar Bondy, Vienna.

Blumka Gallery, New York.

Varya and Hans Cohn, Los Angeles, 1950.

Donated to the Los Angeles County Museum of Art, 1992.

LITERATURE

Cohn 1991, 282–83.

Color plate, page 56

45

ANONYMOUS MAKER

*Plaque: Portrait of a Woman Called
the Duchesse de Montpensier*

Late nineteenth century
Polychrome and grisaille enamel, flesh tones,
gold, and foil on copper
49.5 x 39.1 cm (19 ½ x 15 ⅜ in.);
oval portrait: 29.2 x 20.6 cm (11 ½ x 8 ⅛ in.)
William Randolph Hearst Collection
49.34.3

DESCRIPTION

The central oval plaque is a half-length portrait of a woman identified by inscription as the *DVCHESSE·DE·MONTPENSIER. She wears a large lace ruff and a dress of rose and turquoise richly decorated with gold embroidery and pearls. Her jewelry consists of a pearl-and-gold star in her hair, pearl drop earrings, and an elaborate chain *en sautoir* of clusters of pearls, gold, and purple stones. Over her shoulders are the inscriptions L*L and ·1557·.

Flanking the portrait are two grisaille plaques of women in classical dress bearing on their heads a bowl and a basket of fruit. At upper left and lower right are a coat of arms in a white-rimmed roundel surrounded by grotesques and arabesques, the upper left with a tablet inscribed L·L. At upper right and lower left a white-rimmed roundel of three fleurs-de-lis on a dotted gold field is similarly surrounded, the tablet in the upper right reading 1556.

The plaques are affixed to an elaborate gilded wood frame carved with grotesque heads, griffin's heads, and strapwork.

TECHNIQUE

The ground color of the central oval is black. The design was executed in translucent enamels over foil and opaque white enamel. There was some *enlevage*, specifically in the ruff, face, and hair, but the patterns of hatching were executed in applied black enamel. The flesh tone was produced in the traditional way, with tiny particles of red enamel suspended in clear flux. Turquoise and rose translucent enamels were used for the dress, golden brown for the hair, and mulberry for the necklace. Gold stripes and patterns decorate the dress and jewelry, and gold curls highlight the coiffure.

The side panels were executed in a traditional grisaille style, with far more *enlevage* in a thin opaque white enamel. Gold was used for drapery trim and the basket and vessel borne by the women. The four armorial panels are also in grisaille, with flesh tones, added colors, and gold arabesques. The wooden frame is covered with a heavy gold paint.

On the portrait oval many firing cracks can be seen below the surface, especially across the face and on the lower bodice of the dress. The right side panel has scratches on the legs of the figure. The left side of the upper left armorial plaque has been badly broken, reattached, and covered with thick black paint. The blue in the coat of arms is crizzling. The frame has many small cracks and chips, not to mention the hundreds of tiny holes made in imitation of worm damage.

★

This framed plaque, or, more accurately, composite of a portrait plaque and six smaller plaques, is a magnificent example of nineteenth-century enamel painting. Although the monogram LL, for Léonard Limousin (c. 1505–1575/77) and the dates **1556** and **1557** are spurious, it is no longer possible to judge whether such an object was made to defraud or whether it was a copy of a lost original or even perhaps an "homage" by a *fin de siècle* enamel painter eager to show his skill.

This plaque demonstrates the failings of many historicizing pieces, fraudulent or not: the artists invent what they imagine the period would have produced and do not attain any degree of archaeological accuracy. Thus, at the time the plaque was produced, it may have been a convincing representation of a Renaissance lady. After a few decades, however, it has become obvious to even the least educated eye that the costume is completely wrong for the sixteenth century, that the hairdo is that of a *Belle-Époque* beauty, and that the necklace, although similar to the triple-strand pearl groupings worn by ladies in authentic sixteenth-century portraits, is of the *sautoir* design (literally, "saltire," a rope of precious metal or jewels worn so that the ends cross in front, forming an X) that had recently been made fashionable in Paris by the House of Cartier.

Pierre Lavedan (1913, 104, 107) reported that among the many portraits executed by Limousin—many of them after drawings by François Clouet or his school—were eighteen in the form of an oval plaque framed in wood and surrounded by a number of smaller plaques. Those now extant, including the well-known portrait of Constable Anne de Montmorency (fig. 6; Musée du Louvre, Paris) and a likeness of the duc de Nevers, François de Clèves (Taft Museum, Cincinnati, inv. no. 1931.305; Taft 1958, cat. no. 81), share the formula of full-length classical figures in grisaille flanking the oval portrait, with the other enamel fields reproducing coats of arms, insignia, monograms, or mottos. In the authentic pieces, however, the grotesque heads at the top and bottom of the plaques are not carved wood, but embossed enamels, all clearly by the same hand. The roundels containing the personal devices are similarly embossed.

One of the coats of arms on the Los Angeles plaque is identifiable by its three fleurs-de-lis as the Bourbon arms—the dukes of Montpensier were a branch of that family—but the other escutcheon has not yet been identified. Since the colors of a coat of arms were one of its important identifying features, no sixteenth-century artist would change the color scheme for decorative reasons from one corner of a composition to another, as the painter has done in this plaque, hindering the possibility of identification.

As to the specific duchess depicted in the Los Angeles portrait, it is probably intended to be Catherine of Lorraine (1552–1596), the daughter of François, duc de Guise, who became the second wife of Louis II de Bourbon, duc de Montpensier (1513–1582), in 1570. Embittered by the assassination of her father and two of her three brothers at the hands of the Valois kings and their adherents, Catherine became an implacable enemy of Henri III, and from 1588 onward devoted her considerable energy and power to the downfall of the line and the advancement of the claim to the throne of her third brother, the duc de Mayenne, over Henri de Navarre, later Henri IV. Catherine was painted by Limousin shortly after her wedding in 1570, and the portrait is in the Waddesdon Bequest to the British Museum, London (Read 1902, cat. no. 24). It would have been in Baron Ferdinand Rothschild's collection in Buckinghamshire at the time the Los Angeles "interpretation" was executed, so it is unlikely that it served as a model for the enamel painter, and indeed, other than a great many pearls and a purple gemstone, there is no resemblance between Catherine and the Los Angeles subject. There are other complications: since Catherine was eighteen at the time of her marriage, had the artist painted her in 1557, she would have been only five years old. Also, the second coat of arms is not that of the Guise family. It is possible that the enamel painter intended to

depict the woman who may have been the duchesse de Montpensier in 1557, Louis's first wife, Jacqueline de Long-Vic. Or the portrait may even be an "homage" to a nineteenth-century lady, perhaps the bride of a member of a later branch of the Bourbon family.

The pose, costume, and style of the Los Angeles portrait oval are most reminiscent of those in a putative likeness of the duchesse d'Étampes, painted about 1600 (thus posthumous), and said to be from a mantelpiece in the royal château of Chenonceaux. It was formerly in the collection of the earl of Rosebery pendant to a plaque, by the same hand and with the same provenance, of a woman identified as the duchesse de Nevers (sold Sotheby Parke Bernet, Mentmore Towers, May 20 [day 3], 1977, lots 1099–1100); it is possible that the chimneypiece contained an enamel pantheon of famous duchesses including Montpensier, whose portrait, now lost, may have served as a model for the Los Angeles plaque.

Inaccuracies of technique are even more damning than historical inconsistencies: the solid black ground (not dark mulberry, as in all authentic sixteenth-century enamels), translucent rose, and precise shade of translucent turquoise were not available to sixteenth-century painters; the "gilding" is simply gold paint; and the "worm holes," which only occur on subsidiary areas where no structural damage is caused, contain gold paint (that is, they precede the "gilding"), are all perpendicular to the surface and remarkably uniform in depth and thickness, and are nowhere to be seen on the back of the frame.

The value of such enamels lies primarily in their staggering technical excellence—another clue to their later origin. The nineteenth-century artists who rediscovered and revived the technique of painting on enamel brought the art to a much higher level of technical achievement than had their Renaissance predecessors. They expanded the available palette of colors and worked with a subtlety of modeling and tonality, bringing the surfaces to an extraordinary finish.

PROVENANCE

William Randolph Hearst.

Donated to the Los Angeles County Museum of Art, 1949.

ARDANT 1855.
Maurice Ardant. *Émailleurs et émaillerie de Limoges*. Isle: Ardant frères, 1855.

ARDANT 1860.
Maurice Ardant. "Émailleurs limousins: Jehan Courteys." *Bulletin de la Société archéologique et historique du Limousin* 10 (1860): 147–58.

AVRIL 1978.
François Avril. *Manuscript Painting at the Court of France: The Fourteenth Century (1310–1380)*. Translated by Ursule Molinaro and Bruce Benderson. New York: George Braziller, 1978.

BALDRY 1904.
Alfred Lys Baldry. *The Wallace Collection at Hertford House*. London: Manzi, Joyant, 1904.

BARTSCH 1978–82.
The Illustrated Bartsch. Edited by Walter L. Strauss. New York: Abaris Books, 1978–82.

BERLINER 1925–26.
Rudolf Berliner. *Ornamentale Vorlageblätter des 15. bis 18. Jahrhunderts*. Vol. I, *15. und 16. Jahrhundert*. Leipzig: Klinkhardt & Biermann, 1925–26.

BLUM 1978.
André Blum. *The Origin and Early History of Engraving in France*. Rev. and enl. New York: Hacker Art Books, 1978.

BOHN 1857.
Henry G. Bohn. *A Guide to the Knowledge of Pottery, Porcelain, and Other Objects of Vertu, Comprising an Illustrated Catalogue of the Bernal Collection of Works of Art*. London: H. G. Bohn, 1857.

BONNAFFÉ 1874.
Edmond Bonnaffé. *Inventaire des meubles de Catherine de Médicis en 1589: Mobilier, tableaux, objets d'art, manuscrits*. Paris: Auguste Aubry, 1874.

BOURDERY 1886.
Louis Bourdery. *Les Émaux peints*. Limoges: Ducourtieux, 1886.

BOURDERY 1888.
Louis Bourdery. "Les Émaux peints à l'exposition rétrospective de Limoges en 1886." *Bulletin de la Société archéologique et historique du Limousin* 35 [also ser. 2, 13] (1888): 283–510.

BOURDERY 1895.
Louis Bourdery. "Léonard Limousin et son oeuvre." *Bulletin de la Société archéologique et historique du Limousin* 44 [also ser. 2, 22] (1895): clxii–clxxiv.

BOURDERY AND LACHENAUD 1897.
Louis Bourdery and Émile Lachenaud. *Léonard Limousin, peintre des portraits*. Paris: L. H. May, 1897.

BRECK 1925.
Joseph Breck. "The Aeneid Enamels." *Bulletin of the Metropolitan Museum of Art* 20 (1925): 95–98.

BRITISH MUSEUM 1924.
A Guide to the Mediaeval Antiquities and Objects of Later Date in the Department of British and Mediaeval Antiquities. Oxford: Oxford University Press, 1924.

BRUN 1930.
Robert Brun. *Le Livre illustré en France au XVIᵉ siècle*. Paris: Félix Alcan, 1930.

CHRISTIE'S 1991.
"Enamels from the Virgil Series." *Christie's International Magazine* 8, no. 4 (April 1991): 6–7.

COHN 1991.
By Judgment of the Eye: The Varya and Hans Cohn Collection. Edited by Nancy Thomas and Constantina Oldknow. Los Angeles, privately published, 1991.

COURBOIN 1923.
François Courboin. *Histoire illustrée de la gravure en France*. Pt. 1, *Des origines à 1660*. 5 vols. Paris: Maurice Le Garrec, 1923.

DACOS 1969.
Nicole Dacos. *La Découverte de la Domus Aurea et la formation des grotesques à la Renaissance.* Studies of the Warburg Institute, vol. 31. London: Warburg Institute/Leiden: E. J. Brill, 1969.

DALTON 1912.
O. M. Dalton. *Fitzwilliam Museum, McClean Bequest: Catalogue of the Mediaeval Ivories, Enamels, Jewellery, Gems and Miscellaneous Objects Bequeathed to the Museum by Frank McClean, M.A., F.R.S.* Cambridge: Cambridge University Press, 1912.

DAMIRON 1926.
Charles Damiron. *La Faïence de Lyon.* Vol. 1, *Première Époque: Le XVIe siècle.* Paris: Dorbon-Ainé, 1926.

DARCEL 1865–66.
Alfred Darcel. "Musée rétrospectif: Le Moyen-Âge et la Renaissance. Les Émaux." *Gazette des beaux-arts* 19 (1865): 507–33; 20 (1866): 48–61.

DARCEL 1883.
Alfred Darcel. *Notices des émaux et de l'orfèvrerie exposés dans les galeries du Musée du Louvre.* 3d ed. (with a supplement by Émile Molinier). Paris: Musée National du Louvre, 1883.

DARCEL 1891.
Alfred Darcel. *Notices des émaux et de l'orfèvrerie exposés dans les galeries du Musée du Louvre.* 4th ed. (with supplements by Émile Molinier). Paris: Musée National du Louvre, 1891.

DARCEL AND BASILEWSKY 1874.
Alfred Darcel and A. Basilewsky. *Collection Basilewsky: Catalogue raisonné précédé d'un essai sur les arts industriels du Ier au XVIe siècle.* Paris: A. Morel, 1874.

DEMARTIAL 1910.
André Demartial. *Les Émaux peints: Les Primitifs: L'École de Monvaerni.* Limoges: Ducourtieux et Gout, 1910. Also published in *Bulletin de la Société archéologique et historique du Limousin* 59 (1909): 405–35.

DEMARTIAL 1914.
André Demartial. *Chronique de l'orfèvrerie et de l'émaillerie anciennes de Limoges.* Limoges: Ducourtieux et Gout, 1914.

DEMUS 1955.
Otto Demus. *Byzantine Mosaic Decoration: Aspects of Monumental Art in Byzantium.* Boston: Boston Book & Art Shop, 1955.

DOBROKLONSKAYA 1969.
Olimpiada Dmitrievna Dobroklonskaya. *Painted Enamels of Limoges: XV and XVI Centuries: The State Ermitage Collection.* Moscow: Iskusstvo, 1969.

DREYFUS 1909.
Carle Dreyfus. "Douze Plaques d'émail peint par Monvaerni (Musée du Louvre)." *Bulletin des musées de France,* 1909, no. 4: 51–53.

DUBON 1980.
David DuBon. "A Spectacular Limoges Painted Enamel." *Bulletin* (Philadelphia Museum of Art) 76, no. 329 (1980): 3–17.

DU SOMMERARD 1838–46.
Alexandre du Sommerard. *Les Arts au Moyen-Âge en ce qui concerne principalement le palais romain de Paris l'Hôtel de Cluny...et les objets d'art de la collection classée dans cet hôtel.* 5 vols. Paris: Hôtel de Cluny, 1838–46.

DU SOMMERARD 1883.
Edmond du Sommerard. *Musée des Thermes et de l'Hôtel de Cluny: Catalogue et description des objets d'art de l'antiquité, du Moyen-Âge, e de la Renaissance exposés au musée.* Paris: Hôtel de Cluny, 1883.

EVANS 1969.
Joan Evans. *Art in Medieval France, 987–1498.* 2d ed. Oxford: Clarendon, 1969.

FALIZE 1893–94.
Lucien Falize. "Claudius Popelin et la renaissance des émaux peints." *Gazette des beaux-arts,* ser. 3, 9 (1893): 418–35, 502–18; 10 (1893): 60–76, 426–37, 478–89; 11 (1894): 130–48.

FILLON 1882.
Catalogue des objets d'art et de haute curiosité... composant la collection de feu Benjamin Fillon. Sale cat., Paul Chevallier, London, 1882.

FISCHEL 1948.
Oskar Fischel. *Raphael.* Translated by Bernard Rackham. 2 vols. London: Kegan Paul, 1948.

GARNIER 1886.
Édouard Garnier. *Histoire de la verrerie et de l'émaillerie.* Tours: Alfred Mame, 1886.

GAUTHIER 1972.
Marie-Madeleine Gauthier. *Émaux du Moyen-Âge occidental.* Fribourg: Office du Livre, 1972.

GÉBELIN 1942.
François Gébelin. *Le Style Renaissance en France.* Paris: Larousse, 1942.

GEYMÜLLER 1887.
Heinrich von Geymüller. *Les Du Cerceaus: Leur Vie et leur oeuvre d'après de nouvelles recherches.* Paris: J. Rouan, 1887.

GIACOMOTTI 1974.
Jeanne Giacomotti. *Catalogue des majoliques des musées nationaux.* Paris: Éditions des Musées Nationaux, 1974.

GRAVES 1955.
Robert Graves. *The Greek Myths.* 2 vols. Baltimore: Penguin Books, 1955.

GRAVES 1966.
Robert Graves. *The White Goddess: A Historical Grammar of Poetic Myth.* Rev. and enl. New York: Farrar, Straus & Giroux, 1966.

GRUYER 1864.
François-Anatole Gruyer. *Raphaël et l'antiquité.* 2 vols. Paris: Jules Renouard, 1864.

GUIBERT 1908.
Louis Guibert. "Catalogue des artistes limousins." *Bulletin de la Société archéologique et historique du Limousin* 58 (1908): 119–209. Also published as a book, Limoges: Ducourtieux et Gout, 1909.

GUILBERT 1731.
Pierre Guilbert. *Description historique des château, bourg et forest de Fontainebleau.* Paris: André Cailleau, 1731.

GUILMARD 1880–81.
Désiré Guilmard. *Les Maîtres ornemanistes: Dessinateurs, peintres, architectes, sculpteurs et graveurs, écoles française, italienne, allemande et des Pays-Bas.* 2 vols. Paris: Plon, 1880–81.

HALL 1979.
James Hall. *Dictionary of Subjects and Symbols in Art.* Rev. ed. New York: Harper & Row, 1979.

HAUG 1978.
Hans Haug. *L'Orfèvrerie de Strasbourg dans les collections publiques françaises.* Paris: Éditions des Musées Nationaux, 1978.

HAVARD 1896.
Henry Havard. *Histoire de l'orfèvrerie française.* Paris: Quantin, 1896.

HERNMARCK 1977.
Carl Hernmarck. *The Art of the European Silversmith, 1430–1830.* 2 vols. London: Sotheby Parke Bernet Publications, 1977.

HOOGEWERFF 1945.
Godefridus Hoogewerff. "Raffaello nella Villa Farnesina." *Capitolium* 20 (1945): 9–15.

ILG 1884.
Albert Ilg. "Die limousiner Grisaillen in den kaiserlichen Haus-sammlungen." *Jahrbuch der kunsthistorischen Sammlungen des allerhöchsten Kaiserhauses* 2 (1884): 111–28.

JACQUEMART 1864.
Albert Jacquemart. "La Galerie comte Pourtalès: Objets d'art et de curiosités." *Gazette des beaux-arts* 17 (1864): 377–97.

JONES 1912.
E. Alfred Jones. *A Catalogue of the Objects in Gold and Silver and the Limoges Enamels in the Collection of the Baroness James de Rothschild.* London: Constable, 1912.

KANSAS CITY 1983.
Kansas City, Missouri: Nelson-Atkins Museum of Art. *Medieval Enamels and Sculptures from the Keir Collection.* Exh. cat. 1983.

KJELLBERG 1979.
Pierre Kjellberg. "Émaux et modèles." *Connaissance des arts*, no. 329 (July 1979): 54–63.

LABARTE 1847.
Jules Labarte. *Description des objets d'art qui composent la collection Debruge-Duménil.* Paris: Victor Didron, 1847.

LABARTE 1875.
Jules Labarte. *Histoire des arts industriels au Moyen-Âge et à l'époque de la Renaissance.* 2d ed. 3 vols. Paris: Morel, 1875.

LABORDE 1852.
Léon de Laborde. *Notice des émaux, bijoux et objets divers, exposés dans les galeries du Musée du Louvre.* Pt. 1, *Histoire et description.* Paris: Musée National du Louvre, 1852.

LABORDE 1853.
Léon de Laborde. *Notice des émaux, bijoux et objets divers exposés dans les galeries du Musée du Louvre.* Pt. 1, *Histoire et description* (2d ed.); pt. 2, *Documents et glossaire.* Paris: Musée National du Louvre, 1853.

LA COSTE-MESSELIÈRE 1957.
Marie-Geneviève de La Coste-Messelière. "Les Médaillons historiques de Gaillon." *La Revue des arts* 7 (1957): 65–70.

LADIS 1982.
Andrew Ladis. *Taddeo Gaddi: Critical Reappraisal and Catalogue Raisonné.* Columbia: University of Missouri Press, 1982.

LAVEDAN 1913.
Pierre Lavedan. *Léonard Limosin [sic] et les émailleurs français.* Paris: Henri Laurens, 1913.

LIEURE 1927.
Jules Lieure. *La Gravure dans le livre et l'ornement.* Paris/Brussels: Van Oest, 1927.

LIGHTBOWN 1987.
Ronald Lightbown. "The Migration Period and the Middle Ages." In *The History of Silver*, 37–66. Edited by Claude Blair. London: Macdonald Orbis, 1987.

LIMOGES 1966.
Guide du Musée Municipal: Collection égyptienne, émaux. Limoges: Musée Municipal, 1966.

LONDON 1862.
London: South Kensington Museum. *Catalogue of the Special Exhibition of Works of Art of the Medieval, Renaissance, and More Recent Periods, on Loan at the South Kensington Museum, June 1862.* Edited by J. C. Robinson. Rev. ed. Exh. cat. 1863. The section on painted enamels is by Augustus W. Franks.

LONDON 1874.
London: South Kensington Museum. *Catalogue of the Special Loan Exhibition of Enamels on Metal Held at the South Kensington Museum in 1874.* Exh. cat. 1875.

LONDON 1897.
London: Burlington Fine Arts Club. *Catalogue of a Collection of European Enamels from the Earliest Date to the End of the XVIIth Century.* Exh. cat. by J. S. Gardner. 1897.

LONDON 1926.
Books Printed in France and French Books Printed in Other Countries from 1470 to 1700 A.D. Sale cat., Maggs Brothers, London, 1926.

LOS ANGELES 1953–54.
Los Angeles: Los Angeles County Museum, Art Division. *Mediaeval and Renaissance Illuminated Manuscripts: A Loan Exhibition.* Exh. cat. by Marvin C. Ross. 1953–54.

LYONS 1887.
Catalogue sommaire des musées de la ville de Lyon. Lyons: Mougin-Rusand, 1887.

MAGNE 1885.
Lucien Magne. *L'Oeuvre des peintres verriers français.* Paris: Firmin-Didot, 1885.

MÂLE 1922.
Émile Mâle. *L'Art religieux de la fin du Moyen-Âge en France.* Rev. and enl. Paris: Armand Colin, 1922.

MARLE 1932.
Raimond van Marle. *Iconographie de l'art profane au Moyen-Âge et à la Renaissance.* The Hague: Martin Nijhoff, 1932.

MARQUET DE VASSELOT 1910.
Jean-Joseph Marquet de Vasselot. "Les Émaux de Monvaerni au Musée du Louvre." *Gazette des beaux-arts*, ser. 4, 3 (1910): 299–316.

MARQUET DE VASSELOT 1911.
Jean-Joseph Marquet de Vasselot. "Pour dater quelques émaux de Monvaerni." *Revue archéologique* 1 (1911): 299–306.

MARQUET DE VASSELOT 1912.
Jean-Joseph Marquet de Vasselot. "Une Suite d'émaux limousins à sujets tirés de l'Énéide." *Bulletin de la Société de l'histoire de l'art français*, 1912, 6–51.

MARQUET DE VASSELOT 1914.
Jean-Joseph Marquet de Vasselot. *Musée National du Louvre: Catalogue sommaire de l'orfèvrerie de l'émaillerie, et des gemmes du Moyen-Âge au XVIIe siècle.* Paris: Musée National du Louvre, n.d. [1914].

MARQUET DE VASSELOT 1921.
Jean-Joseph Marquet de Vasselot. *Les Émaux limousins de la fin du XVe siècle et de la première partie du XVIe: Étude sur Nardon Pénicaud et ses contemporains.* 2 vols. Paris: Auguste Picard, 1921.

MARYON 1971.
Herbert Maryon. *Metalwork and Enamelling: A Practical Treatise on Gold and Silversmiths' Work and Their Allied Crafts.* 5th ed., rev. and enl. New York: Dover Books, 1971.

MEISS 1968.
Millard Meiss, with Kathleen Morand and Edith W. Kirsch. *French Painting in the Time of Jean de Berry: The Boucicaut Master.* National Gallery of Art: Kress Foundation Studies in the History of European Art, no. 3. London/New York: Phaidon, 1968.

MICHAELS 1964–65.
Peter E. Michaels. "Technical Observations on Early Painted Enamels of Limoges: Their Materials, Structure, Technique and Deterioration." *Journal of the Walters Art Gallery* 27–28 (1964–65): 21–47.

MIROT 1918–19.
Léon Mirot. "L'Hôtel et les collections du connétable de Montmorency." *Bibliothèque de l'École des Chartes: Revue d'érudition* 79 (July–December 1918): 311–413; 80 (January–June 1919): 152–229.

MITCHELL 1910.
H. P. Mitchell. "Good-Bye to Monvaerni?" *The Burlington Magazine* 17 (1910): 37–39.

MITCHELL 1911.
H. P. Mitchell. "The Limoges Enamels in the Salting Collection." *The Burlington Magazine* 20 (1911): 77–89.

MITCHELL 1917.
H. P. Mitchell. "Some Limoges Enamels of the Primitive Schools." *The Burlington Magazine* 30 (1917): 219–25.

MOLINIER 1891.
Émile Molinier. *L'Émaillerie.* Paris: Hachette, 1891.

MOLINIER 1898.
Émile Molinier. *Collection Charles Mannheim: Objets d'art.* Paris: E. Moreau, 1898.

NATANSON 1954.
Joseph Natanson. *The Wernher Collection, Luton Hoo: Catalogue, Medieval and Renaissance Art in the Collection.* 1954.

NOEL 1882.
G. Noel. "Les Collections de Benjamin Fillon." *L'Art* 28 (1882).

NORWICH 1985.
Norwich: Castle Museum. *Norfolk & the Grand Tour: Eighteenth-Century Travellers Abroad and Their Souvenirs.* Exh. cat. by Andrew W. Moore; enamel entries by Hugh Tait. 1985.

ORLÉANS 1828.
Explication des tableaux, dessins, sculptures, antiquités et curiosités exposés au musée d'Orléans ouvert pour la première fois le 4 Septembre 1825. Orléans: Musée d'Orléans, 1828.

PANOFSKY 1958.
Erwin Panofsky. *Early Netherlandish Painting: Its Origins and Character.* 2 vols. Cambridge: Harvard University Press, 1958.

PANOFSKY 1969.
Erwin Panofsky. "Comments on Art and Reformation." In *Symbols in Transformation: Iconographic Themes at the Time of the Reformation,* 9–14. Exh. cat. Princeton: Art Museum, Princeton University, 1969.

PARIS 1867.
Paris: Exposition universelle. *Catalogue général: Histoire du travail.* Exh. cat. 1867.

PARIS 1880.
Paris: Union centrale des arts décoratifs. *Catalogue de la 6° exposition: Le Métal.* Exh. cat. 1880.

PARIS 1884.
Paris: Union centrale des arts décoratifs. *Catalogue de l'exposition de l'Union centrale des arts décoratifs.* Exh. cat. 1884.

PARIS 1889.
Paris: Palais du Trocadéro. *Exposition rétrospective de l'art français au Trocadéro.* Exh. cat. 1889.

PETIT 1843.
Catalogue de la collection d'objets d'art formée à Lyon par M. Didier Petit,...précédé de deux notices, l'une sur le crucifix, l'autre sur les émaux de Limoges. Paris/Lyons, 1843.

PINKHAM 1972.
Roger Pinkham. "Attributions to the Aeneid Master." *Apollo* 95 (May 1972): 370–75.

PINKHAM 1975.
Roger Pinkham. "The Art of the Limoges Enameller." *Country Life,* June 5, 1975, 1443–46.

POPELIN 1866.
Claudius Popelin. *L'Émail des peintres.* Paris: A. Lévy, 1866.

POPELIN 1881.
Claudius Popelin. "Collections Spitzer: Les Émaux peints." *Gazette des beaux-arts,* ser. 2, 24 (1881): 105–31.

RACKHAM 1921.
Bernard Rackham. "Limoges Enamels of the Aeneid Series at Alnwick Castle." *The Burlington Magazine* 38 (1921): 238–44.

READ 1902.
Charles H. Read. *The Waddesdon Bequest: Catalogue of the Works of Art Bequeathed to the British Museum by Baron Ferdinand Rothschild, M.P., 1898.* London: Trustees of the British Museum, 1902.

RICHTER 1970.
Jean Paul Richter, ed. *The Literary Works of Leonardo da Vinci.* 3d ed. 2 vols. New York: Phaidon, 1970.

ROBERT-DUMESNIL 1865.
A.-P.-F. Robert-Dumesnil. *Le Peintre-graveur français ou Catalogue raisonné des estampes gravées par les peintres et les dessinateurs de l'école française.* 11 vols. Paris: Georges Duplessis, 1865. Reprint. Paris: F. de Nobèle, 1967.

RONDOT 1897.
Natalis Rondot. *Bernard Salomon: Peintre et tailleur d'histoires.* Lyons: Mougin-Rusand, 1897.

ROSS 1939.
Marvin Chauncey Ross. "Notes on Enamels by Pierre Reymond." *Journal of the Walters Art Gallery* 2 (1939): 77–103.

ROSS 1941.
Marvin Chauncey Ross. "The Master of the Orléans Triptych, Enameler and Painter." *Journal of the Walters Art Gallery* 4 (1941): 9–25.

SCHERER 1964.
Margaret R. Scherer. *The Legends of Troy in Art and Literature.* 2d ed. New York: Metropolitan Museum of Art/London: Phaidon, 1964.

SCHNITZLER 1965.
Hermann Schnitzler, Peter Bloch, and Charles Ratton. *Sammlung E. und M. Kofler-Truniger Luzern.* Vol. 2, *Email, Goldschmiede- und Metallarbeiten: Europäisches Mittelalter.* Lucerne/Stuttgart: Räber, 1965.

SMITH 1987.
Rika Smith, Janice H. Carlson, Richard M. Newman. "An Investigation into the Deterioration of Painted Limoges Enamel Plaques c. 1470–1530." *Studies in Conservation* 32, no. 3 (August 1987): 102–13.

SNELL 1982.
Robert Snell. *Théophile Gautier: A Romantic Critic of the Visual Arts.* Oxford: Clarendon, 1982.

SOMERS COCKS 1980.
Anna Somers Cocks. *The Victoria and Albert Museum: The Making of the Collection.* London: Victoria and Albert Museum, 1980.

SPITZER 1891.
La Collection Spitzer: *Antiquité—Moyen-Âge—Renaissance.* Vol. 2, *Les Émaux peints.* Entries by Claudius Popelin and Émile Molinier. Paris: Quantin, 1891.

STRONG 1984.
Roy Strong. *Art and Power: Renaissance Festivals, 1450–1650.* Woodbridge, Suffolk: Boydell, 1984.

SZABÓ 1975.
George Szabó. *The Robert Lehman Collection: A Guide.* New York: Metropolitan Museum of Art, 1975.

TAFT 1958.
Taft Museum Catalogue. Cincinnati: Cincinnati Institute of Fine Arts, 1958.

TAIT 1981.
Hugh Tait. *The Waddesdon Bequest: The Legacy of Baron Ferdinand Rothschild to the British Museum.* London: Trustees of the British Museum, 1981.

TEXIER 1842.
Abbé Texier. "Essai historique et descriptif sur les argentiers et les émailleurs de Limoges." *Mémoires de la Société des antiquaires de l'ouest* 9 (1842): 77–347.

THEOPHILUS 1979.
Theophilus. *On Divers Arts.* Translated and edited by John G. Hawthorne and Cyril Stanley-Smith. New York: Dover, 1979.

VASARI 1906.
Giorgio Vasari. *Le opere.* Edited and annotated by Gaetano Milanesi. 9 vols. Florence: Sansoni, 1906.

VERDIER 1961.
Philippe Verdier. "A Medallion of the 'Ara Coeli' and the Netherlandish Enamels of the Fifteenth Century." *Journal of the Walters Art Gallery* 24 (1961): 8–37.

VERDIER 1967.
Philippe Verdier. *The Walters Art Gallery: Catalogue of the Painted Enamels of the Renaissance*. Baltimore: Trustees of the Walters Art Gallery, 1967.

VERDIER 1977.
Philippe Verdier. *The Frick Collection: An Illustrated Catalogue*. Vol. 8, *Limoges Painted Enamels, Oriental Rugs and English Silver*. New York: The Frick Collection, 1977.

WADDESDON 1977.
Waddesdon Manor: The James A. de Rothschild Collection. Glass and Stained Glass; Limoges and Other Painted Enamels. Enamel entries by Madeleine Marcheix and R. J. Charleston. London: The National Trust, 1977.

WEISS 1953.
Roberto Weiss. "The Castle of Gaillon in 1509–10." *Journal of the Warburg and Courtauld Institutes* 16 (1953): 1–12.

WIND 1968.
Edgar Wind. *Pagan Mysteries in the Renaissance*. Rev. and enl. London: Faber and Faber, 1968.